Metaphysical Song

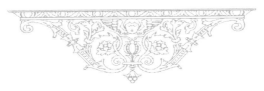

PRINCETON STUDIES IN OPERA

CAROLYN ABBATE AND ROGER PARKER
Series Editors

GARY TOMLINSON

Metaphysical Song

An Essay on Opera

PRINCETON UNIVERSITY PRESS • PRINCETON, NEW JERSEY

COPYRIGHT © 1999 BY PRINCETON UNIVERSITY PRESS
PUBLISHED BY PRINCETON UNIVERSITY PRESS, 41 WILLIAM STREET,
PRINCETON, NEW JERSEY 08540
IN THE UNITED KINGDOM: PRINCETON UNIVERSITY PRESS,
CHICHESTER, WEST SUSSEX

LIBRARY OF CONGRESS CATALOGING-IN-PUBLICATION DATA

TOMLINSON, GARY

METAPHYSICAL SONG : AN ESSAY ON OPERA / GARY TOMLINSON.

P.   CM.

INCLUDES BIBILIOGRAPHICAL REFERENCES AND INDEX.

ISBN 0-691-00408-0 (CLOTH : ALK. PAPER).

ISBN 0-691-00409-9 (PBK. : ALK. PAPER)

1. OPERA. 2. MUSIC—PHILOSOPHY AND AESTHETICS. I. TITLE.

ML 3858.T66 1998

782.1—DC21   98-25780

THIS BOOK HAS BEEN COMPOSED IN SABON

PRINCETON UNIVERSITY PRESS BOOKS ARE PRINTED
ON ACID-FREE PAPER AND MEET THE GUIDELINES FOR
PERMANENCE AND DURABILITY OF THE COMMITTEE ON
PRODUCTION GUIDELINES FOR BOOK LONGEVITY
OF THE COUNCIL ON LIBRARY RESOURCES

PRINTED IN THE UNITED STATES OF AMERICA

1 3 5 7 9 10 8 6 4 2
1 3 5 7 9 10 8 6 4 2
(PBK.)

For Jonny

CONTENTS

PREFACE

THIS IS NOT a history of opera. Neither is it a history of writings on opera or philosophies of opera, if such may be said to exist. (Although I will have much to say about a number of philosophers, several of them had nothing to say about opera.) It is instead something more tentative, a series of brief and rather specific forays into operatic history. Or it is something at once less and more than that: a set of descriptions of intersections between operatic creativity and reception, on the one hand, and the cultural production of models of subjectivity, on the other. I aim here to single out particular historical moments when the functions of operatic voice seem to me expressly to manifest current conceptions of the human subject. I have chosen moments that I believe represent major stages within the historical flux of such conceptions. The historical locales I linger over are not, then, arbitrary; but it will be obvious from the first that they are also not comprehensive.

The specificity of this essay turns on the particular issue of operatic comprehension that I wish to bring to light, to describe, and, in a preliminary way, to historicize: the hearing of the operatic voice as a medium putting its listeners in touch with invisible, supersensory realms. The specific ways operatic hearing has done this have not stood unchanged over the last four hundred years. Instead they have shifted fundamentally in interplay with the hidden regions characteristic of their broader cultural contexts. These shifts reflect deep-level changes in Western conceptions of the human subject and its relation to metaphysics. They call for a historicizing of opera's relations to invisible realms, gauged against changing modes of subjectivity and metaphysics. It is the barest outlines of such historical changes that I have aimed to sketch.

I have tried here to put down some very basic and simple thoughts on opera. But it will be clear at once that they must turn back, for their sense, on issues that are by no means simple. They raise questions of how Western cultures since the Renaissance have conceived of the individual subject, how they have defined its relations to sensed and unsensed worlds around it, and what powers they have granted or denied it.

Along the way to giving shape to these thoughts, I have benefited from the advice of friends and colleagues who read all or part of the manuscript and tried to steer me clear of misconceptions and irrelevancies (their attempts reflect well on them when they succeeded, badly on me when they failed): Susan Golomb, Joseph Kerman, Ellen Rosand, Ruth Solie, Peter Stallybrass, and Wendy Steiner. Alexander Nehamas and Roger Parker read the manuscript for the Princeton University Press; their efforts were extraordinary and their comments abundantly helpful. Elizabeth Hudson and Mary Ann Smart, finally, deserve thanks for the invitation to speak at a memorable opera conference of their devising, which induced the first skeletal formulation of the ideas fleshed out here.

Metaphysical Song

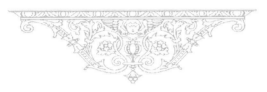

I

VOICES OF THE INVISIBLE

J UST as the operatic voice has fascinated us, in the West, continuously for four hundred years, so we have felt the need again and again to formulate explanations of its force. Two recent scholarly developments suggest that the time may be ripe for a new such formulation. First, the notion of *voice* in opera has grown increasingly complex and rich in recent years. It has been scrutinized from enough perspectives—from narratology to post-Freudian and post-Lacanian psychoanalysis, from feminist theory to queer sensibility—that we must think twice before presuming to know just who expresses what as a singer portrays for us a dramatic role. Musicologists in particular have tried out on the operatic voice a wide array of the approaches to utterance and self that have emerged from other academic disciplines. In the process voice has seemed at times almost to displace the musical score at the heart of operatic study. It has done so provocatively and, often, productively.

The second development is the anthropological impulse, broadly speaking, that drives many of the human sciences these days, which I would sum up as the quest for a knowledge of others that can alienate even as it illuminates, a knowledge that is of ourselves in its being of others. In musicology, in the wake of this impulse, an assertion such as Carl Dahlhaus's from some years back that "the task of historical hermeneutics is to make alien material comprehensible"[1] no longer seems self-evident. The prevailing winds have shifted, far enough indeed that the historian's aim may at times seem fully the opposite of Dahlhaus's—an aim, precisely, of making comprehensible material alien. At the very least the hermeneutic task seems now to require a joining or reconciliation of the two trajectories, a distancing of materials that somehow brings with it new familiarity in them and new knowledge of ourselves.

This defamiliarizing impulse has grown strong enough in musicology that we may now see that our tendency to describe our operatic commitment as "fascination" is no happenstance choice of words. It signals processes set in motion by operatic singing and enactment that remain for us mysterious in their distance from our self-conscious, rationalized conceptions and in their proximity to some more atavistic wellspring in us of sensibility and emotion. We tend to forget the precisely magical entailments of *fascination*, its invoking of hidden forces that inhabit the history of the word and characterize the phenomena it has conveyed at least as far back as the Latin *fascinum* of late antiquity. As we overcome this forgetfulness, we might begin to sense—or sense anew, since it is a connection that has been more often noted than ignored over the last four centuries—that opera is inevitably and rightly implicated in a magical history. "Fascination" is an apt watchword for the genre's links, throughout its history, with extravagance, un- or hyperreality, and irrationality.

In global perspective this association connects opera to a wide, deep, and cross-cultural mainstream of vocal functions. The effects of operatic singing constitute one subspecies within a huge family of human experiences brought about by heightened utterance—chanting, shouting, singing, incantation, whatever. These experiences are found in countless different cultural settings—probably, indeed, they are determining features of all cultural settings. They extend across a span of time that, were we in a position to measure it, would likely be found to equal the whole history of human society. In them, voice, employed in exceptional ways and in special, carefully demarcated circumstances, opens to perception invisible realms. Voice connects its bearers and hearers to ordinarily supersensible realities.

The essay that follows in the first place advances a claim that opera, through its history, has been a chief staging ground in elite Western culture for a belief in the existence of two worlds, one accessible to the senses, the other not. Operatic singing has supplied for the elite societies of early modern and modern Europe a potent experience of a metaphysics as well as of a physics, of an immaterial as well as of a material world.

Opera, needless to say, was not the first and has not been the only important European singing to bring about such an experience. Another, the liturgical chant of the Middle Ages, always walked a fine line between the revelation of a Christian supersensible and some other, more mundane display. (In the religious context this was a problem. Augustine worried famously about the tightrope act, and a millennium later Erasmus and many others were still worrying.) But opera is unique in elite European culture of the last four centuries: unique in its extraordinary history of sustained creativity from the late Renaissance on; in the central, ritualistic functions that changing societies have accorded it across that time; and even (if we include under its aegis various outgrowths such as musical comedy) in the dramatic staging altogether of the act of singing.

Across this influential history, opera has not always envoiced the same invisible realms or envoiced them in the same ways. Instead the genre has witnessed, registered, and indeed helped to define several fundamental changes in the arrangement of perceived and imperceptible worlds. Opera, in other words, has embodied not one Western metaphysics but several. As Adorno once put it (in a gnomic tone reminiscent of his colleague

Walter Benjamin), operatic metaphysics "is absolutely not a realm of in-
variance which one could grasp by looking out through the barred win-
dows of the historical; it is the glimmer of light which falls into the prison
itself."[2] The four-hundred-year history of the genre is measured off by
these shifting, shimmering metaphysics. Though we habitually conceive it
as a unitary progress, operatic history might rather be rethought as a set
of diverse manifestations, differing at fundamental levels of cultural formation, of the older, deeper, and broader impulse to voice an ordering of
the world that includes invisible terrains. Opera's history can be mapped
and partitioned according to the various supersensible realms it has
brought to audible perception and the changing ways it has done so.[3]

These differing hidden realms, it should be understood, are posited
here not as absolute supersensible realities but as cultural constructions.
They are what is presumed by a particular society to lie beyond the limits
of its sensate perception. But by virtue of this marking of boundaries, this
setting-off of a place beyond the liminal extremes granted to perception,
the hidden realms become real indeed. They answer to deep conditions of
possibility of knowledge, imagination, and aspiration in the cultures that
give rise to them. They reflect the deepest ways in which a culture plots its
place, and the places of the individuals that constitute it, in the world.

And, to repeat, these realms are time and again rendered to the senses
and to cognition especially through extraordinary manipulations of voice
and its supporting minions. An approach to the fascinations of opera,
then, requires a historicizing of its different voices, an attempt to sketch
the deep-level transformations that operatic voices have undergone since
1600. An approach that will highlight our own immersion in the most
recent of these transformations calls in particular for a characterization of
the new operatic voice that emerged around 1800. We remain, in basic
ways, in the thrall of this post-Enlightenment voice, whatever the transformations it has more recently undergone. It militates against our gain-
ing access to a place where we might have leverage to think it critically—
to hear it, so to speak, from a distance—and thereby to hear the different
voices that preceded it.

Perhaps it has always been obvious (but it is especially clear in an era
whose thought grants to utterance an extraordinary, volatile constitutive
force) that the uses of voice are fundamental features of an individual
subject's self-definition in interaction with others and the world around.
The historicizing of opera according to its different fashions of envoicing
supersensible realities, then, will be a story also of the genre's expression
of changing models of subjectivity. The operatic voice provides a compelling capsule history of the realization of these shifting subjectivities in
Western expressive culture. In setting the borderlines between sense and

the supersensible, it taps the deepest subjective expectations of the elite echelons of Western society that created and appreciated it. For these strata of society the operatic voice, among other forces, locates the subject in the world.

Here again, in this general function of envoicing subjectivity through song, opera is no different from the practices of countless other cultures. The chanting of Brazilian *candomblé* or Haitian *voudun,* in which particular gods are summoned to possess the singers; the frenzied recitation of Plato's poet, flushed from on high with divinity; the song-journey of a Tungus shaman to unseen regions where life-and-death struggles are fought for human souls; the sung astrology of the European Renaissance, bringing health and well-being to the magus through concord with the celestial spheres; the dream songs of tribal Malaysia, in which souls of trees, animals, and places convey messages through the singer—all these well-studied cases and many others have begun to tell us much about their respective models of subjectivity. More specifically, all these acts of song delineate the subject by at once defining and breaching borders between it and other, external forces, both sensible and supersensible. They reveal non-Western or premodern intuitions of subjectivity in the same way that the history of opera traces the changing picture of envoiced subjectivity in the early modern and modern West.

In the broadest division, in the deepest shifting of envoiced hidden worlds, the history traced below falls into three eras. The first, the late Renaissance, extends back well before the creation of recitative, the single most important technical innovation marking the moment about 1600 when musicologists conventionally locate the "birth" of opera. This first period embraces many varieties of Renaissance music drama, including works like Poliziano's *Orfeo,* Romain Rolland's *opéra avant l'opéra;* it reaches forward to include the mythological court music dramas of the early 1600s. The second period extends from the middle of the seventeenth century through the era of dominance of Lullian *tragédie en musique* and its outgrowths and of Metastasian opera seria. And the third reaches from sometime near the end of the eighteenth century through the nineteenth century and, with momentous internal shifts of its own, to the present day.

Each of these eras of opera projects in voice its own distinctive subjectivity. Each can be understood, in general terms, according to its characteristic construction of the human individual, according to its conception of the visible and invisible realms of the broader cosmos, and its location of the individual in them, and according to the idiosyncratic use it makes of voice onstage in manifesting those views. These differing constructions of the subject circulate, without doubt, more widely in their respective eras than in opera alone. They may be posited as foundational structures for (at least) the elite cultures of their eras. As such they might well be traced in other contemporaneous media and genres.

And, more important here, they can be described with the assistance of broad philosophical currents of their times that are congruent with them—those philosophies especially that aim to spell out or summarize a view of the human organism, its physics, and its metaphysics. Thus we find in Ficino a portrayal of the human subject that matches in fundamental regards the subjectivity given voice in late Renaissance opera; in Descartes a model captured in opera seria and its immediate antecedents; in Kant a subject that has haunted the operatic stage for the last two centuries; and in Nietzsche a reconceiving of subjectivity that challenges Kantianism and limns an opera that perhaps has never been.

It must not be thought, however, that these philosophers are put forward here as theorists of opera itself. Among them only Nietzsche might qualify. Neither do I maintain that they determine or control by specific lines of influence the profile of the operas of their respective ages. They are linked to opera in a relation of analogy, not causality. There is no specifically Cartesian brand of opera, much less a Ficinian or a Kantian one. (This is true notwithstanding the fact that it might be feasible to locate a work that more or less explicitly moots issues raised by an influential philosopher of its day. *Tristan*, whose reliance on Schopenhauer is as unquestionable as it is elusive, is the most famous—and perhaps a singular—example.) Instead Ficino, Descartes, and Kant express ways of experiencing subjectivity, each of which pervaded a particular, historically situated society. They are theorists not of opera but of the human subject. Instead of acting as agents of operatic history, they give us cogent, discursive analyses of modes of subjectivity that are voiced as well (through different means) in opera. The widely divergent views they offer of the self in the world capture in some small measure the shifting experience of subjectivity in the West over the last half-millennium.

Put the matter the other way around: These different subjectivities can be witnessed in much of the elite expressive culture of each period, including its philosophy. And they are given voice, perhaps preeminently, in opera. So although there is little or no Cartesian opera as such, nevertheless opera from the mid-seventeenth to the mid-eighteenth century repeatedly broached a model of subjectivity congruent with Descartes's *cogito* and the particular dualism it entailed. Although the court music dramas in the years around 1600 may not, in most cases, amount to explicit projects of white magic in song, they nonetheless embody a sense of the centrality of voice in the matrix of the individual and world that is akin to Ficino's. And whereas Kant's transcendental subject may not be broached self-consciously in Verdi, Meyerbeer, or even (usually) in Wagner, still the themes, topoi, and most of all the uses of voice in these composers' works (and in the works of countless of their contemporaries) resonate with an approach to the world and self that Kant also had expressed with unprecedented clarity in the realm of epistemology.

It is the representativeness of each of these philosophers in their visions of subjectivity that justifies their invocation in an essay on the uses of operatic voice. Other essays could certainly be written along more or less similar lines, I believe, using other theorists of subjectivity: Campanella or Pomponazzi might be substituted for Ficino, Spinoza or Leibniz for Descartes, and Hegel or Schopenhauer for Kant. Nietzsche is a special case: no one else, probably, could substitute for him, though the idea of summoning Wittgenstein in his place is intriguing.[4] Any such study would necessarily raise other issues and bring different emphases than this one, but it might well not differ in its broadest outline. Such is the range and general import of the conceptions of the self that Ficino, Descartes, and Kant described.

II

LATE RENAISSANCE OPERA

W HEN OPERA BEGAN, voice, psyche, and the subject as a whole were at one with the hidden regions of the world. By virtue of this conjunction there was no unconscious in early opera, no psyche at odds with itself. Instead there was only an extension of human powers into parts of the world hidden from the senses. Similarly, we see no symbolism in these works, but only a voicing of connections between perceived and supersensible realms in a unified cosmos. Symbolism, in its modern sense, at least, entails a metaphorical leap from one realm to another, unconnected realm. Renaissance significance instead comes from something more like a tracing, at root metonymic, of connections out from a center point to adjacent things. The voice of late Renaissance opera effects just such a tracing. Its ability to do so says much about both its place in the human organism and that organism's place in the broader cosmos.[1]

The late Renaissance experience of the universe and the place of humankind in it as an immense web of connected entities is expressed most clearly in the revival and dispersion of Platonic and Neoplatonic modes of thought. In such thought, at least as the sixteenth century interpreted it, the fertile mind of God imbues all things lower than itself, from the highest angel to the lowliest stone, with formal simulacrums of its divine ideas. This ineffable fertility guarantees the connection of things to one another, ultimately because of the unified nature of God's mind. In principle, all things must therefore be connected in a more or less mediated and circuitous fashion. This web of relations, this cosmos, manifests intricate patterns of similitude among things, similitudes crossing whatever more directly related things fill the ontological distance between them. And, because the power of these connections arises as a function of God's ultimate creative efficacy—his pouring forth of ideas from the divine mind— all things have the potential to influence and operate on all other things.

Bisecting this web of related things is the borderline between a higher, immaterial realm and a lower, material one. The connections of things, founded in godly ideas, extend with no impediment from the higher realm to the lower. The boundary between the two realms is so permeable as almost to be no boundary at all. And it is further blurred by an ontology that posits a smooth continuum stretching from the hardest, most stolid materials through less and less dense matter—vapors and the like—to sheer immateriality. In such a gradient the substantial and supersubstantial worlds are not categorically distinct. They are joined at the point of the least substantial materials, the least immaterial nonsubstances.

At the very center of this inconceivably intricate web sits the human organism. Its powers arise from this central positioning. Pico della Mirandola's God speaks thus to Adam: "I have set you at the center of the world so that from that position you may search about you with the greater ease upon all that is in the world contained"; from this power to choose to range freely higher toward divinity arises the human dignity Pico championed. Some years later Pietro Pomponazzi echoed Pico's view. "All agree," Pomponazzi wrote, "that man is intermediate between eternal things and generable and corruptible things; and he is put in the middle not so that he may be excluded but truly so that he may participate. Whence he may participate in all extremes."[2] Human knowledge and understanding take the form of the mapping of connections, extending out from body and soul, that are always known to be present, as by a priori postulate, but that are often hidden from all but the most persistent and demanding scrutiny. Also, human efficacy on others and the world around is folded over onto knowledge. The God-given connections are operative in their essential nature, so knowing and doing are in some measure conflated.

The central position of the human organism is evidenced, as Pomponazzi specified, by its habitation of the borderline between material and immaterial worlds. Unlike all higher things, it has a coarse, congealed material body; unlike all lower things, it has an immaterial soul. In merging material and immaterial worlds it repeats the structure of the cosmos in miniature; it is microcosm to the macrocosm of the cosmos. There is no human feature that does not replicate features external to the human organism. There is no physiology that does not echo a wider ontology, no psychology that is not also a cosmology.

In keeping with its blurring of the borderline between substantial and non-substantial worlds, Renaissance thought is not dualistic. It locates the human organism at the border of the two realms, but also posits it as the bridge making them one. The "unbreakable connection between mind and matter" that one writer has found to be characteristic of Pomponazzi's thought is a basic tenet of late Renaissance ontology of many persuasions.[3] If the cosmic midpoint joining material and immaterial things would, by the late seventeenth century, come to appear ineffable, Renaissance philosophers still worked hard to pin it down.

To do so they had recourse to a long and complicated history of pneumatology and the human *spiritus* it described. For Pomponazzi the bridge between realms took the form of the soul's immersion in thinly substantial phantasmic images, an immersion so complete it proved the soul itself to be mortal. For Bacon it was an attenuated substance, corporeal yet identical with the lower regions of a soul whose upper regions were immaterial.[4] For Bernardino Telesio and Tommaso Campanella it was a hot and subtle substance, perhaps overlapping with soul, that pervaded the world. For Ficino, whose interpretation helped to authorize all these other, later accounts, it was a bivalent spirit, not to be confused with soul, which he discussed at length in various writings. This Ficinian spirit at the heart of the human organism, bonding body and soul (and hence material and immaterial realms), is emblematic of the whole Renaissance evasion of a dualism that would only later erupt with full force.

If it has seemed to at least one modern observer that Ficino "redefines spirit in every treatise," this is because the locating of spirit between cosmic realms makes it notoriously difficult to describe with precision.[5] In attempting a definition Ficino has constant recourse to qualification, circumlocution, and pleonasm. Spirit is "almost not a body but a soul; or again, almost not a soul but a body," he tells us.[6] It is an extremely subtle, vaporous, or airy substance; or perhaps it is no substance at all, a congealed nonsubstance. Distributed through the body, it operates in two directions, conveying the animating force of the soul to the body and the stimuli received by the corporeal senses back to the soul. These stimuli it brings to the soul in the form of "images" that must be understood not only as visual formations but also as sonic motions and as stimuli from the lower senses as well. The soul thus comes in contact with "colors through the spirit of the eye, sounds through the spirit of the ears, and so forth"; then "it conceives anew in itself the entirely spiritual images of colors, sounds, etc."[7] Cognition is this process of striking a correspondence between sensual images and the soul's immaterial images. Spirit extends between the two.

In its airy nature, spirit has a special affinity to voice, song, and music. The ontological basis for this is evident when Ficino describes the continuum of material and immaterial things, for instance so as to enumerate correspondences of the sublunar world to the heavens. Words, song, and sounds—*verba, cantus, soni*—"occupy the middle position and are dedicated to Apollo," whose greatest creation, Ficino informs us, is music. Harder, more solid materials are arrayed beneath them, from stones and metals through plant matter to fine powders and vapors. These correspond respectively to the lower planets: the moon, Mercury, and Venus. Immaterial things stand above them: the conceptions of the imagination, such as passions (aligned with Mars), the deliberations of discursive reason (Jupiter), and the remote or hidden operations of the mind, almost motionless and divine (Saturn).[8]

The rational harmonic motions of song in particular underscore the affinity between spirit and sound. Song constructs images not of material things but rather of human gesture, affect, and moral characters. (Here Ficino looked back knowingly on Platonic and ancient Neoplatonic sources that he had translated from Greek to Latin and lengthily glossed.)

Song points upward toward the passions and other mobile conceptions of the imagination, aligned with Mars. It forms these moving, sonic images with a precision that makes it "the most powerful imitator of all things." The images bring song near to the heart of the imagistic process of cognition, which itself turns on the similitude of images one to another, mediated through the spirit. They make song, as Ficino was to affirm, "almost nothing other than another spirit." And they give it an extraordinary operative potency gained by interacting thus with the soul: song "imitates and enacts everything so forcefully that it immediately provokes both the singer and the hearers to imitate and enact the same things."[9]

In this fashion the airy and mimetic motions of song marked out a liminal place for it, close to spirit, in the Renaissance cosmos of interconnected forms. Both song and spirit traverse material and immaterial realms alike; they bring to perception otherwise invisible images of affect and ethos and operate on souls through the powers gained in this revelation. The psychology of musical affect, through the late Renaissance, is conceived as this manifestation of transsensual forms, while the mechanics of musical effect is a question of the mimetic capabilities of harmonic sounds and the affinity of voice to spirit. The human subject, whose place and special status in the cosmos are determined not so much by a dualism of body and soul as by the spiritual mechanism that assuages it, finds in voice and particularly in song the most potent bodily medium of this unique mechanism. (It is because the powers of song thus sit near the center of the late Renaissance experience of subjectivity that the efficacy of the ancient Orphic and Davidic voices could attain the sweeping prominence as cultural emblems that they enjoyed throughout the sixteenth century.) Voice resides at the center of the Ficinian subject in the form of spirit.

And harmony, lodged at the center of man, inhabits also the cosmos at large. In this too, microcosm reflects macrocosm. The music theorist Zarlino, who sums up so much else in his encyclopedic treatise, *Istitutioni harmoniche*, summed up this aspect of the Ficinian subject as well:

> If the world was composed by the creator in such harmony, why should we believe man himself to be bereft of it? And if the soul of the world is (as some say) nothing other than harmony, could it be that our soul is not a cause of all our harmony and harmonically joined with the body? This is certainly reasonable to assume, especially since God created man according to the plan of the larger world, called by the Greeks "Cosmos" that is, "ornament" or "ornate," and made him similar to the world but of lesser quantity, whence he is called "Microcosmos" or "small world."[10]

In such a world the human subject could best experience fullness of connection to the broader cosmos by conceiving patterns of his own similar to larger patterns of correspondence. He could reveal ties to invisible realms by assaying his harmony with them. He—or she, indeed, for the pattern was not culturally delimited to men—could do this by giving voice to song.

Late Renaissance song conveys this Ficinian subject. The driving force behind song repertories of this period is most often the attempt to strike up systems of correspondence among different levels of sonic and verbal significance. In this these repertories construct a musical voice that seeks its efficacy in the tonal mimesis of other, nontonal and nonverbal formal patterns. They embody the emotional and ethical patterns that give song access to the supersensible realm.

This is true of the repertories of solo song that played so important a role in elite music making of the time. The best singers of such music, men like the late-fifteenth-century poet and musician Serafino Aquilano, could be praised for "reciting his poems so ardently and concerting music and words so judiciously that the souls of his listeners, whether wise or mediocre or plebeian or female, were equally moved."[11] And it is true, signally, of the Italian madrigal and the French, German, and Elizabethan repertories that reflect its values. Madrigal composers employed many means to bind tones and words: subtle declamatory rhythms and melodic aria, iconic word painting, affective harmonic dissonance or chromaticism, reflection of verbal syntax in textural play or in the shapes and interaction of musical phrases, or even the most general rhythmic pacing, formal organization, and tonal orientation of a work. All these devices constructed sonic images of psychological states, images that could claim to reach beyond the psyche to the world by virtue of the connections and correspondences of micro- and macrocosmos. The songs that employed such means gained potency through the correspondences struck up between the patterns of their vocal spirit and similar images in the soul and the world.

The "measured" chansons advocated by French composers near the end of the sixteenth century, likewise, looked to imitate the patterns of ethical states in their additive rhythmic scansion. The letters patent of the academy that Baïf established to promote such music are explicit concerning the broad ethical aspirations and civic powers of these songs. The letters also assert that those powers will be gained precisely through the correspondence of song and soul:

> It is of great importance to the morals of the citizens of a city that the music current and heard there should be governed by certain laws, since the souls of most men conform to and behave in accord with it (so that, where music is disordered morals are easily depraved, while where it is well ordered men are well chastened).[12]

This Platonic sentiment, expressed on the eve of cataclysmic and horrifying religious wars in France, is only one of the more pragmatic and poignant attestations of an efficacious correspondence widely expected of late Renaissance song styles.

Perhaps it is true, as a number of scholars have urged, that some madrigalists responded in creating such music-word correspondences to the linguistic doctrines of Pietro Bembo.[13] Bembo's *Prose della volgar lingua* of 1525 represents a particularly explicit and influential entry of the Ficinian subject into theorizing about the verbal arts. Bembo believed that the power of well-wrought poetic and rhetorical speech arose from an "occult force . . . residing in each word." This force, sufficient to ravish the souls of listeners, was the product of natural correspondences between affective states of the soul and the sounds of letters, combinations of letters, words, and phrases. A *spirito* of decidedly Ficinian cast played a central role in it, so much so that Bembo could rank the effects of the letters of the alphabet according to the fullness of spirit given out in their pronunciation. Whether or not the madrigalists looked knowingly to Bembo for guidance, there can be no question that they shared with him a larger view of verbal utterance and its powers. For all of them the voice, properly used, could create correspondences, through the soul, to the harmonic concord of the cosmos.

We need to tread carefully in interpreting these correspondences. In discussions of the madrigal they are customarily understood as iconic representations in tones of the meanings of words. But this is to reverse, anachronistically, the equation. The effectiveness of correspondences between word and tone in late Renaissance song was conceived as arising from an innate harmony within words that was muted in normal speech. It was not a question of music assimilating itself to signifying words but of *words disclosing, in song, the hidden harmony that underpinned their significance.*

It is essential to distinguish thus between the operative correspondences of the late Renaissance and more recent conceptions of representation, especially since it is all too tempting to see these later conceptions as coalescing already at the end of the Renaissance. They seem to do so particularly in the extensive body of literary debate published through the late sixteenth and early seventeenth centuries, debate stimulated by, above all else, the recovery and exegesis of Aristotle's *Poetics*.[14] The innumerable accounts of representation, imitation, or mimesis broached in this literature prepared the way for post-Renaissance understandings of imitation in the expressive arts. But simply to read those later understandings back into the earlier accounts is to distort them.[15]

Most late Renaissance accounts of verbal imitation do not purport to offer an epistemology or psychology of literary expression. Instead they are technical guides for writers: primers laying out, in pragmatic detail, the kinds of external subjects, actions, and ways of describing them appropriate to this or that literary genre. Tasso clearly expressed this exter-

nal, sensate view of imitation in an "Allegory" published with his
Gerusalemme liberata in 1581:

> Imitation concerns the actions of man which are subject to the external
> senses, and laboring mainly over these, it tries to represent them with effec-
> tive and expressive words and ones apt to place clearly before the physical
> eyes the things represented; nor does it consider characters or passions or the
> discoursings of the mind insofar as these are intrinsic, but only insofar as
> they issue forth and accompany action by manifesting themselves in speech
> and in actions and deeds.[16]

In the modern senses of the terms, such accounts of poetic imitation are
not exercises in literary theory at all, but rather prescriptions for literary
praxis. It is not their aim to connect the similitudes at the heart of verbal
mimesis to deeper ontological or cosmological premises. They have little
power to explain the spiritual or psychological force of such external similarities, because these arise from the operation of innate, mostly hidden
correspondences that they ignore.

When, occasionally, such accounts aimed to offer a full theory of expressive psychology, they had recourse to the cosmos of operative affinities and the Ficinian subject's place in it. Thus, for Agnolo Segni, poetry
participated, by virtue of its imitation, in a Platonic chain of being extending from divine ideas to objects and images of them. It was necessary to
distinguish two kinds of truth in poetic imitation: the accurate reflection
of sensible things, and the ultimate truth of the divine ideas standing
above them. The authenticity of this latter, higher imitation was not ra-
tionally attained but rather guaranteed by man's access to a supersensible
and divine inspiration: Plato's poetic furor. And this furor was a product
of the divine "symmetry, proportion, and harmony" that ruled the cosmos.[17] Campanella also relied on the frenzied poet's attunement to supersensible concords to explain the powers of verse. For him poetry
gained these powers not principally through its relation to external objects but through its songlike imitation and stimulation of the motions of
the spirit; these could "use our spirit like an instrument to bring forth
auguries from the soul."[18]

Pragmatic, nontheoretical views of imitation, when applied to song,
cut it off from the features of the world that were seen, in a fuller psy-
chocosmology, to be the wellspring of its power. As a result they system-
atically likened the relation of tones and words to external, sensible similitudes like those of Tasso's imitation, above all to the relation of words
and painting. They maintained—and we tend still to believe mistakenly
that they could do no more than maintain—that tones explicate objects
referred to by words just as words might describe objects depicted on a
canvas. This was, for example, the starting point for Vincenzo Galilei's
famous attack on what he saw as the pictorial abuses of madrigal com-

posers. Such a view uproots song from its connection to a supersensible world; it detaches song from soul. Galilei himself suggested an alternative view when he urged musicians to pattern their settings after the natural tonal and rhythmic elements of speech: the pitch, volume, gesture, accent, and speed of words spoken in one situation or another. In this way, he believed, instead of merely titillating the ear, song might reach deep inside its listeners to foster affections like the singer's.[19]

Teodato Osio, another of the writers who broaches a full-fledged theory of poetic imitation, points up the superficiality of the pragmatic, iconic view. Following such writers as Tasso and Segni, he distinguishes external similitudes among sensed things from a deeper, more internal connection to supersensible things. He calls the first "representation" and the second "imitation," and he offers imitation as the true, musical aim of the poet:

> The specific difference between the poet and the painter will not be verse itself, but rather verse as the medium introducing imitation by means of its musical proportion. The office of the painter and the actor is, by representing signs and figures, to make visible with those signs and figures the external semblance of the object represented; of the poet [the office is] to convey with the expression of one ethos or another an understanding of what must be inside. So that the difference that exists between representation and imitation will be the same as the difference between the painter and the poet. Which perhaps distances greatly the operation of the poet, who introduces himself through the ears and insinuates himself into the soul by means of musical movements, from that of the painter, who simply represents to the imagination by means of figures and signs and through the eye.[20]

Osio's representation portrays external outlines of things similar to those present to the senses. Imitation brings us into contact with the supersensible, operative force behind such surface likenesses. While representation stands at one remove from the harmony that resonates through the cosmos, imitation, instead, taps that harmony and puts it to emotional use. It is the music of words themselves, not pictures of things drawn in tones, that allows word and tone to be merged. And it is the reflection in this human harmony of higher concordances that allows song to attain ethical and emotional powers.

· · · · ·

Late Renaissance opera marks a culmination of sorts of this view of the voice and its powers. The invention of recitative in the court music dramas of the 1590s and early 1600s was, by any measure, the crucial technical achievement distinguishing these works from earlier musico-dramatic entertainments. But it is important not to overstate the novelty of the new style. Recitative was a synthetic idiom, an amalgam of musical and poetic techniques that were familiar from other song styles of the late Renaissance. Its solo texture was prevalent at court and in elite society throughout the later Renaissance; it looked back to the likes of Serafino Aquilano and beyond. The ways recitative merged music and word came largely from the madrigal, though in a solo texture they could be deployed with a declamatory freedom rarely attempted in polyphonic song. Recitative took its staged presence and its stock of characters from the many sung mythologies presented at court, in the form of *intermedi* and other entertainments, from the late fifteenth century on. It derived its practice of envoicing a persona not the singer's own from these and also from the polyphonic madrigal, where five-voice renditions of what seem to modern ears the most individual complaints, amorous ecstasies, and so forth had become commonplace. (Indeed this last congruence may help to explain a certain expressive interchangeability of solo and polyphonic textures in this period, curious to modern perceptions. It is witnessed most famously in Monteverdi's recasting of Ariadne's recitative-like solo lament, from his music drama *L'Arianna* of 1608, as a cycle of five-voice madrigals.)

In all these features recitative showed itself to be yet another demonstration of song's power to mimic invisible spiritual and psychological motions. In this it linked late Renaissance opera not only to the song styles from which it was descended but also to all those that rested on the same cultural foundation and that envoiced the same human subject, fully engaged in a world of harmonious similitude. The new recitative did not, then, pose a novel musico-dramatic dilemma to be solved. It is not, except in a predictable fallacy of historical hindsight, the beginning of a problematic teleology that would exercise Gluck, Mozart, Wagner, and the rest. There is no "problem" of joining word and tone in early opera at all—except in the minds of those who wish that it had manifested different cultural formations and aspirations than its own. There is only a rich culmination of the many ways in which a culture had sung its place in the world in the preceding decades. In this culture word and tone were always already joined in nature. It was merely a question of letting each be heard in equal measure, of sung rather than spoken speech.

Some of the pragmatic accounts of the creation of recitative even hint at this. Jacopo Peri was the first master of the style. His brief narrative of its creation, in the foreword to the score of his opera *L'Euridice*, is necessarily cast as a tale of his musical response to the words presented him by the aristocrat-poet Ottavio Rinuccini. Nevertheless, and in spite also of his rejection of the notion of a far-off historical age when men spoke in song ("without doubt no one ever spoke singing," he says), Peri based his practice on the recognition of an intrinsic tonality in speech: "I knew . . . that in our speech some words are so intoned that harmony can be founded upon them and that in the course of speaking we pass through many others that are not so intoned until we return to another capable of moving to a fresh consonance." He realized as well that an essential task of the new style was to capture, in its musical rhythms, the internal rhythms of the soul's passions as they are reflected in speech: "And having in mind those manners and accents that serve us in our grief, in our happiness, and in similar states, I caused the bass to move in time to these, now more, now less, according to the passions." These rhythms were, then, synchronized with the shifts of pitch determined by the intrinsic musical elements of speech: "I held [the bass] firm . . . until, running through various notes, the voice of the speaker came to [a word] that, being intoned in normal speech, opens the way to a fresh harmony." The whole complex was intimately attuned to the natural features of the Italian language: "And therefore, just as I should not dare to affirm that this is the singing used in the fables of the Greeks and Romans, so I have come to believe that it is the only one our music can give us in accommodating itself to our speech."[21]

Peri's recitative itself reveals the innate musicality of words even more pervasively than his description of it suggests. Orpheus's famous response to the news of Euridice's death is a case in point (one that is not, however, at all unique in *L'Euridice*; see example 1). The musical rhythms reflect, from moment to moment, the declamatory rhythms of speech. At a broader level, across the soliloquy, they trace the natural rhythms of Orpheus's changing emotions: from catatonic despair (mm. 1–17, "Non piango. . . .") through a gradually rising anger and desperation (mm. 18–26, "Ohimè, chi mi t'ha tolto. . . .") to a final, rousing determination to retrieve Eurydice (mm. 27–35, "Tosto vedrai ch'invano. . . ."). Dissonance and unexpected harmonic shifts are especially pronounced in the abject misery of the opening measures. Thereafter they are more fleeting or employed (in the manner of countless madrigals) to capture the emotional gesture of a single word or phrase (the E major-to-G minor harmonic shift introducing "Ohimè," mm. 17–18, for instance).

Throughout the passage Peri's melody and harmony match the sonorous aspects of the words, themselves linked intimately to the sense and emotion of the situation. Thus ponderous consonantal clusters and dark vocalic sounds—the *a* and *o* assonance that Bembo had pronounced spiritually apt for a grave situation such as this one—predominate throughout, piling up resonantly at the moment of Orpheus's greatest determination ("Non son, non son lontano," m. 32). (Contrast with these sounds, for example, the light-footed consonants and *e* and *i* assonance, redolent

Example 1. From Peri, *L'Euridice*

of Bembo's pleasantness or *piacevolezza*, that dominate a happy song like the shepherd's that begins *L'Euridice*; see example 2.)

Perhaps most strikingly, Peri mirrors also the syntactic, rhetorical structures of Orpheus's words, the symmetries and asymmetries that played a crucial role, in the Renaissance Ciceronian traditions represented by a writer like Bembo, in conveying the changing passions of the poet. Peri's attention to these details is evident in the first four lines of the speech (see example 1), carefully balanced by the poet Rinuccini in sense, syntax, scansion, and rhyme: in the free melodic resemblances of the settings of "Non piango e non sospiro" and its counterpart "Ché sospirar, ché lacrimar non posso" (mm. 1–4 and 8–10); and in the rhythmically similar phrases that subtly capture the paired vocatives "O mia cara Euridice" and "Cadavero infelice" (mm. 5–7 and 11–13). Peri's musical rhetoric is manifest as well in the phrasing of "o pace, o vita" as a reflective expansion—a kind of musical *peristasis*—on the preceding "O mio

Example 2. From Peri, *L'Euridice*

Pastore del coro

Nin - fe, ch'i bei crin d'o - ro scio-glie-te lie - te al - lo scher-zar de' ven - ti, e

voi, ch'al - mo te - so - ro den-tro chiu - de - te a' bei ru - bi - ni ar-den - ti,

_ e voi, ch'all' al-ba in ciel to-glie-te i van - ti, tut - te ve - ni - te, o pa-sto-

rel - le a - man - ti,   e per que - ste fio - ri - te al - me con - tra - de ri-

core, o mia speme" (mm. 14–17); and in the rising sequence for the re-peated questioning at "Chi mi t'ha tolto, ohimè, dove sei gita?" (mm. 21–25).

Features such as these have often enough been admired in Peri's recita-tive, and the point of exemplifying them here is not merely to repeat the gesture. It is, instead, to situate this recitative in a broader cultural con-stellation within which song was understood to tease out of words their natural harmonic connection to supersensible forces and realms. The re-lations of the nascent recitative to the song repertories that had preceded it and, indeed, its very emergence at this moment have everything to do with this constellation. Conversely, as we shall see, a later transformation of this cultural formation would recast the meanings available to recita-tive styles, even though they still shared many musico-poetic features of Peri's.

The manifestation in recitative of a natural alliance between word and tone is described again in the treatise *Il corago*, written by an unknown author about 1630.[22] *Il corago* treats a broad range of theatrical issues, both for spoken and sung plays. But its paramount energies, and approximately half its text, are devoted to the nature of recitative. It amounts to the fullest contemporary statement we have on the aims and requirements of the new song style.

Throughout these pages the author's central concerns are to ensure the comprehensibility of the words, to achieve a variety of pacing and effect that will not bore or tire the listeners, and, above all, to create a natural expression of the passions. The sung delivery of recitative does not by any means contravene this naturalness. Instead recitative's highest attainment will be found in its matching of melodic gesture or aria to the sentiments of the text—a correspondence that is, itself, a natural relation:

> I conclude therefore that, inasmuch as any concept or affection expressed in words with suitable meter is more proportionate to one progression than to another, the excellence of the composer of this sort of music will consist in discovering among all *arie* that which most appropriately and with the greatest naturalness suits the sense, affection, meter, and order of the words given him by the poet.[23]

To discover this natural bond *Il corago* recommends not so much a recitative that imitates everyday speech as one that captures in song heightened recitation, "the reciting of those who are esteemed by all the best actors or affective speakers." Such recitation itself, *Il corago* explains in a chapter devoted to spoken theatrical delivery, is a difficult matter of finding a *naturalezza* above and beyond ordinary speech that will "accommodate the voice, from moment to moment, to the variety of affections" conveyed by the words.[24]

Thus *Il corago* recognizes in all theatrical recitation, spoken or sung, a correspondence between utterance and passion that exceeds common speech. Pushing only lightly at the borders of what the treatise's author enunciates, we may sense that he conceives theatrical recitation not as a mirror of sensible reality but as an adumbration of higher ontological orders, less efficaciously evident in everyday discourse than in heightened versions of it. *Il corago* comes close, in other words, to an explicit affirmation of a supersensible realm to which theatrical recitation gives some access.

In this light must be understood the treatise's recommendation that the most appropriate characters for music drama will be the ancient gods, semigods, heroes, and, above all, the musicians among them, such as Orpheus and Amphion. Such personages either reside in or are nearer to supersensible regions than ordinary mortals; they have a more direct and natural access to the hidden accords extending between speech and song:

> As it is obvious to every listener that ordinary people do not speak in music but instead plainly, at least in the more familiar parts of the world, speaking in music therefore conforms more with our conception of superhuman characters than with our conception and manifest knowledge of everyday men; because harmonic discourse is higher, more masterful, sweeter, and more noble than everyday speech, we attribute it, by means of a certain connate sense, to the more sublime and divine characters.[25]

The representation of supernatural beings in late Renaissance opera was not, as it has often been portrayed in recent years, an expedient to justify the unnaturalness of sung theater.[26] This suggests, as will emerge more clearly below, a relation of the human subject to supersensible realms that came into its own only after the Renaissance. Instead the supernatural personages of late Renaissance opera functioned in a way almost diametrically opposed to this modern conception. They affirmed the existence of higher orders of expression that are a supersensible part of the natural order itself. It is these orders of expression that resonate in recitative, this aspect of the higher, invisible cosmos that recitative makes palpable. The deities of early opera, far from an apology for singing, confirmed its supersensible naturalness and truth.[27]

·   ·   ·   ·   ·

In this use of the singing voice to uncover natural correspondences binding the visible and invisible regions of the cosmos, finally, recitative realized the specific goals of pastoral drama, a type of Renaissance spoken drama whose relation to the first operas has always posed a complicated historical problem.

According to the measures that have usually been invoked in comparing them, the earliest operas are evidently not pastoral dramas. The typical pastoral play depended on regular *cinquecento* comedy for its plot structures and for some of its stock characters. Its plot was built of the intertwined, multiple love affairs, the disguises and mistaken identities, and the intrigues of comedy (opera would wait till its second age to see the incorporation, under the influence of spoken comedy, of these devices). The pastoral drama's protagonists were mortal rustics, ranging in refinement (often in the same play) from barely countrified nobility to Bottomed-out buffoonery.[28]

Late Renaissance operas showed none of these features. Their protagonists were not Arcadian mortals but instead the gods, demigods, and heroes of Ovid's *Metamorphoses*: Orpheus and Euridice; Daphne and

Apollo; Ariadne, Theseus, and Bacchus; Cephalus and Aurora. Their plots were utterly straightforward in structure, relating their simple, affective tales without peripeties, disguises, recognitions, or intrigues. For this reason, no doubt, the most common generic designation their authors applied to these works was not the *favola pastorale* or *favola boscareccia* so frequent in the tradition of spoken pastoral, but rather a stripped-down epithet rarely if ever encountered there: *favola*, meaning simply "mythological story" or "fable," or, more simply still, "plot."[29] Moreover, the first opera librettos differ utterly from spoken pastoral plays in their typical length, much less than half that of even shorter pastoral plays like Tasso's *Aminta*. They employ a prosody different from that of spoken pastorals, one which often assumes the pacing of a series of closed lyric forms: *madrigali, ottave rime, terze rime,* and *canzonette* (these last, miniature strophic songs in the novel metric arrangements championed by the Savoyard poet Gabriello Chiabrera). At the level of literary and dramatic techniques there is no case to be made for the dependence of early opera on spoken pastoral.

There is, nonetheless, an important relation between the two genres. It lies not in borrowed dramatic techniques or even in broader patterns of intergeneric influence but at a deeper level of cultural formation. What binds the two genres is precisely the relationship they enact between sensible and supersensible realms. Both genres were manifestations in drama of the inclusive, interconnected world of the late Renaissance.

Louise Clubb recognizes this vision in the spoken pastoral when she writes of the large role magic played in the genre. She sees the spoken pastoral as attempting the mimesis of an "invisible reality." The effort renounces the down-to-earth definition of imitation offered by Tasso; indeed it cuts against the grain of all the pragmatic literary authorities:

> The imitation of reality, the aim of drama throughout the early sixteenth century, remains valid . . . but the reality imitated is not only that which presents itself to our eyes or can be grasped by the five senses. The theorists of drama do not state this goal; instead they obscure it, continually holding forth on the "natural" and the "verisimilar." . . . The texts of pastoral dramas, on the other hand, manifest the aspiration to a reality not directly accessible to the physical senses.[30]

Where late Renaissance opera presents a supersensible reality through the spiritual manipulations of voice, spoken pastoral attempted to body forth that invisible reality in the form of a magic repressed in the Aristotelian dramatic genres of comedy and tragedy. It did so, in Clubb's view, first in its insistent exploration of human emotions, especially love, which in the wake of Ficino's own, immensely influential amorous theories was one of the most fertile grounds throughout the sixteenth century for the exploration and definition of the Ficinian subject. It did so also in its reference to an invisible reality guided by a harmony of which humans were a part but that eluded the grasp of their reason.[31]

These pathways toward an invisible reality appear also in Richard Cody's interpretation of Renaissance pastoral drama. For him, too, the essence of Italian pastoral is its reconciliation of "this-worldliness and other-worldliness," its "Socratic compromise between . . . transcendence and immanence." This is accomplished in ways similar to those discerned by Clubb: in the depiction of the pastoral landscape as a sensible reflection of supersensible perfection (corresponding to Clubb's allusions to an invisible reality); and in the practice of Socratic speech, especially the erotic speech of Plato's most pastoral dialogue, *Phaedrus* (Clubb's exploration of love).[32] Cody adds, however, a third path through pastoral to an invisible reality: Orphic song. In his view, the history of Renaissance pastoral begins more than a century before the first operas, with the portentous, substantially or even primarily sung performance of Poliziano's *Orfeo*.[33]

Only a sung drama could most confidently traverse Cody's third path. The role of song in *Orfeo* weakens the case for a connection between it and the small tradition of mythological dramas it gave rise to about 1500, on the one hand, and, on the other hand, the spoken pastoral drama of the late 1500s, anxiously looking over its shoulder for Aristotelian sanction. Instead the connection of those earlier mythological dramas runs, in general profile and specific technique, more directly to the first opera librettos of Rinuccini and his epigones.[34] In fashioning itself after regular Aristotelian drama, rather than after Polizianesque music drama, the pastoral play of the waning sixteenth century cut itself off from its third means of access to supersensible realities. Late Renaissance opera recuperated this loss, and in this sense it may be seen to realize a fundamental pastoral aspiration that the spoken drama of its time could not.

With some exasperation and with Hegelian teleology at the ready, de Sanctis long ago pronounced the seventeenth century and its opera to be the culmination of an increasing musicalization of language through the late Renaissance: "The word, no longer being anything more than music, had lost its *raison d'être* and ceded the field to music and song."[35] The image is not all right, to be sure; but neither is it all wrong. In contrast to the late Renaissance pastoral play, opera gave full voice to an Orphic song that manifested an invisible harmony—one which the spoken genre had everywhere aspired to but voiced only in its Orphic prehistory. With respect to the varieties of late Renaissance song from which it emerged, the recitative style provided one more demonstration, and perhaps the ne plus ultra, of humanity's privileged access to a cosmos of harmonic operation. Peri's recitative, in this sense, amounts to a musical *Oration on the Dignity of Man.*

But de Sanctis was wrong to perceive a dissolving of language's significance in music stretching into the seventeenth century. The invention of opera represents not dissolution but culmination: the culmination of a Renaissance culture in which the significance of language and human utterance arose, itself, from human access to cosmic harmony. The new recitative was devised to be faithful to hidden harmonies of speech that were a peculiar preoccupation of the Renaissance. In making them audible recitative took its place in traditions of Renaissance song that had given voice to the operative affinities of sensible and supersensible worlds. Its deep cultural significance was to affirm human participation, through voice, in the supersensible realm.

This significance would disappear when, at the end of the Renaissance, the spirit was reconceived and the perceptual link of the human organism to the supersensible was broken. The period from 1650 to 1750, the great era of operatic production, standardization, and fervor, was an age in which the word, far from becoming music, grew distant from its audible harmony and even came to regard it with curiosity and suspicion.

Excursus 1

A COSMOS OF APOLLINIAN HARMONY

Manuals asserting the enduring significance of ancient mythology enjoyed a long-lasting vogue through the late sixteenth and early seventeenth centuries. Many were printed with deluxe woodcut illustrations or had them added in later, expanded editions. Natale Conti's *Mythologiae. sive explicationis fabularum libri decem* (*Ten Books of Mythology or Explanations of Fables*, 1551) and Vincenzo Cartari's *Imagini de gli dei de gli antichi* (*Images of the Gods of the Ancients*, 1556) were two of the most influential and often reprinted of such works. The editions of them published in Padua in the early seventeenth century shared the same engraved illustrations.

In these editions both Conti's and Cartari's manuals begin with a rendering, reproduced here (figure 1), of the graded scale of the mythological cosmos. It extends in unbroken fashion from supersensible gods, through the celestial spheres and the orders of angellike beings around the sphere of the moon, to the material realms of air, earth, water, and underworld flames.

The central planetary sphere here, the sun, had been associated by Ficino with music because of Apollo's legendary invention of the art. The connection was repeated and elaborated by most late Renaissance mythographers. From Conti it helped to elicit a general celebration of the sun's potent illumination, warming sustenance, and harmonious operation across long distances:

> What opens the way to the truth and disperses the dark shadows from human things more than the sun?. . . It is the sole artificer of the generation and corruption of things. . . . From very far away in the heavens it casts its rays, hardly weakened, to earth, whence it is called by the poets *ekaergos*, that is, working at long distance. . . . It alone determines sickness or health, since the life and health of living things are contained in the universal symmetry of its heat. It holds the midpoint, as of the leader, among the planets, whose motions the Pythagoreans believed to create a harmony of incredible sweetness, whence it is considered the inventor of music. They attributed to it the invention of the lyre, which at first was strung with seven strings. . . . The number of these strings matched the number of planets.

For Cartari, too, Apollo's lyre signified the celestial harmony. Apollo's placement in the midst of his daughters, the nine Muses, pictured here

Figure 1: The graded mythological cosmos. From Natale Conti,
Mythologiae (Padua, 1637).

Figure 2: Apollo among his daughters the Muses. From Natale Conti,
Mythologiae (Padua 1637).

(figure 2) from the same editions of Cartari and Conti, mirrored his place
at the center of the heavens and signified the all-pervading diffusive
power of his harmony.

A strong conviction of the relevance to contemporary life of ancient
mythological conceptions is apparent here—of the effectiveness of
Apollo's harmony, in this case, as a conceptualizing trope for knowledge
against ignorance, health against pestilence, and generation against cor-
ruption. Indeed, the starting point for projects like Cartari's and Conti's
was the belief that, as Conti put it, the ancients personified in their gods
quite real "forces of nature and the stars, and actions of God on high in
human things." Such thinking refutes the modern tendency to view the
late Renaissance revival of ancient myth as little more than the pastime of
idle metaphor-mongers and disengaged antiquarians. The mythographers revealed what they considered to be the truths hidden in ancient
myths, but in so doing they also gave expression to a contemporary ethics
and discovered a new efficacy for the old fables.

The truths they found could be given fresh ethical and political force
through the reenactment of the myths in which they found them. Thus the
Apollo of the mythographers, assuring the world's health and vitality
through his harmony, is the guiding presence of the *intermedi* performed
at the Medici court in Florence in 1589. These, among the most extrava-

gant such *tableaux vivants* from the whole sixteenth century, were commissioned to celebrate the Grand Duke's wedding—and political alliance—to Christine of Lorraine. (They involved some of the same musicians and poets who would later create the earliest operas, notably the composer Jacopo Peri and the poet Ottavio Rinuccini.) In the first intermezzo the harmony of the spheres, guided by Apollo (as Conti had said), is enacted in the version related in Plato's Myth of Er (*Republic* 614ff). Harmony herself introduces the Fates and the singing Sirens, celestial souls who accompany the planets on their harmonious rounds, to celebrate the Grand Duke and his bride. In the second intermezzo the Muses, daughters of Apollo, win their singing contest against the Pierides, as in the story from Ovid. In the third, Apollo himself descends to slay Python, an episode, Conti and Cartari explain, representing the sun's drying of the earth, avoidance of humid putrefaction, and revitalizing of life after the Flood. In the sixth and climactic intermezzo Apollo intervenes once more, now with his personified attributes Harmony and Rhythm, to confirm the bond of heaven and earth in the new Golden Age being inaugurated by the Duke and his bride. Apollo is not pictured in the engraving reproduced here (figure 3), representing this last intermezzo, but his operation from afar through an ontology extending continuously from immaterial to material regions—touted by Conti—is evident. His gleaming rays dominate the uppermost stratum of the picture, and his harmonious effects rain down through celestial musicians to the mortals below.

Apollo was also father to Orpheus, legendary musician who moved all things and even prevailed over the gods of the Underworld with his song. In the last act of Claudio Monteverdi's *Orfeo* of 1607, Apollo descends *ex machina* to bring harmony to earth, much as he had in 1589. There is this difference, however: whereas the harmonizing force he conveyed from the heavens in 1589 was aimed at Florentine and broader society, ushering in a new Golden Age, here he harmonizes a single discomposed soul, that of Orpheus himself, who has lost Euridice to the Underworld for the second time, now irrevocably.

Apollo's harmonizing therapy accorded easily with the psychology and medical practices of the later Renaissance, steeped as these were in theories of humoral balance and proportion derived from Galen and other ancient authorities. Here Apollo calls his son back from a desperation (amply demonstrated in Orpheus's lament, just before Apollo descends) that is the product of emotional excess and, hence, humoral disharmony. He delivers a minilecture on the ethics of psychological harmony:

> Why do you give yourself over, my son,
> to misery and anger?
> It's not the course of wisdom

Figure 3: The descent of Harmony and Rhythm in the sixth *intermedio* of 1589.
Engraving by Epifanio d'Alfiano. Credit: Civica Raccolta delle Stampe Achille
Bertarelli—Castello Sforzesco, Milan.

> For gen'rous souls to serve
> naught but their own emotions.
> On this count, shame and danger
> already I see threat'ning you,
> wherefore from heav'n I come to give you aid.
> . . . .
> Too much, too much you savored
> your happy fortune; now you rue too much
> your harsh and bitter fate; don't you yet know
> that nothing here below delights and lasts?

Apollo's admonishments bring home the perceived necessity of moderation, balance, and proportion—of harmony, in a word—for well-being in
the late Renaissance. They underscore also the broader, social and religious entailments of this internal, psychic harmony: without it one is
ungenerous, prey to the passions, and an object of scorn; attaining and

maintaining it depends on affirming one's connection to heaven and repudiating overreliance on mundane things.

The stagey apotheosis at the end of *Orfeo* has sometimes been judged harshly as an unfortunate bow to the spectacular "special effects" of the *intermedio* tradition. It has been disparaged in comparison with a different, plainer ending for the opera that was printed in Alessandro Striggio's libretto but for which no musical setting survives. In this alternative ending a chorus of bacchantes threatens Orpheus and sings praises of Bacchus, without recourse to elaborate machinery.

Such criticism, however, overlooks the heavy cultural baggage that Apollo's role carried. His appearance, his words, and his song together assert a psychology and an ethics of congruence, proportion, and moderation. They stage the immersion of human souls in a broader play of forces extending from immaterial to material realms. And they enact once more the force of Apollinian harmony over all sublunar souls. In 1607 no medium could have seemed more appropriate for the conveying of such messages than the novel dramatic song of recitative.

III

EARLY MODERN OPERA

ABOUT THE MIDDLE of the seventeenth century, an ostensibly demystified operatic voice led to a superficial scepticism and to doubts as to the propriety of sung drama. A librettist of that time complained that "musical recitation is improper altogether, since it does not imitate natural discourse," and the allegation of unnaturalness was to be repeated often enough over the following century to come to seem self-evident.[1] But the complaint, viewed from the vantage point of earlier opera, was startlingly novel. The guiding principle of that earlier repertory, whether evinced in the words or music of Peri or by the author of *Il corago*, had been the pursuit of an exalted but natural order. Now, however, musical recitation was coming to seem unnatural, and its practice and theory would be preoccupied for a hundred years with the conditions of its artificiality. The new complaint reflected a new relation of voice to the highest, supersensible realms of the cosmos. It was the product of a new construction of the subject. If it was not heard in the late Renaissance, this is because it would not have been fully comprehensible then.

In the seventeenth century the operatic voice was not, in truth, demystified—if by this we mean rendered neutral in regard to immaterial realms. Indeed, under this definition the operatic voice has never lost its metaphysical powers. The impression of demystification, however, is symptomatic of new functions accorded to voice. Where late Renaissance opera celebrated the link of visible and invisible worlds, opera revealed ever more clearly across the late seventeenth century a void between them. Where the older operatic voice had indicated the fulness of connection between material and immaterial realms, the new voice stood as a cipher of their troubling separation. It traversed the abyss between them—in this resided its persistent metaphysical force—but could do so only by means of a representation that was not conceivable. This new voice embodied a new ordering of signification that was thought to underlie all perception and communication. The political principle it carried, as I shall suggest, was absolutism; the experience of subjectivity it conveyed was one of unresolved dualism.[2]

When the relation of Cartesian dualism and rationalism to early modern opera is raised at all, it is usually treated as a question of the *Affektenlehre* or "Doctrine of Affections." This schematic categorization of emotions and the musical means to depict them is, to be sure, a marked feature of musical and especially operatic expression in the period. But it is no more than a symptomatic reflection of the new subjectivity. Its cultural significance cannot be gauged without an analysis of the physical and metaphysical conditions under which the Cartesian subject operated in the world.

Similarly, the relation of dualism to the new operatic voice is not sufficiently explained as one of mechanism, in which the systematicity of musical technique, the consistency of musical rhythm, or, indeed, the categorical stylistic distinction of emotional states is seen somehow to mirror a new mechanically conceived operation of the human organism. Mechanism *in toto* is too blunt a tool to make necessary historical distinctions. It is not a novel feature of the Cartesian model of the subject, but rather is inherited by it from earlier models, which had their own mechanical workings (as even the summary in chapter 2 of Ficino's psychology and epistemology reveals). The distinction between Cartesian and pre-Cartesian subjectivity is not the difference between a mechanism and something nonmechanistic that preceded it. Rather the change is from a mechanism whose workings were thought to be fully explicable—a mechanism that seemed in the workings of its spirit to span physical and metaphysical realms—to one whose central operations had become opaque.

The name this opacity assumed in the seventeenth century is *representation*, which we define simply, for now, as the presenting over again of one thing in another place. To see how so seemingly straightforward a process could grow mysterious requires looking more closely at the novel features of Cartesian subjectivity. These emerge especially as the new thought breaks down the continuous ontology, with spirit at its midpoint, of the Renaissance. The warding off of dualism, which characterized Renaissance thought in the form of its many more or less Ficinian doctrines of spirit, finally ceded the field to an embrace of dualism and an attempt to analyze it. This shift in the concerns of philosophers enunciated a new experience of subjectivity, one manifested also in other areas of discursive and expressive culture.

The unified cosmos, pictured in the late Renaissance as a smooth gradient from utter immateriality to the most stolid material substances, is ruptured in the new philosophy. Matter and nonmatter, and with them the human body and mind, are henceforth out of touch with one another, categorically distinct, and irreconcilable. Extension through space is the essential attribute of the body, while thought is the essence of the mind. "Everything else which can be attributed to body presupposes extension, and is merely a mode of an extended thing; and similarly, whatever we find in the mind is simply one of the various modes of thinking."[3]

Cognitive experience of the material world was for Descartes, as for the Renaissance, mediated by spirit. The *esprits animaux* that in their motions brought about Descartes's passions of the soul look back through Renaissance pneumatology to ancient forebears. But in comparison with their Renaissance precursors they have been profoundly altered. They have lost the characteristic bivalence of Renaissance spirit. The participation of Ficino's subject in an integrated cosmos had depended on a spirit that was half material, half immaterial—almost not a body but a soul, almost not a soul but a body, as he had said. This spirit gained its powers from its unique ontological placement, sitting at the very center of the human organism and, hence, of the cosmos.

Descartes's spirits, instead, are fully materialized: "What I name spirits here are nothing but bodies; their only property is that they are bodies which are very small and which move very rapidly."[4] From the traditions of pneumatology that Ficino also had exploited, Descartes took over only the physical, medical spirits, thought to be the finest parts of the blood. He left aside the spirits that claimed metaphysical properties and approached more closely to soul.

In this Descartes distanced the spirit and its body from the soul in a way that undoes the earlier wholeness of the world. Where there was once spirit at its central point, there is now an abyss with material spirit hovering at one edge, immaterial mind at the other. This abyss henceforth divides the cosmos. Moreover, it divides it by a distinction that is, finally, inseparable from Descartes's most famous achievement, his dispelling of doubts of his own existence. In the *Meditations*, the assertion of the cogito as utterly distinct from bodily substance is a necessary corollary of the proof of being.

The intractable and fundamental dualism posed by this division was immediately recognized by Descartes's contemporaries. If mind has no extension, they asked, how will it communicate with body? How, conversely, will the purely material spirits move or be moved by an immaterial thing? Puzzling over Descartes's cogito, Pierre Gassendi remarks, "We cannot grasp how you impress a motion upon [the spirits], you who are yourself in a point, unless you are really a body, or unless you have a body by which you are in contact with them and at the same time propel them."[5] Descartes's definition of the subject as thinking substance will not allow mind to merge in Ficino's seamless union with body. But at the same time the interactions of mind and body will apparently not allow their categorical distinction either.

The analysis and assuaging of this dualism became, it is safe to say, a primary project of philosophy through the century after Descartes. Descartes's own answer to Gassendi's objection relied on a natural correspondence between mind and body that stands outside both. In discussing the interaction of body and soul at the pineal gland, where he believed passions to be aroused, Descartes pronounced the soul to have "such a nature that it receives into itself as many different impressions—that is, has as many different perceptions—as there are different movements which take place in this gland." Meanwhile, on the other hand, "the machine of the body is so composed that, merely because this [pineal] gland is moved diversely by the soul or any other cause there may be, it drives the spirits that surround it toward the brain's pores, which guide [the spirits] through the nerves into the muscles, by means of which it makes them move the members."[6] Or again, more ineffably, he states, "Simply in virtue of entering these pores [of the brain], these spirits excite a particular movement in this gland which is *instituted by nature* to make the soul feel this passion."[7]

In the sixth *Meditation* Descartes suggests the cause of this natural institution, this innate correspondence between mind and body. When we feel pain in our foot, it is because of particular movements of nerves (and spirits in them) and because "nature has laid it down that this motion should produce in the mind a sensation of pain, as occurring in the foot." Every movement stands thus in a natural correspondence to a sensation of the mind. "It is true that God could have made the nature of man such that this particular motion in the brain indicated something else to the mind." But in that event we would not have moved our foot to escape more injury. Anything other than the particular God-given correspondence that connects the sensation of the soul represented as foot-pain to injury of our foot would not "have been so conducive to the continued well-being of the body."[8] God's supreme beneficence, then, acts as guarantor of the system of correspondences he has established between mind and body. Ficino's leap of faith was to an animating substance that could be, mysteriously, both material and immaterial and could thereby underwrite the continuities of the cosmos. Descartes's, on the other hand, takes the form of an affirmation of God's goodness in a world irreparably sundered. Reason can discover no other foundation for the harmonious correspondence of body and soul.

Approaches to Cartesian dualism throughout the later seventeenth and early eighteenth centuries similarly relied on broad systems of harmony or correspondence between the irreconcilable realms of matter and nonmatter. These systems tended, like Descartes's, to take the form of a theological principle or presence. And this presence continued to resist full rational explanation. For Baruch Spinoza, mind and body are parallel attributes of an infinite God, unified only in him. "Substance thinking and substance extended are one and the same substance, which is now comprehended under this attribute, now under that," he writes; through whichever attribute we conceive of the world, we discover the same sequence of things and chain of causes. Nicolas Malebranche's occasionalism evaded the problem of a causal relation between mind and body altogether by attributing causality only to God. Meanwhile another occasionalist, Arnold Geulincx, saw God as manipulating two instruments, mind and body, so as to reveal, miraculously, a perfect harmonic accord between them. God causes the two to coincide so that thought and sensation are perfectly reflected in bodily actions, and bodily actions in thought. The properties of Leibniz's monads, also, harmonize with one another in a manner that he posited as a fundamental "hypothesis of concomitance"; only this correspondence allows some systematicity to the phenomenal appearances of the world. Even Hume's radical empiricism could not escape hypotheses of correspondence between nature and human nature—and within human nature, between impressions and ideas. In this, Gilles Deleuze has observed, can be seen its proximity to earlier rationalisms.[9]

These projects to analyze dualism disclose a fundamentally new way of experiencing subjectivity in the West. Ostensibly, the Cartesian subject remains the intermediary at the center of the cosmos that it had been for Ficino and other philosophers of the Renaissance. And the system of correspondences that allows interactions of mind and body is descended from and superficially resembles the harmonic cosmos of the Renaissance. But in the Renaissance the human organism had found knowledge along paths of similitude leading out in both directions from the meeting point, within it, of sensible and supersensible realms. Now the subject is essentially defined in its immateriality and is cut off from direct access to matter. The Ficinian subject forged a central link in an integral chain of being. The Cartesian subject is left to contemplate a void between it and the material world. And where, in the Renaissance, perception had come about by virtue of human participation in the harmonic integration of the cosmos, now it depended on correspondences beyond the grasp of the intellect, congruencies of the sorts described by Spinoza, Leibniz, and the rest that could not be perceived because they were the medium itself of perception. The subject did not participate in these congruencies; instead its defining feature, the interaction of mind and matter, was made possible by them. The Cartesian subject was, in short, transcended by a divine system of harmonious similitudes.

Later, in the period of Kant, a new dualism would mark the advent of yet another model of subjectivity. Kantian dualism would see the categories, principles, and schemata involved in cognition not as transcending the subject but as structures within a transcendental subject who unites them with sense perception—and only thus comes to know. The history of Western subjectivity since the Renaissance might be written as this story of the shift from a *participating* subject, in contact with a unified cosmos extending smoothly from materiality to immateriality; to a *transcended* subject, whose knowledge depends on an unknowable harmony granted by a loving God between material and immaterial realms utterly out of touch with one another; and finally to a *transcendental* subject, encompassing within itself all the material and immaterial means necessary in order to know.

The Cartesian void between body and soul is never really crossed. Instead sensation and cognition come about when movements at one verge of the abyss summon congruent impressions at the other. This process is *representation*. Where no contact is possible, there remains as the only means of our perception the presenting-over-again of one thing in a different thing. The soul, in a mysterious exercise of innate powers arising from a transcending harmony, represents the qualities of objects and thus brings them into cognition. Or the body, tapping the same system of correspondences through the motions of the animal spirits, represents to the soul external stimuli that result in appropriate sensations. This representation no longer is understood in the manner of Renaissance imitation as an action brought about by contact, by operative contiguities in a graded universe of similitude. Both the void between mind and body and the transcendence of mind by the divine correspondences repudiate any such view. The efficacy of the new representation, its conformity to the conditions of Cartesian subjectivity, consists exactly in its operation in the absence of contact. It presents imitation in a new guise: not an experienced, participatory imitation but a likeness founded on unknowable harmonies; not a tracing of connections built into the fabric of the world but a correspondence of utterly unconnected things whose affinity to one another surpasses analysis.

This is what Foucault meant when he concluded, in his analysis of representation in the French classical age, that no theory of signification was possible at this time. To construct such a theory would not, as in the Renaissance, have involved an awareness of the meticulous, arithmetic process by which human beings moved from place to place in a world of which they were part. Instead it would have amounted to making visible something that the human organism was not part of: the very conditions of possibility of its theorizing consciousness. For Foucault the classical sign and signified were joined together not by a third element, as in the Renaissance, when a worldly similitude, palpable and preexistent to knowledge of it, extended between them. They were connected, rather, in an unmediated way that could be conceptualized only as the product of the act of knowing per se. The force of signification resided in the analytic comparison of two things that had no humanly conceivable relation between them other than the action of re-presenting one another at different levels of being. Each sign, Foucault writes, "posits itself in its transparency as the sign of what it represents; and yet—or rather, by this very fact—no specific activity of consciousness can ever constitute a signification."[10]

But if the relation within representation was beyond human comprehension, the shifting of signification from one correspondence to another (predicated always on this mysterious relation) was feasible and within grasp. Descartes, in the *Passions of the Soul,* anticipated this human potential in what Stephen Voss has called his "principle of habituation." Descartes explains, "Although the movements—both of the [pineal] gland and of the spirits and brain—which represent certain objects to the soul are naturally joined with those [movements] which excite certain passions in it, they can nevertheless by habituation be separated from them and joined with other quite different ones." This is evident, Descartes elaborates, in the example of speech. In speaking, the disposition of the soul necessary to enunciate certain words is linked by habituation with the conventional meanings of the words to be spoken. It passes over bodily motions more naturally connected with it: the motions of tongue and lips, brought about by the spirits, that are needed to form the words in the first place.[11]

Such conventional representation operates just as natural representation does. It is not to be understood as standing somehow outside the representational order, but rather as allowing some space within it for the accumulation of experience, memory, and learning in a human lifetime. Hence we must include conventional representation under the umbrella of faith that covers natural representation: both are founded on unknowable correspondences between mind and body willed by a beneficent God.

Where conventional representation may differ from natural representation, however, is in revealing needs deeply felt by the Cartesian subject. Here the subject may find some modicum of control over the relations of the sign to what it signifies and of the material sign to immaterial concepts and passions. These relations may no longer be experienced as grounded in human participation in the world. Instead they may now reflect a province of divine correspondences not so much corroborated by reason or experienced in perception as guaranteed by faith. But through habituation they can come to be located in a repetitive, stable, and finally reassuring system of human meanings.

·   ·   ·   ·   ·

The voice of early modern opera sings from within the condition of representation. As it had been in the Renaissance, this voice is assimilated to spirit; but now it is the material spirit of Descartes that it resembles. Indeed the connection of voice to spirit can be all the more palpable than it was in the Renaissance, inasmuch as spirit has relinquished any claims to immateriality. Both voice and spirit are now pure (if tenuous) matter set in motion. The early modern voice conveys a dualistic subjectivity in which it does not touch the soul. Its materiality will not permit it to cross the Cartesian divide. Its power over the soul, then, consists only in presenting itself at one side of the mind-body divide. At the other side, soul re-presents its motions in the forms of sensation or passion.

In taking on this operation, voice becomes an avatar of a new subject, distinct from the one embodied in Renaissance song. Early modern voice realigns the subject in relation to metaphysical realms. Its effectiveness arises, as the effectiveness of all representation now arises, from a divine harmony whose existence must be granted, as it were *a priori*, in order for voice to be perceived by soul in the first place. Voice relies, as representation now relies, upon the supersensible correspondence that is the unknowable foundation of human perception. So the early modern envoicing of the supersensible realm is equivocal, at once indicating its presence for the subject and its transcendence of the subject. The voice of the dualistic subject, hovering at the edge of the void at the center of being, signals the existence of an inconceivable harmony.

We may hear this voice in both the recitative and aria of early modern opera. But by a self-consciously propelled process of national stylistic distinction, it came to sound loudest in the recitative of French opera, on the one hand, and the aria of Italian and Italianate styles, on the other. In French recitative the representational voice took the form of an unprecedented difficulty in joining words and music, an aporia created when some of the opacity of representation came to inhabit the relation between speech and musical tone. In Italianate aria it came to be heard as a predominantly musical sign of affect that reduced strikingly the importance of recitative and finally diminished the signifying role of words altogether.

At the close of the Renaissance in Italy, recitative had embodied the motions of a spirit that was both physical and metaphysical, in a language that was unified by virtue of the natural harmonies shared by word and tone. Now the challenge of forging a musical language of dramatic recitation was taken up afresh in France in a series of experiments, a quickly coalescing canon, and an accompanying series of pamphlets and polemics. Often enough, these all seem to replay Italian developments from seventy years earlier. But the aura of familiarity is superficial only, a question of general trans-Alpine technical influences and the limited range of options open to those who would create a speechlike song within elite European musical norms. At a deeper level, the French recitative of Lully's *tragédies en musique* was conceived and experienced differently than its Italian ancestor. Its tones and words were thought to stimulate passions through a purely tangible force, revealing its hidden correspondences with immaterial realms via the obscure process of representation. The joining of harmony and word in Lullian recitative is a materialistic affair. "It is not a question of treating the music as a mysterious force of immaterial psychic evocation, but rather as a real power of mechanical excitation," Catherine Kintzler has written of the style. The means by which the music of *tragédie en musique* arouses emotions in the spectator, she argues, must be understood as "a sympathetic transmission of vibrations" of the sort described by Descartes.[12]

There are several implications and consequences of this materialization. With the disappearance of an ontology connecting sensible and supersensible realms—or to turn the matter around, with the appearance of a world in which relations across the divide between matter and nonmatter depended on representation rather than contiguity and contact—the operations of tones and words grew more and more distinct from one another. While words aroused passions through a signification that relied primarily, as Descartes had said, on conventional associations to immaterial movements of the soul, the effects of tone and harmony could not be thus understood, at least not fully. The lack of signifying precision of musical tones alone gave them an equivocal status, and if they partook of some measure of conventionalism, they seemed as well to tap rich natural correspondences no longer understood to inhere in words. (It is no happenstance that the Cartesian era marks the final decline of the theories of natural language that had remained powerful through the Renaissance or that debates began in this era over the relations of music and language that would ultimately help determine nineteenth-century musical ideologies.)

Discerning the places where the functions of words and tones did not overlap came to be the first step in conceiving of recitative. The style ceased to be one that revealed a (normally occult) *sameness* and came instead to entail the mitigation of the innate *difference* between the signifying operations of words and tones. The "problem" of recitative was born, a problem nonexistent in the participatory metaphysics of the late Renaissance from which the style had first emerged. It is not saying too much to add that this problem is an early symptom of the emergence of a new, general category of discursive practice in the West, a category independent of words that would commandeer for its name the age-old term *music*.

In the face of the new differences of musical and verbal expression, some of the opacity of Cartesian representation was transferred into the purely material relation of words and tones. Just as each of these languages aroused passions in the soul through a re-presentation there that could only allude to an unknowable correspondence, so the relation between the languages themselves came to seem another, parallel correspondence, which was at least in part mysterious. Their harmonious merger involved the representation of the signification of one language in another. It replicated in the material realm some measure of the ineffability of the representation that related each language separately to the immaterial soul. So the problem of recitative involved not only the mysterious re-presentation of its gestures in the soul that aroused appropriate passions but also the relations between words and musical tones that allowed the second to re-present the conventional meanings of the first. Solving the problem entailed understanding the nature of the bond between two distinct languages.

A complete understanding of this correspondence could not be sought within the structures of early modern subjectivity, for to do so would have required analysis of the inscrutable representation at its heart. The impossibility of such analysis is apparent in the debate that Rousseau and Rameau waged in the 1750s over Lully's recitative. Rousseau was happy to disparage this ornate French style in favor of what seemed to him more expressive and natural Italianate melody. Rameau, in springing to Lully's defense, however, found himself hampered by an inability to discuss the joining of music and poetry except in the context of a broad harmonic theory that emphasized the *discreteness* of the two. As a result, his defense of recitative as an expressive musico-poetic amalgam always seems to veer toward an assertion of the independent, extraverbal, and inscrutable expressive powers of music alone.[13]

Indeed the very ornamentalism of Lully's recitative, its myriad of small graces that was one of the features Rousseau criticized, is a point of eruption in the style of pure tonal powers distanced from the power of words. Here the parallel and untouching signifying trajectories of words and music, bound up now in their own interrelation of representation, appear; here the new problem of recitative crystallizes as a technical and expressive conundrum. The Italian recitative that Rousseau championed, instead, did not assert so prominent and independent a musical component. (In Italianate opera, we shall see, this assertion was left to aria. For this reason it is in aria that Italianate music and words drifted apart, posing a problem of representation generally similar to that of French recitative.)

Kintzler stresses the new problem of recitative from a different perspective. In her account it takes the form of an inability, Foucauldian in tone, "of French classical thought to comprehend theoretically the literary effect—the effect of sense—produced by music."[14] In the light of this limitation—or, as I have understood it, of the representational opacity that is transferred into the relation of music and words—the creators and critics of French recitative whom Kintzler scrutinizes are pushed by their materialism to conceive the relation of tones and words as one of analogy. They view music's effect as a result of its structural and formal parallels to words. Music's powers are not doubted (often just the opposite), but they are narrowly bound to the powers of words.

Inevitably, this bond takes the form of a hierarchy. Because music is weakly semantic at best and gestural only in a fashion restricted by rules of voice leading and harmony, it is subordinated in the pursuit of passionate expression to the freer gestures and fuller, more specific signification of speech. Where the natural, hidden harmonies of words had been revealed in late Renaissance recitative, now the situation is turned on its head. Now French composers bind music to words in a relation of subordination and imitation. Musical tone responds to commanding word instead of merging with it to discover its inmost expressive nature.

Jean Léonor le Gallois de Grimarest described this subordination in his *Traité du récitatif* of 1707: "We must establish in principle that passion can only be expressed by the accents, pronunciation, and gestures appropriate to it. Now it is impossible to convey these things in music while still conserving its rules; only dramatic speech [*déclamation*] can do this. Therefore any passion fixed in the intervals and measures of music loses some of its force." Here the Cartesian harmony enabling representation lurks in Grimarest's confident notion of a propriety between passions and speech; music is a constrained, second-order approximation of this correspondence. Pierre Perrin, too, at the very beginning of French music drama, affirmed a similar scheme. He wrote of the expression of the sentiments of the soul in speech (*par le discours*), of his attempt to capture these sentiments in the poetry of his librettos, and in turn of the musician's obligation to reflect the changing sentiments of the poetry in a varied setting.[15]

For Kintzler, this strict hierarchy of words over music—the *modèle lullyste*, she calls it—is fundamental to the attempts in the decades around 1700 to define what she calls a "poetics" of French opera.[16] She argues that it loosened only in the middle of the eighteenth century. It did so (or appeared to do so) first in the non-recitative music of Rameau: *divertissements*, ballets, symphonic passages, and airs. This music struck its listeners as so superabundant in complexity, detail, pictorial power, and effect that it threatened, to the outrage of the *lullystes* who rose up against it, to make of itself an autonomous force, free of words.[17] But Rameau's musical "special effects" labored in the context of his own ambivalent adherence to the Lullian model, evident in his problematic defense of his predecessor's recitative. Moreover, they revealed a misconstruing of Cartesian rationalism that enabled him to finesse altogether its mind-body dualism through the concoction of a metaphysical body, his *corps sonore*. Representation would not so easily be theorized: Rameau himself, in attempting such a theory in his late writings, wandered ever more deeply into a musical ontology that no longer rested on the cultural foundation that had supported it in the Renaissance. For his pains he was ridiculed by the philosophers around him, not least by his former adherent d'Alembert.[18]

A new paradigm for the understanding of musical effect would begin to take shape in the *Essay on the Origin of Languages* of Rameau's enemy Rousseau. Here music and language would still be tightly bound to one another, as in the *modèle lullyste*, but in a new arrangement: not a subordination of music to words (and not, as in the Renaissance, a natural alliance of music and words in a seamless, harmonious cosmos), but a *historical* discovery of the primacy of tone as the first language behind all words.[19] Rousseau's *Essay*, along with some other writings of this period (the most important, Vico's *New Science*), forged something akin to the Renaissance union of word and tone—the union that had been broken in the early modern era. It remade this bond not, however, as a contemporary (if revived) reality but as a longed-for, mythic, and unregainable place in humanity's early history—a place rife with philosophical conundrums, as abundant commentary on the *Essay* has shown in recent years.[20]

The subordination of music to language and the functioning of both by means of representation together help explain why early modern writers relied on theories of imitation to analyze musical effect. As understood in these theories, imitation did not have the contact with metaphysical forces that Teodato Osio had granted it when he distinguished it from representation; this was the imitation characteristic of late Renaissance opera. Early modern imitation was instead more pragmatic, a play of structural and gestural analogies circulating in the material world alone: analogies between pictures and things, musical motions and the articulations of language, or actions in the world and reenactments onstage. It did not function, as it had for Osio, to differentiate the representative arts of painting and acting from the imitative, metaphysical arts of music and poetry. Instead it connoted the mechanistic, material functioning of all arts, regardless of their means. It answered the problem of Cartesian mind-body dualism only by ignoring the immaterial world, hence by a wholesale evasion. For music especially this conflation of the arts under the banner of a materialist imitation raised more questions than it answered: what things in the world did music imitate, and how? Such questions would be debated productively through the eighteenth century, especially by philosophers of expression, and ultimately lead to new, nonmimetic conceptions of musical effect.

In debates over the nature of French opera, carried on always in the long shadow of Aristotle's *Poetics*, concerns about musical imitation were particularly pressing. They echoed the worries of the Italian librettist quoted earlier that musical speech was improper because it imitated

no "natural discourse." In order to legitimate itself in the context of spoken drama of the French classic era, this practice of reciting a play in
song, now experienced as an empirical impossibility, needed to attain its
own generic space of operation in which to define its particular manners
of dramatic verisimilitude. Opera required a niche among the pigeon-
holes of Peripatetic dramatic theory. Its proponents sought this niche, as
Kintzler elaborates, by gradually defining a separate register of an unreal
dramatic realism, a "verisimilitude . . . of the marvelous." This alternative verisimilitude differentiated *tragédie en musique* from its spoken
counterpart by inverting most of the features of spoken drama; in this
way it justified stage song. The first, crucial step of French opera toward
this marvelous verisimilitude was its "absorption," as Kintzler puts it, of
spoken pastoral drama, the Italian Renaissance genre that had persisted
into the French classical age. Here was a fabulous stage space where singing in place of speaking and actions impossible in the everyday world
could seem real.[21]

In this early modern assimilation of spoken pastoral and opera, we
seem again to be retracing Italian developments of seventy years earlier.
But once more the duplication is illusory. Indeed, the early modern
French convergence of pastoral drama and opera is something like the
mirror image of its Renaissance Italian counterpart, and in the reversal of
the image we glimpse the epistemological divide that separates the earliest
operas from their early modern followers. The connections of pastoral
and opera in the late Renaissance took the form of opera's envoicing of a
relation of subject and supersensible worlds that pastoral could express
only in a more muted form. The metaphysical goals of Renaissance pastoral found their fullest achievement in the singing of opera. In early modern France, instead, pastoral drama opened a rent, so to speak, through
which opera could sneak into the big tent of Aristotelian dramatic theory.
Now pastoral drama offered an apology for opera, an absolution of its
evident sins against empirical, material reality. The earliest operas had
fleshed out a true reality only foreshadowed in pastoral. Now pastoral
located a place where the otherwise grating spectacle of sung drama, imi-
tating nothing in the world, could be assuaged—a stage on which miracles could for a moment take material form. True to the void at the center
of the new subjectivity, there is no contact here with invisible worlds,
only a justification for trying—through song—to imitate them.

In these differing relations of pastoral drama and opera we see
reflected, once more, the expressive gap between late Renaissance and
early modern recitative. In the earlier period, recitative could attain the
goals that pastoral drama had aimed toward but fallen short of, pulled
back to earth by its spoken medium. Pastoral magic was realized in the
linguistic metaphysics of song. In the Lullian period, by contrast, pastoral

supernaturalism alleviated the burden of verisimilitude that weighed un-
bearably, now, on the artifice of sung speech. Song-speech, a medium
savored but no longer believed in, took refuge in a realm accepted only as
an unreal reality.

.   .   .   .   .

Early modern opera exhibits the working of the representational voice in
these features of its French dialect. Some of them are specific and limited
to the French style, especially its emphasis of ornamental recitative, which
works in tandem with its relatively slight stylistic distinction of air from
recitative. Other features, instead, extend across a broader operatic
range, even across the whole of European music drama of the period.
Aristotelian concerns over the dramatic legitimacy of opera, for example,
are certainly not limited to France, and the issues arising from them were
widely appreciated. A clear expression of such concerns elsewhere is
Francesco Algarotti's *Saggio sopra l'opera in musica* of 1755, preoccupied throughout with opera's verisimilitude.[22]

Most broadly, perhaps, the operatic voice conveys an early modern
experience of subjectivity in its effort to reassure of the efficacy of a representation founded in incomprehensible correspondences. This effort
comes to the fore most pervasively and generally in the gradual crystaliza-
tion, across all operatic repertories of the period, of stock musico-
dramatic gestures. These constitute, to our ears and eyes as they did to
those of the seventeenth and eighteenth centuries, an array of eminently
serviceable operatic conventions. They look back, in some cases, to late
Renaissance antecedents; but even when they do so, they manifest in relation to those anticipations a proliferation and hardening of expressive
categories.

These conventions cut across operatic space, dividing it according to
different (if interconnected) measures. They may take the form of stan-
dardized personae: kings and queens, generals and the women who love
them, refined shepherds and shepherdesses (especially in the Arcadian period about 1700), and (until they were banished, also about 1700) comic
characters, such as hunchbacked stammerers and libidinous old women.
Conventionalism is evident in such recurring tableaux as allegorical pro-
logues, infernal or heavenly choruses, tempests at sea, and ballets. It appears also in commonly found dramatic situations: the recognition of a
disguised protagonist, an invocation of gods or demons, a sleep scene
with lullaby, a lament. The conventions assume pictorial form in the consolidation, across the late seventeenth century, of a collection of stylized
scenic spaces that would remain influential in opera staging long after:
various indoor spaces, from throne rooms to private chambers, outdoor

perspectives on monumental architecture, gardens, untamed grottoes, and so forth. And finally, especially in Italianate styles, the conventions are expressed in the rhythmic and melodic motion, tonal orientation, or orchestration of arias.[23]

The deployment of such conventions creates a system of representational codes. It builds a lexicon of stable patterns whose gestures (or motions) come to stand in conventional, habitual, and assured relations to passions (or emotions) of the soul. In this they present a hugely dispersed doctrine of affections. Such codes answer the need, in the new representative order, for predictable patterns of signification. They are a musico-dramatic exercise in Cartesian habituation. (And, for an analysis of representation in opera, it is telling that a particular use of voice—speech—comprises Descartes's chief example of habituation and its reorientation of the representational relation between soul and body.)

In the broadest perspective, also, these conventions set the trajectory of the subsequent evolution of music drama, which will unfold after the early modern period as a series of meditations on, reactions to, and more or less fierce departures from early modern conventionalism. But to condemn this conventionalism as antidramatic in itself, to see the repertories that embodied it only as failed preliminaries to later dramaturgies (Kerman's infamous "dark ages" of opera), is not only to indulge in feeble teleologies; it is also to ignore the conditions of subjectivity, different from later ones, that they express. For the Cartesian subject, conventionalism is a necessary source of compelling representation and, hence, of both sense and expressive power in drama.

In Italianate opera, the most important of the new conventions concerns the manipulation of voice in what is now the musico-dramatic crux: aria. The rise to dominance of aria and the concomitant decline of recitative across the 1600s together constitute the most important stylistic change in this first century of Italian opera. This evolution traces the emergence and envoicing of a new subjectivity. It does so just as clearly as Lullian recitative, if along a different musical path; a synoptic view of opera in the later seventeenth century would perceive a dichotomous response to late Renaissance recitative, tending on the one hand toward the French problematizing of it and on the other toward the Italian minimizing of it in favor of aria.

Late Renaissance recitative had been conceived in a world of innumerable signifying connections extending out from the human organism. Its variety of pacing was the key to its ability to convey these connections in song. Italian aria came to function as a primary operatic expression of a different subject in a different relation with the world; uniformity and consistency were its métier. At first approximation, the difference at the heart of the genre between late Renaissance and early modern Italian opera appears as a shift from the fluidity and flux of recitative to the single-mindedness of aria.

Monteverdi provided an emblematic instance of this shift in two pieces he composed at opposite ends of his later career to portray mostly similar dramatic situations. The lament from his early music drama *L'Arianna* and his later *Lament of the Nymph* differ essentially in the lability of Ariadne's emotions and the stasis of the nymph's. Through the interplay of melodic designs with the strict ostinato bass that accompanies them, the nymph can eloquently present musical motions that correspond to a single attitude of her mind. Unlike her, however, Ariadne can *change her mind*. The madrigalian flexibility of every element of her musical language allows for wholesale redirections of the emotions she expresses. The distance between these two works is something of a measure of the gap between expression by participation and expression by representation.[24]

Recitative did not vanish in early modern Italian opera, of course. It lived on, but with diminished aspirations and altered capacities. By the late 1600s it came to serve as little more than a bridge between arias. It was heard as an idiom repeated by rote, hardly constituting song. Indeed it embodied not diversity and variety but a dulling uniformity. "It's the same throughout and can't properly be called singing," wrote François Raguenet, otherwise a staunch defender of Italian opera, of its recitative. Recitative provided a context for the affection elaborated in the aria that followed, but it could no longer pretend to be the center of gravity of operatic expression. For such a librettist as Barthold Feind, even though the aria needed to refer to the preceding recitative—to "function almost as explanatory notes" for it—it was nonetheless the "spirit and soul of the entertainment" and represented "whatever is most charming and artistic in the poetry."[25]

The uniformity that Raguenet and other early modern listeners found in Italian recitative marks most clearly its new reduced status. Here a paradox seems to arise, since uniformity is also the preeminent expressive advantage that underwrites the ascendancy of early modern aria. But the paradox is not real. The perceptions of uniformity in recitative and in aria are of different orders. The first is a consequence of the rise of aria itself, stimulated by its increasing musical elaboration, which casts recitative, finally, as something tantamount to nonsong. Aria came to function, as Bianconi has put it, as the "minimum semantic unit" in early modern opera.[26] In doing so, aria altered the scale of operatic signification altogether, so that meaningfulness came to be measured in units too broad to register the smaller, local gestures of recitative. The semanticity itself of the recitative style was drowned out by overwhelming musical forces within the aria.

The uniformity of aria offered something different from this monotony of a style whose individual motions were indistinguishable because they had ceased to be meaningful. It comprised the internal consistency of a singular, self-sufficient, and indivisible sign. (Indivisible in principle: this does not rule out the possibility of a slightly less uniform expression within aria, in which the second section of a da capo aria represents emotions distinct from those represented in the first. A famous example is Rinaldo's "Cara sposa, amante cara" from Handel's *Rinaldo*. In such a case, Bianconi's minimal semantic unit is no longer the aria as a whole but instead the large, constitutive sections of the aria. This slightly smaller unit then represents in precisely the same fashion as the whole of a more uniform aria.) The features that allowed aria to be experienced in this fashion were unavailable to recitative: orchestral ritornellos, marking it off from the surrounding music; propulsive rhythmic consistency; uniformity of melodic motion and motivic design; and harmonic coherence brought about by the predictability of its modulations.

These traits made aria an ideal musical sign of a single spiritual motion and hence the ideal presentation of a single, discrete passion. They enabled aria to answer, in a way that the recitative around it could not, to the felt need for representational standardization that characterizes the Cartesian subject. The totalizing expression of an aria simplified and schematized the presentation of passions, reassuring the listener of a coherent and significant representational order. It warded off the abstraction and arbitrariness of expression haunting the margins of the ineffable process of representation. Moreover, it facilitated the construction in music of easily recognizable expressive conventions, since a group of arias similar in both affect and means could by a process of habituation (like the one envisaged by Descartes) solidify the musical representation of a passion.

This is not to say that aria presents an explicit working out in song of Descartes's discrete categories of passion. Neither is it to conceive aria as the standard-bearer of some culturewide doctrine of affections. If early modern aria is never far from such a portrayal of affect, we should nonetheless remember, with Bianconi, that eighteenth-century typologies of aria tend to be based not on affect alone, but also on technical, vocal, and stylistic criteria.[27] Aria's portrayal of categorical emotion was symptomatic rather than essential. Aria revealed deep cultural formations not so much in its lexicon of specific passions, or even in its characteristic approach to the passions all told, as in its urge to conventionalism per se. It conveyed a Cartesian view of discrete passions because its significance, achieved through a conventionalized representational crossing of the void between mind and body, could be clear and assured only in this way.

To achieve this representation the aria needed to rely on words to identify the nature of the passion it represented. Significantly, this reliance narrowed in early modern aria to the point of becoming minimal. The function of words was reduced to one of labeling, and the aria was able to represent effectively through *almost purely tonal means*. The possibility of creating through repeated usage conventional connections of sign to signified, of motion to emotion, permitted a manner of sung expression that reduced to almost nothing the signification of individual words. Their semantic specificity, which in French recitative had granted them hierarchical rule over musical tone, was overwhelmed, like the local gestures of recitative, by the larger semantic scope of the "aria-sign." The hierarchy of word and tone affirmed in French recitative—the reliance of tone on word—was not broken, but rather explored and exploited in different ways. The very consistency of the music of aria enabled it to rely on words in new ways—and thereby arrogate to itself new powers.

This expanded role that purely tonal means played in aria's representation was one current in the broader cultural shift, noted earlier, that began to separate out notes from words and the tonal from the verbal elements even within voice. It is the Italianate analogue of the problematic of Lullian recitative and of the almost autonomous musical force, still tied to the Lullian model, that appears in the works of Rameau. Rousseau might have recognized this force in aria and worried, had his championing of Italian opera against Rameau been less ardent, for it militated toward the separation of singing from speech and of harmony from vocal inflection that for him had deprived song of its ancient ethical force.[28] In moving away from the native origins of song, Lully's recitative, the historical development Rousseau sketched, and Rameau's harmonies (which Rousseau opposed) all took part in the formation of the new cultural and ideological category, music. The minimizing in early modern aria of the semantic function of words was another important gesture in the same broad development.

The possibility of an almost purely tonal representation of passions—again, a possibility that needs to be understood as an outgrowth of the dualism of the Cartesian subject or, more specifically, of the urge to conventionalism that arises with it—affords early modern aria new and epochal opportunities for orchestral expression. In late Renaissance recitative, voice and continuo had formed a single, indivisible unit, in which the expressive operation of the instrumental support was determined at the most precise level by the tones and meanings of the voice. The instrumental accompaniment of early modern aria carries different capabilities. It can survey as a whole the significance of the vocal utterance it accompanies and represent it in synoptic fashion. It can synthesize meanings that the voice must unfold across the space of its discursive, semantic operation. In its generalizing semantic import, as I have said, it can operate on a different scale than the semantics of words. This power enables the accompaniment to function as an emblem or symbol, focusing representational powers necessarily dispersed in words. Tone works as a kind of semiotic distillation, reducing to a musical essence the tropes of aria verse—which had become commonplaces by the period of Metastasio, the premier early modern librettist, tracing their ancestry back through Chiabrera's ditties to sixteenth-century Petrarchism.

The *ariette* of late Renaissance opera—brief, strophic tunes of which Orpheus's "Vi ricorda, o boschi ombrosi" from Monteverdi's *Orfeo* is the most famous instance—had already begun to explore such synoptic expression. In these songs, however, it was invested primarily in the voice, rather than in a conventional, representational instrumental accompaniment. (Indeed it is possible to interpret the new-found prominence in the late Renaissance of the concept "aria," by then an important if vague category within more general ideas of melos, as signaling a broad realization of possibilities of a synoptic melodic ethos that formed a counterpart to the particularistic tendencies of the text-music relation in the period.) The author of *Il corago* precisely described this difference between recitative and aria, seeing expression "in particular, according to each word and figure" as characteristic of the first and a "broader and more generic" expression as a hallmark of the second.[29]

Nevertheless, the cultural divide is large between the *ariette* of late Renaissance opera, or late Renaissance aria in general, and the arias of early modern opera. It can be measured partly in technical changes: in the substantial shift to the orchestra, in early modern arias, of the new representational power. But it also needs to be perceived in a broader, ideological context, against the backdrop of evaluative systems by which the differences of recitative and aria were gauged. The generalized expression of the *ariette* rendered them secondary to recitative in fulfilling the operatic aims of the earlier period, while early modern arias could, by exploiting related means in the context of a revised subjectivity, overwhelm recitative and move to the heart of the new musico-dramatic experience.

Numerous ostinato basslines in lament arias of the mid-seventeenth century exemplify the new emblematic powers of instrumental music.[30] Such basslines—we have already encountered a nonoperatic example in Monteverdi's *Lament of the Nymph*—provide an almost pure experience of Cartesian conventionalism. Their consistency of motion, brevity, and very tautology facilitate the representational crossing of the mind-body divide. This is evident in Cassandra's lament from Cavalli's *Didone* (see strophe 1 in example 3). No instrumental support more responsive to the individual gestures of the voice—no support, in other words, closer to the recitative style—could embody the synthetic representational power evident here in Cavalli's mobile, but repetitive, descending chromatic bass.

Example 3. From Cavalli, *La Didone*

In comparison to late Renaissance recitative, the emblematic function of this accompaniment is especially marked, because Cassandra sings a melody that is declamatory throughout and shifts, at the end of each strophe, into straightforward recitative. But even this final declamation does not work as earlier recitative had. It, too, is underlaid by the ostinato, in a slowed-down version; hence, its expressive force is a function not so much of its local movement in time with its continuo accompaniment as of a distinction between the two, which grants the whole an independent mode of signifying that is differentiated from speech.

This new emblematic representation enables instruments, for the first time, in a condition of substantial independence from voice, to take over the envoicing of subjectivity. Independent instrumental representation in this period is not, however, a question of emancipation from and transcendence of verbal language. This would come later, along with the emergence of a different subjectivity. Instead instruments encroach on vocal powers in the same way, and to the same extent, as the voice's own tonal qualities are separated from, displace, and take over the signifying role of its meanings. Tonality of voice and tonality of instruments move together to the verge of dispensing with words, to the asymptote where the signaling of habituated affect would no longer require any verbal enunciation. This tendency encourages the stylistic assimilation, or even seeming equivalence, of voice and instruments in arias of the early eighteenth century, a feature everywhere apparent in the seria style but egregiously displayed, from time to time, in the famous musical contests between singers and soloists from the orchestra.

De Sanctis's view, again, needs to be rethought. It is not a question of a seventeenth-century musicalization of the word, for word and tone had been more fully merged in the spiritual powers of voice during the Renaissance. Instead the representational function that operates in words can now be fulfilled also and in new ways by musical tones alone—or almost alone. In the early modern era, instrumental melody and song come close to being equivalent in function and, because of this equivalence, they are able to operate independently of one another. Their equivalence arises from the conventional representational capabilities they share.

But, because of the minimal function still accorded the semantic values of words in this musical representation, the expressive capabilities of instruments are displaced slightly from a perfect duplication of vocal powers. This displacement is evident in the ostinato of Cassandra's lament, focusing in its reiterated gesture a kind of symbolic representation difficult to achieve in the voice's discursive plenitude and declamatory variety.

The displacement is clear also in countless early eighteenth-century arias in which the gestures of voice and instruments are not identical or nearly so but instead seem to offer two subtly distinct versions of the passions signaled in the words. In the aria "Figlio! Tiranno! O Dio!" from Alessandro Scarlatti's *Griselda*, (see example 4), Griselda's agitated despair at the threatened murder of her son is represented in her vocal line by short, exclamatory phrases, long leaps, and (once, to close the first section of the aria) scalar coloratura. The string band shares these features, and together with the voice it offers a compelling representation of the passion seizing Griselda at this moment. But the orchestra also moves independently of voice. It elaborates on Griselda's one thirty-second-note scalar flourish, and it adds to the other expressive features of the aria an idiomatic tremolo at the beginning and end of the passage as well as quick, repeated notes throughout, which the voice does not attempt. The orchestra, in its motions, enhances the representation of the ruling passion identified by the words and represented by the vocal line.

The obverse in this displacement of instrumental from vocal expression is also significant. In distinguishing its functions from those of voice, the orchestra reveals that the voice still has something of its own to contribute. It reveals, in other words, that the independence of tone from verbal enunciation is not complete and that instruments cannot alone offer a full and specific representation. Though the orchestra in Scarlatti's aria, in Cassandra's ostinato lament, and in early modern aria in general can tell us much, it can only offer enhanced, altered, or synoptic versions of what the voice signifies in its own conjunction of tones and enunciated words. The autonomy of musical expression here remains as incomplete—and as dependent on words—as it would in Rameau's spectacles. The aria orchestra can fill in the sketch that voice offers of what the soul knows of itself, but it cannot represent things about the soul not represented also by the voice and its words.

The new horizons of tonal and instrumental expression afforded by early modern representation are thus not equivalent to the language-transcending instrumentalism of the nineteenth century. But with hindsight we may see that they nonetheless point in its direction. The ineffable nature of representation in Cartesian subjectivity marks the starting point from which the new, different ineffability of romantic and postromantic musical expression could emerge. The conventionalism at the heart of Cartesian musical expression enables an exploration of musical powers not heretofore prominent. It suggests that the designs and motions of music through a process of habituation might themselves come to signify eloquently, if not specifically, and even in the absence of words. In doing so the instrumentalism poses again, from a different vantage point, the question raised by Lullian recitative: from what manner of formal or structural analogy could purely musical imitation—and hence representation—arise?

One way of addressing this question was to moot the possibility of an ever more complete usurpation of vocal expression by instrumental music. This possibility would take determinate shape only as the expression of a post-Cartesian subjectivity, of the nineteenth-century, transcendental conceptions of both program music and absolute music. And these conceptions are seen, at this level of analysis, to be two versions of the same thing, two parallel avenues along which music approaches its romantic birthright of an affinity with the soul emancipated from the down-dragging bondage of words. Their difference amounts only to a question of how—that is, in what precise relation to verbal language and its specific concepts—transcendence is achieved.[31]

Example 4. From Scarlatti, *La Griselda*

ran - no, ti - ran - no,   ti - ran - no!   Che far pos - s'i - o?

Here she looks at her son,
then speaks angrily to Ottone

Ti - ran   -   no, ti - ran   -   no!

tutti con cembalo

So by the late eighteenth century the powers accorded to instrumental expression in opera could expand occasionally onto new terrain. The orchestra in this later opera sometimes gains expressive capabilities that move beyond those of voice. It comes to be able to know and represent even states of the soul opposed to those given in the voice. Its powers seem almost to grant it access, independent of voice, to the soul. Thus, in the most famous of instances, from Gluck's *Iphigénie en Tauride*, the syncopated figure played by the violas attests to an agitation that Orestes denies or cannot sense (see example 5).

Such new orchestral powers are one of the early intimations in opera of the advent of a new subjectivity, one whose soul can be divided at fundamental levels. They foreshadow the introjection into the soul of mysterious regions that had been conceived to lie outside it. It is not surprising that Gluck's passage, first singled out in reactions to the premiere of *Iphigénie*, would be cited long into the nineteenth century and celebrated by Madame de Staël, the fountainhead of so much romantic creed.[32]

Nevertheless, it is important to observe once more that these new opportunities for instrumental expression find their limit, in early modern opera, in the voice. The working of operatic voice in this period, its tapping of correspondences in the particular supersensible world implicated in Cartesian dualism, can be seconded, enhanced, and epitomized—but not utterly surpassed by the orchestra. Just as in French recitative, in Italian aria the fundamental connection between matter and mind is a voice that joins tone and word, a voice whose tones operate in a manner explicable only by some reference, even if minimal, to its words.

This insistent vocalism reverberates through the political climate that supported and was reflected in early modern opera. Recently Martha Feldman explored this broader resonance, for Italianate opera seria, from

Example 5. From Gluck, *Iphigénie en Tauride*

the perspective of ritual theory.[33] She sees in the archetypal plots of Metastasio's librettos, and exemplifies in an analysis of his *Artaserse*, a structure of early modern absolutism stable enough (and repeated often
enough) to attain the status of myth. In this myth the resolution of conflict
and the moral and social orders themselves are referred ever higher until
finally they reach the magnanimous ruler. But this king is, as Feldman reminds us, a divided figure, human in person but divine in office and power.
His power, too, is dualistic, divided between physical and metaphysical
realms. So the reference of societal order back to him in fact looks beyond
him to an invisible and mysterious divinity that underwrites his authority.

The repeated framing of this myth in the form of Metastasian music drama has the effect of emptying out the narrative content of the work—of casting the drama onto a metaphysical stage, so to speak. Opera seria "in its classic form asserts a social order that exists naturally, inevitably, and endlessly," Feldman writes. "Seria's characters . . . are abstract actors of a transcendental truth, divine messengers of absolutist metaphysics. . . . The claims of seria exceed the possibility of representation in the material world."[34] This situation recalls the French verisimilitude of the marvelous, analyzed by Kintzler. As in the French version where the singing voice found its appropriate place on the realistic (but unreal) pastoral stage, so in Italian opera the metaphysical dimension of dramatic representation—the mythic claim of divine authority—was linked to singing and operatic spectacle. It was associated especially with singing: in the climactic lyric moments at the end of each scene—that is, in the arias that all observers by now agreed were the center of gravity of Italianate operatic experience—the voice "worked to dissolve narrative into lyric magic, as recitative culminate[d] repeatedly in outbursts of unfathomable, mystically empowered song."[35]

The magical virtuosity that Feldman describes here is the métier of the representational voice. Its powers are magical not in the operative, participatory manner of Renaissance voice, and not through the assertion of a transcendental subjectivity that would come only later, but because they refer to a system of divine correspondences that underpins the dualistic subject and cannot, from its perspective, be perceived. This dualism is reflected in the dualism of absolute kingship that reached its apogee, in the West, in the age of Cartesian subjectivity. Absolutism was the political figuration of dualism (embodied in the figure of the king) and of the mystery of representation (the correspondence of physical and metaphysical in the king's power and authority). Even as the dualistic subject found its political reflection in absolutism, it found an embodiment of its representational perception in early modern voice. In a situation in which mythic plot structures absolved words of much of their narrative burden, vocal sonorousness stepped forward to affirm the general, invisible connection of phenomenal opera to the immaterial soul. The convergence of absolutism and voice in Metastasian opera, then, marks a doubly characteristic expression of Cartesian subjectivity.

. . . . .

Both the convergence and the subjectivity grow unstable in the operas of Mozart. We may recognize in this repertory, in a manner shrewdly sketched by Ivan Nagel, an ambivalence that divides it between two sorts of works: those that betray the exhaustion of absolutism (with its rituals of kingly clemency) as the ground for operatic vocalism—*Idomeneo* and *La clemenza di Tito*—and those that push beyond absolutism to foreshadow new possibilities for subjective autonomy—in different ways, *Figaro, Don Giovanni,* and *The Magic Flute*.[36] Nagel's approach has this strong argument in its favor: in describing Mozart's ability to envoice for the first time a subjectivity that is decisively close to us, it illuminates both the expressive sublimity we continue to find in Mozart's music and, more specifically, the steadfast suasion his operas continue to exert on modern sensibilities. Nagel's explanation reaches deeper, at any rate, than the more customary appeals to the technical details of Mozart's operatic craft: to displays of his musical wit, to his merger of sonata structures with dramatic pacing, to the novel character-types and situations he explored, and so forth.

In its most robust form the new voice Mozart presents comes to grips with a metaphysics that had been out of the reach of its predecessors. Its novelty consists in its attempt to bridge through willful, unmediated vocal assertiveness the abyss of representation. It offers a song whose forcefulness threatens to short-circuit the parallel wiring of early-modern body and soul. It clasps to itself the immaterial realm of Cartesian transcendence and forecasts the new relation to that realm of Kantian subjectivity.

The characters of opera buffa, throughout its long eighteenth-century genesis, do not fully reveal this new voice. Their bourgeois stance is one that gains, from John Gay's *Beggar's Opera* and Pergolesi's *La serva padrona* through Mozart's *Figaro,* much power to lampoon the myths and pretenses of seria aristocracies, whether by explicit reference or implicit contrast. In this they look back on their forebears, the singing comedians who had shared the stage with serious characters before late-seventeenth-century efforts to purge them. The subversive stance of buffa characters has considerable power also, in Nagel's terms, to transform the authoritarian mercy of seria into a humbler, more humane forgiveness among equals.[37]

These powers arise from a resistance to seria metaphysics. The characters of opera buffa attempt to articulate a steadfastly mundane vision, circulating and defining themselves in a purely material human interaction. It is true, they may not offer any resolution or basic reorientation of Cartesian dualism and its puzzles of representation. But their alternative to the subjectivity of opera seria, if not fundamental, is nevertheless noteworthy. Their portrayal of emotion seems not to pay homage to the discrete, internal, monadic passions of seria characters and arias, with its focusing of attention on the mysterious meeting of mind and body. Instead, buffa emotions turn outward to be defined in an intersubjective matrix of social relations. They melt down and meld Cartesian passions, juxtaposing once inert materials and mixing them in new, volatile compounds. Buffa portrayal, far more than seria, reflects the world of exteriorized, interactive emotion connoted in such characteristic eighteenth-century terms as sentiment, sensibility, and expression.[38]

Opera buffa does so especially by resisting the relations of voice and transcendence staged in the arias of opera seria. This resistance seems to be constitutive of opera buffa, and reveals itself in the avoidance of seria virtuosity—Feldman's unfathomable, mystical force—that characterized buffa singing from the first. But, again, such avoidance only puts aside, but does not force, the issue of Cartesian dualism.

Because a truly new voice would need to be founded, unlike the buffa voice, in a new relation to metaphysical realms, it is Don Giovanni who issues its manifesto. Giovanni proclaims his own selfhood with a violence that challenges, if it cannot quite overthrow, the power of any other force to transcend him. He has no truck with the clemency of kings, and he attempts to put off even their higher manifestations, avenging ghosts. He represents, as Slavoj Žižek has commented, elaborating Nagel, "the emergence of an autonomy so radical that it leaves no space open for mercy."[39] Giovanni's autonomy is such that it assumes, as Kierkegaard recognized in his essay on *Don Giovanni*, the form of a singular force or principle rather than of a variegated psyche. For this reason, only heaven itself is a match for him (were he less than this, Kierkegaard quips, it would be "ill-advised to use such strong measures").[40]

But heaven's intervention does not make of Mozart's opera a morality play, no matter the intent of earlier tellings of the Don Juan story, Mozart's halfhearted gestures in this direction, or the accounts of his opera that (from romantic celebrations of Giovanni to recent condemnations of him) have gauged its action against this backdrop. Don Giovanni's indomitability stands in essential opposition to the morality tale. His power seems never to be brought low, even as he descends in smoke and hellfire. (His last, characteristic response to the Commendatore: "No! No! No! No! No! No!" Had any operatic character before him ever sung such words?) Instead Mozart's opera affords a glimpse, unsettling at deep levels, of a human desire and willfulness that threatens because it claims to sidestep morality altogether. (The vision is, in hindsight, almost Nietzschean, and Nietzsche would ask, apropos of Don Juan in hell, "Has it been noticed that in heaven all interesting men are missing?")[41]

Don Giovanni presents the intuition of a subject radically different from the seria and buffa characters of early modern opera, and different even from the novel versions of them that populated the *dramma giocoso*, a mixed operatic genre forged in the 1750s, which Mozart and Da Ponte built upon in their opera.[42] Against these character types, Giovanni evokes a self that confronts with senses alone the transcendent realms of early modern representation and refuses, almost successfully, to be transcended. (Another unique operatic line is Giovanni's "Mi pare sentir odor di femmina." What other singer in the repertory celebrates female allure through sense of smell?) The grasp of the Commendatore is also Don Giovanni's countergrasp: a confident and firm grip that comes close to refuting metaphysics itself.

This prehensile approach to invisible realms is, in other words, the counterforce that the opera exerts to the moralizing heritage that pulls at its sleeve. It is the nexus of the drama, and it marks Giovanni as a character whose claim to absolute self-possession not only moves far from early modern operatic subjectivity but even obviates procedures that elsewhere might seem the glory of Mozart's mature operas. Forty years ago Joseph Kerman was not willing to grant Giovanni this power. In *Opera as Drama* he enumerated the procedural lapses of *Don Giovanni* in comparison to *Figaro* and *Così fan tutte*: especially, a thoughtless, improbable, even cynical organization of the plot and a vacuous main character. Kerman rejected Kierkegaard's judgment that the opera comprises a perfect merging of form and content, sensing in that view typically romantic "daydreams and idealizations" that attributed to Mozart an unwonted "demonic" nature. But Kerman's polemic seems to misconstrue Kierkegaard's assertion. He never called Mozart a demonic composer; he only described *Don Giovanni* as a work of classic perfection in a medium, music, that was in and of itself demonic. His gesture was not biographical, that is, but instead ontological and aesthetic (in the idiosyncratic way he employed that latter term).[43]

Kierkegaard's gesture parallels other nineteenth-century strategies for understanding music: Schopenhauer's (in conceiving the special power of music as an abstraction that grants it a unique access to cosmic forces and distances it from reflective consciousness and its ideas); at the same time, Nietzsche's (in his break with Schopenhauer, since for Kierkegaard the only idea sufficiently abstract to match music perfectly is an eroticism or "sensuous-erotic genius" akin to Nietzsche's anti-Schopenhauerian, anti-idealist, somatic will to power).[44] It is not whimsical to note that in his logic Kierkegaard also anticipates another later philosopher, Jacques Derrida. Kierkegaard defines music as demonic only by virtue of its special relation to the erotic sensuous genius, in turn defined by its exclusion from and opposition to Christianity. Music is thus "a Christian art, or rather . . . the art which Christianity posits in excluding it from itself, as being a medium for that which Christianity excludes from itself, and thereby posits." Or again: "Music is . . . the medium for that species of the immediate [i.e., sensuous immediacy] which, spiritually determined, is determined as lying outside of the spirit." With lingering traces of a Hegelian dialectic, the place of both music and the sensuous in relation to Christianity approaches the locale of Derrida's supplement.[45]

Kierkegaard does not, then, posit *Don Giovanni* as a perfect joining of form and content because of the matching of the structure of Da Ponte's libretto to Mozart's musico-dramatic technique or because of the careful portrayal of dramatic character and its move to self-knowledge. These are the forms of perfection Kerman seeks, but does not find, in the opera. Instead Kierkegaard finds the classical luster of *Don Giovanni* in its conjuncture of music with the *only subject matter that could be the absolute object of music*. He hears *Don Giovanni* as the perfect expression of the irruption of the sensuous nonrational in the modern subject.

We may well balk at the heady, sweeping generalizations behind this conception, and we certainly may find repugnant the mysogynist sentimentality that views only subtly different would lead Nicolaus Lenau or Richard Strauss to. But we should at the same time remember that Kierkegaard's analysis led him to judgments that have, ever since the general proliferation of his essay around the turn of the century, articulated the terms of our involvement with *Don Giovanni*. It led him to the central proposition, as I have noted, that Don Giovanni is not so much a dramatic character as a principle, a power, a force, a *passion*; to the assertion that he can be called a "seducer" only after an exacting qualification of that term that recognizes this passion in him and its absence from those we commonly call "seducers"; to the view that all the other characters in the opera, with the exception of the Commendatore (a crucial exception!), are hardly independent figures but little more than reflections of Don Giovanni's animating force; to the recognition of Leporello's erotic dependency upon Giovanni; to the specification, even, of Giovanni's preemptive-strike "champagne aria" ("Finch'han dal vino") as the lyrical epicenter of the opera.[46]

For Kierkegaard, *Don Giovanni* boiled down to the unassuageable confrontation of the protagonist, embodiment of sensuous immediacy, with the only other character who truly matters, the Commendatore, representing reflective consciousness.[47] These two realms define one another by exclusion; they are bound together (remember the clasped hands) in a supplementary relation in which neither can know the other, but, by the same token, neither can be defined without the other. (Because of this supplementary play, for Kierkegaard, the Commendatore had to remain a dark and indistinct character—read: musically inflexible and ponderous—to grant free rein to the sensuous musicality of Giovanni.) This opposition is not a preliminary move in a dialectic in which all will be ameliorated at a higher, synthetic level; Kierkegaard scorned such a Hegelian outcome. Instead it is more like an existential playing-out of the enduring Kantian opposition, at the heart of the modern subject and reflected through it in countless ways, of phenomenal and noumenal realms. In his own fashion Kierkegaard recognized in *Don*

Giovanni a parable of modern subjectivity. He certainly continues to point the way for us to find it there.

Of course parables are not the stuff of Kermanesque music drama. It is indubitable that Kierkegaard's approach to *Don Giovanni* deals out of the account long stretches of music and stage action, and so it will not satisfy fully if we share Kerman's worries—or those of other exegetes, from Abert and Dent to Heartz—about an integrated and developing drama. But these worries are, after all, in good part pronouncements of local, romantic and postromantic dramatic criteria. We might glimpse, alongside or behind them, the possibility of a parable being sung onstage to potent and deep effect. *Don Giovanni* is such a sung parable, perhaps the most potent we have.

And its singing is entirely to the point, for the parable comes into its own most of all in the unyielding, brute pitting of one voice against another. ("We must open our ears," Nagel says, "to the unprecedented vocal character" of Giovanni, "fusing mellifluence and brutality.")[48] The baritone-bass confrontation when the statue arrives is the sonorous heart of the opera, the sound that resonates long after it is over. Its reverberant force is prepared in many ways: by the plot itself, that is, by the loosely strung, paratactic sequence of events leading up to it (here again, the heritage of the morality play, with its rhythm of repeated misdeeds calling for repentance or punishment); by the lunar reflection—lunar in its captivating dimness—of Giovanni's power in the seria and buffa characters around him, most movingly in Elvira; by, famously, the anticipation of the statue's music in the overture.

But most of all the force of the confrontation is prepared by the feature of Giovanni's character—of his *voice*—that has often been seen as a limitation of the opera: its steadfast, unself-conscious, unknowing, and unknowable nature.

This is why Kierkegaard was right to name "Finch'han dal vino" the lyric center of the work. This piece of lightning-quick bravura may be all the things that commentators have called it in recent years: a "panicked rage pulsat[ing] under the zest of the words and the bravura of their declamation," "a crude expression of the phallic," "a feverish explosion of sheer sexual drive," a menacing display of "unmotivated anger . . . associated with, about, at, or in sex."[49] But whatever else, it is also the clearest and most demonstrative of a number of points in the opera when Giovanni summons the vocal force that reveals his frightful power and that he will rely upon in his encounter with the Commendatore.[50] (Other kindred but lesser vocal gestures occur throughout Giovanni's role: in his frequent violent rejoinders to Leporello in their recitative exchanges; in his leading of the acclamation "Viva la libertà" in the act 1 finale; in the trio "Ah, taci, ingiusto core," when he forces the tonality from E major to

C, so as to try out on Elvira the serenade he has prepared for her maid; in the cemetery scene, accompanied by the same sideslip from E to C in the orchestra, when Giovanni himself finally addresses the statue; and at the beginning of the act 2 finale, "Già la mensa è preparata.") "Finch'han dal vino" is the moment when Don Giovanni musters a voice that can try to grasp, or at least grapple with, metaphysics. It was, in its several variations, a voice opera would endeavor to stage all through the modern era.

EXCURSUS 2

THE BORDERS OF THEATRICAL SPACE

From the heyday of Renaissance *intermedi* to the high point of Metastasian opera seria—roughly the late sixteenth to the early eighteenth century—the history of musico-dramatic staging reveals a gradual, uneven,
but finally inexorable circumscribing of theatrical space. This setting of
ever clearer boundaries reflects in several ways the emergence of early
modern subjectivity and its novel relation to metaphysical regions.

The stage of the late Renaissance was most often a mobile, provisional,
and impermanent *luogo teatrale*, a place for specific presentations created
in princely gardens, chambers, or larger halls, or indeed on the streets and
plazas of the city itself. In these provisional spaces scenographers and
engineers lavished the prince's funds on ingenious perspectival sets, novel
mechanisms for instantaneous scene changes, and machines for all manner of spectacular effects. Already in this period, however, a tendency
grew toward greater stability and fixity of theatrical space, a trend most
famously preserved in Palladio's harbinger of permanent theaters-to-
come, the Teatro Olimpico at Vicenza (1580–85). Through the seventeenth century the two conceptions—of occasional theatrical space and
permanent theater—would coexist, with the latter finally coming to dominate, especially through the proliferation of public opera houses.

Jacques Callot's engraving after Giulio Parigi of a Florentine *intermedio* of 1617 renders a Medici theater-hall, apparently more or less permanent, within the Uffizi. (Callot's perspective much exaggerates the size of
the chamber, perhaps in the interest of asserting Florentine ducal gran-
deur.) The room had first been used for theater in the 1580s, just after the
completion of the Uffizi, and was the site of the spectacular *intermedi* of
1589 (see excursus 1). Callot's engraving could almost be a self-conscious
depiction of subjective involvement, through theater, in a continuous Renaissance cosmos. The spectators are drawn by the dancers in the orchestra area up the ramps, onto the stage, and thence into the celestial orders
perched at back on clouds. The liminal space between audience and performers seems unfixed and permeable, as does the distance between mundane dancers onstage and heavenly hosts behind them, traversed easily by
the gods and goddesses hovering on marvelous machines. Altogether, the
view suggests an unbroken connection extending from the audience
through the ontological levels portrayed onstage.

The second engraving represents one of Giacomo Torelli's sets for
Venere gelosa, performed in Venice in 1643, early in the years of perma-

Figure 4: The Medici theater in the Uffizi. Engraving by Jacques Callot after Giulio Parigi, 1617. Reprinted from Howard Daniel, ed., *Callot's Etchings* (New York: Dover Publications, 1974), p. 6.

Figure 5: Giacomo Torelli: Stage set for *Venere gelosa*, Venice, 1643.
Credit: Biblioteca Nazionale Marciana, Venice.

nent opera houses. In respect to Callot's engraving, it suggests a somewhat altered relation between stage and hall. The massive proscenium
may or may not correspond to some related structure in the theater itself,
but in any case it marks off the audience from the illusionary world onstage in a manner that soon would become the rule. The permeable space
of the late Renaissance between spectators and performers gives way to a
modern "fourth wall" separating them, transparent for the spectators but
impenetrable. Within Torelli's stage world, however, a portrayal of contiguity persists between heaven and earth, reminiscent of the late Renaissance. It is maintained by means descended from the *intermedio* tradition:
the god-bearing stage machines, for which Torelli was famous in Italy
and France alike. The continuous chain from audience to celestial regions
is broken, perhaps, but the "natural magic" of the machines (as one con-

Figure 6: Ferdinando Galli Bibiena: A stage set for a hall. Reprinted from
James Scholz, ed., *Baroque and Romantic Stage Design* (New York:
Dutton, 1964), 01. 24.

temporary described it) asserts continuity at least *within* the staged world.

In Torelli's nonbucolic scenes, and in those of his late seventeenth-century followers, a predilection for monumental architectural presence begins to manifest itself. This taste culminates in the stage designs of opera seria and, more specifically, in those of the Bibiena family, active in operatic centers across Europe (excluding France) through much of the eighteenth century. The sets of Ferdinando and Francesco Galli Bibiena, the founders of the clan who rose to prominence in the years around 1700, take for granted the separation of hall and stage, now standard. But they move a large step beyond Torelli in severing physical and metaphysical worlds. In them there seems to be no possibility of the enactment of direct, palpable contact with the heavens. (Indeed stage machines, the primary mechanisms for portraying such contact in the past, have themselves fallen out of favor, the victims of a taste for verisimilitude that Metastasio would later express when he protested, "Our opera and our reason are not incompatible things.") The immense, looming architectural vistas of the Bibienas cut off not only the audience from the actors onstage but the actors from the heavens above. Or, more precisely, they signal in their fantastic proportions the presence of a beyond that their materiality does not allow them to present but only to re-present. They are avatars of a metaphysics that cannot touch the material world but can only be configured in it by enigmatic correspondence. In this the Bibienas' architecture adumbrates metaphysics in the same way as does the vocal virtuosity displayed in front of it. The scenographic assertion of the early modern, dualistic subject is complete.

IV

MODERN OPERA

THE OPERATIC VOICE had always been powerful, but before the early nineteenth century it was not uncanny. Since that time, on the other hand, its uncanniness has seemed inescapable. This historical distinction is not usually noted in our narratives of opera history. Instead, handed the results of twentieth-century musicological efforts at exhumation and revival of premodern operas, we tend to apply the fascinations with voice peculiar to modern culture to the entire four-hundred-year history of the genre. This extension has encouraged a historical and performative uniformity that imputes to the operatic voice a force little changed throughout its history. And if, for reasons that will emerge soon, a defining trait of the modern operatic voice is its uncanniness, then we have tended to infer this trait to premodern voices as well.

But this universalism is unwarranted, as the analysis in chapters 2 and 3 of differences between late Renaissance and early modern opera has already suggested. Freud may be right to link the experience of uncanniness to an "animism" living on in the modern psyche, if we understand his animism to mean a belief in the existence of supersensible realms and of our interaction, in some manner, with them.[1] The very linkage, however, grounds uncanniness in the conditions and nature of the modern psyche, against which background it functions as a kind of unsettling nostalgia. We have no reason to presume that uncanniness extends any farther, across time or space, than this modern foundation.

Neither can we any longer see animism, in Freud's Frazerian fashion, as a huge, little-differentiated wellspring of prescientific thought. Instead cultures create their own, distinctive animisms. The coalescing of Ficinian and Cartesian subjectivities, with their particular consolidations of the relations between subject and supersensible world, may be seen as two (broadly conceived) moments of such creation in the West. The late eighteenth century marked a third, when supersensible realms and human access to them were reshaped once more. There emerged in the decades around 1800 a new subject, one that could, as a consequence of its other novel capacities, recognize for the first time an experience we have come to call the *uncanny*.

Kantian knowledge describes this new subjectivity as clearly as any other discourse of the time. For Kant, knowing is a combinatory process. It inevitably involves a joining of sensible intuition and understanding: "Without sensibility no object would be given to us, without understanding no object would be thought. Thoughts without content are empty, intuitions without concepts are blind. . . . The understanding can intuit nothing, the senses can think nothing. Only through their union can knowledge arise."[2] Because of this nature, knowledge stands in a different relation to the world than it had in earlier rationalist or sceptical models. It will henceforth be a product of the perspective of the consciousness that attains it. The faculties of knowledge will in basic ways determine the natures of things known. This is the "Copernican revolution" that Kant proclaimed in the preface to *The Critique of Pure Reason*:

> Hitherto it has been assumed that all our knowledge must conform to objects. But all attempts to extend our knowledge of objects by establishing something in regard to them *a priori*, by means of concepts, have, on this assumption, ended in failure. We must therefore make trial whether we may not have more success in the tasks of metaphysics, if we suppose that objects must conform to our knowledge. (*Critique*, p. 22.)

Kant's analysis of the components of this combinatory, perspectival model isolates *a priori* conditions within the subject that enable both intuition and understanding: for intuition, the forms of space and time; for understanding, the famous categories of relations among objects—substance, causality, unity, plurality, limitation, necessity, and the rest. The discernment of these *a priori* elements brings to the Kantian subject new powers, new limitations, and new temptations. The presence in understanding of innate conditions, prior to experience, that enable knowing marks the soul's transcendental status relative to the world of nature. It allows—what Cartesian meditation could not—a critical distance from which the mind can analyze its own processes of representation. In scrutinizing the innate backdrop of knowledge, Kant's critical science seeks not empirical but *transcendental* conditions; it is "occupied not so much with objects as with the mode of our knowledge of objects in so far as this mode of knowledge is to be possible *a priori*." (*Critique*, p. 59) Only through this recognition of transcendentalism can Kant's Copernican reversal be effected. If the soul contains no *a priori* knowledge, it will have no means of shaping external objects according to itself; instead the more passive models of understanding associated with rationalism or empiricism, models in which our knowledge conforms to nature, will reemerge.

In submitting to the transcendental *a priori* aspects of the soul, things do not come into knowledge innocently represented as they are in themselves. Instead they arrive as appearances always already under the aegis of space, time, and the categories. Kant reserved the term *phaenomena* for these appearances, "so far as they are thought as objects according to the unity of the categories." (p. 265) We have no access to things in themselves. Such access would be at root inimical to Kantian subjectivity, once again forcing our knowledge to conform to things in their actuality. The attempt to explain the nature of a putative access of this sort is now judged to be a chimerical goal of rationalism and empiricism. In the transcendental subject, time, space, and the categories instead plot out, in the form of phenomena, the conformity of appearances to our knowledge. Time and space "apply to objects only in so far as objects are viewed as appearances, and do not present things as they are in themselves." (p. 80) Similarly, the objects to which the categories are applied "are only appearances, for it is solely of appearances that we can have *a priori* intuition." (p. 164)

In this unbreakable linkage to phenomena, *a priori* knowledge also sets the limits of its own operation:

> Space and time, as conditions under which alone objects can possibly be given to us, are valid no further than for objects of the senses, and therefore only for experience. Beyond these limits they represent nothing. . . . The pure concepts of understanding [i.e., the categories] . . . are mere forms of thought, without objective reality. . . . Only *our* sensible and empirical intuition can give them body and meaning. (*Critique*, p. 163)

Kant's examination of the *a priori* conditions of knowledge—of its transcendentalism—must thus always circle back to the objective limits within which these conditions are realized. It sets the boundary of our knowledge at the far edge of the comprehended appearance, the phenomenon. Kant's transcendentalism should not be thought to invest the subject with rational powers outstripping those of the Cartesian mind. Rather the reverse: the critical philosophy and its transcendental analytic pose sheer limits beyond which human understanding cannot properly range. In relation to the Cartesian subject, the transcendentalism of the new subjectivity takes the form of a narrowing and a specification of the purview of knowledge. The *a priori* conditions, the very mark of this transcendentalism, are bodied forth only in relation to perceived objects.

Haunting this transcendental subject, however, is an insistent impulse to extend understanding beyond appearances. This is a force of fundamental importance in determining the outlines of the modern subject and its knowledge. (The analysis of its grounds, Kant's "Transcendental Dialectic," might be said to comprise his *apologia* for the nonobjective knowledges of rationalism.) Notwithstanding the warnings of critique, we fall prey to a *"transcendental illusion"* that "carries us altogether beyond the empirical employment of categories and puts us off with a merely deceptive extension of *pure understanding*." (*Critique*, p. 298) This illusion is more than a case of faulty judgment or muddled logic. It "does not cease, even after it has been detected and its invalidity clearly revealed by transcendental criticism." (p. 299) Instead we are deceived by the very structure of reason, a faculty of knowledge separate from understanding, endowed with its own *a priori* conditions. In accepting a premise of syllogistic inference as the condition of a logical conclusion, we set ourselves on an inevitable, regressive course: for each premise of a syllogism, reason seeks the condition that in turn makes it true and so spirals backward toward the asymptote of an utterly *unconditioned* premise. The seeking of this unconditioned knowledge is "the principle peculiar to reason . . . in its logical employment." (p. 306) Thus the "*unconditioned*, which reason, by necessity and by right, demands in things in themselves, as required to complete a series of conditions, . . . necessarily forces us to transcend the limits of experience and of all appearances." (p. 24)

What awaits us beyond those limits is Kant's *noumenon*. This counterpart to the phenomenon is "a thing which is not to be thought of as object of the senses but as a thing in itself, solely through a pure understanding." (p. 271) Of it we can have, by definition, no objective knowledge, and it would seem to have no positive existence but only arise as an inconceivable "intelligible object." (p. 272) Less ambiguously, the noumenon operates negatively, as a limit beyond which sensibility, and with it objective knowledge, cannot proceed. It is, in Kant's terminology, "problematic": a conception that is neither objectively real nor a mere logical fallacy, but instead "connected with other modes of knowledge that involve given concepts which it serves to limit." (p. 271) But its status remains mysterious, encouraging a venturing of our thought into realms beyond its proper positivity and objectivity:

> What our understanding acquires through this concept of a noumenon, is a sort of negative extension; that is to say, understanding is not limited through sensibility; on the contrary, it itself limits sensibility by applying the term noumena to things in themselves (things not regarded as appearances). But in doing so it at the same time sets limits to itself, recognizing that it cannot know these noumena through any of the categories, and that it must therefore think them only under the title of an unknown something. (*Critique*, p. 273)

Or again: "The problematic thought which leaves open a place for [intelligible objects] serves only, like an empty space, for the limitation of empirical principles, without itself containing or revealing any other object of knowledge beyond the sphere of those principles." (p. 275)

· · · · ·

Since the early nineteenth century, the noumenon has been an issue of pervasive dispersion, notorious interpretive difficulty, and extraordinary interpretive licence. We see reflected in the difficulty an essential ineffability invested in the Kantian subject. In the licence we witness a growing tendency within Western culture to assimilate all forms of invisibility, all gestures toward metaphysics, to the noumenal limit Kant described. And in the dispersion we see the intellectual tip of a submerged cultural formation that comprises, in its totality, the modern subject. This new subject incorporates, more fully than earlier models, the framework of its knowledge. The fundamental conditions of knowing no longer lie beyond the mind's borders, as they had in the divine harmonies governing Cartesian thought. Instead they make up the innate, internal equipment necessary for individual consciousness and knowledge in the first place. The accord governing knowledge is now a harmony of faculties within the subject. The system of representation involved in knowing is folded wholly into the soul, and this soul is no longer *transcended* but is in itself *transcendental*.

All this does not resolve the mysteries posed by Cartesian subjectivity. Instead it transfers them to a new locus and transforms them. The correspondences that govern knowledge might do so now from within the subject, but the origin of these correspondences remains mysterious. Kant "rejected the idea of a pre-established harmony between subject and object, substituting the principle of a necessary submission of the object to the subject itself," Deleuze has written. "But does he not once again come up with the idea of harmony, simply transposed to the level of faculties of the subject which differ in nature?"[3] Kant himself was certainly aware of the persisting mystery of correspondence. In writing of the mediation involved in the joining of *a priori* categories with sensibility, for instance, he invoked certain schemata active in the imagination, but he conceded that this schematism "is an art concealed in the depths of the human soul, whose real modes of activity nature is hardly likely ever to allow us to discover, and to have open to our gaze." (*Critique*, p.183) The evolution of the Western subject from the Renaissance on moves from a harmony of the world in which it finds a pellucid place, to a transcendental harmony that guides but excludes it, to a harmony of the objects of knowledge with the very means the subject brings to its knowing of them.

Above all, then, both the familiar features and the mysteries of the Kantian subject are determined by this unknowable aspect of knowledge, the noumenon toward which the mind is impelled by its own motions. For this reason the advent of the noumenon signals the fixing of a modern relation between the subject and the supersensible. Unperceived realms—which in the Renaissance had taken the measure of human participation in the world and in the early modern era had posed the abyss between mind and body as an enigma of representation—now have been introjected into the forms of subjective knowledge. The division of perceived and unperceived realms, which had once structured a cosmos that could be mirrored in the human microcosm, is now encompassed within understanding itself. The Renaissance supersensible was a region hidden from perception but accessible through spirit; the early modern supersensible moved, in its transcendent harmony, to a place utterly beyond (but fundamental to) human conception. Now the supersensible is adumbrated as the nonappearances and nonobjects that limit and tempt our knowledge. The noumenon becomes the modern cipher of the supersensible world.

The transcendentalism of the new subjectivity, then, assumes the dual form of, first, a setting of boundaries, within which positive knowledge is found and beyond which mysteries lie, and, second, the powerful impulsion to breach those boundaries so as to know the unknowable. Indeed, knowing the unknowable, experiencing the noumenon that was for Kant beyond experience, will gradually in his wake take the form of an urge played out across a whole range of modern cultural discourses, from philosophy to the arts.

This non-Cartesian dualism is what Foucault had in mind when he labeled the modern subject a "strange empirico-transcendental doublet."[4] The subject is now determined by the ambivalence of the liminal noumenon, at once the *terminus ante quem* of understanding and an impossible, yet sought-after, transcendental objectivity, the experience of the *Ding an sich*. The positive nature of Kantian knowledge denies us access to metaphysics, in what Foucault calls its "analytic of finitude." But this finitude—the limit of knowledge at the margin of the phenomenon—"is outlined in the paradoxical form of the endless; rather than the rigour of a limitation, it indicates the monotony of a journey which, though it probably has no end, is nevertheless perhaps not without hope."[5] It is a journey, indeed, that knowledge always and necessarily undertakes.

The modern *cogito* takes shape not against a background of doubt and within a matrix of divine harmony, as it had for Descartes, but in a motion of thought that impels it beyond positivity toward an "unthought." This new *cogito* "will not therefore be the sudden and illuminating discovery that all thought is thought," as it had been for Descartes and those who followed, "but the constantly renewed interrogation as to how thought can reside elsewhere than here, and yet so very close to itself; how it can *be* in the forms of non-thinking." This unthought, Foucault asserts, has followed us, "mutely and uninterruptedly," since the nineteenth century.[6]

Because of its fundamental nature, rooted at the heart of the transcendental subject, glimpses of noumenalism will gradually come to form a guiding trope of Western culture. By the twentieth century the psychic mechanism operating in such glimpses is far more widely dispersed than any specific reference to the noumenon itself, spreading like some underground root system beneath sprouting psychological mysteries. Thus Proust's narrator, at the famous moment of madeleine-induced awakening of memory, can describe his inchoate sensations as an inward-turning, noumenal quest: "What an abyss of uncertainty, whenever the mind feels overtaken by itself; when it, the seeker, is at the same time the dark region through which it must go seeking and where all its equipment will avail it nothing." Or, in a religious mode, C.S. Lewis can place heaven itself, "the secret we cannot hide and cannot tell," at the pivot-point of noumenal and phenomenal interchange: "We cannot tell it because it is a desire for something that has never actually appeared in our experience. . . . We cannot hide it because our experience is constantly suggesting it."

For an earlier period Foucault provided a suggestive analysis of the dispersion of this noumenal mechanism through selected areas of knowledge. In his view major shifts in the taxonomy of natural things, the analysis of wealth, and the study of language occurring about 1800 marked the advent of the modern era. All these shifts reflect the Kantian revolution in epistemology in that they represent this quintessentially modern feature of the subject: its capacity to analyze the transcendental conditions of its own knowledge while inevitably attempting to carry knowledge beyond its proper limits toward metaphysics. Foucault writes:

> Where there had formerly been a correlation between a *metaphysics* of representation and of the infinite and an *analysis* of living beings, of man's desires, and of the words of his language, we find being constituted an *analytic* of finitude and human existence, and in opposition to it (though in correlative opposition) a perpetual tendency to constitute a *metaphysics* of life, labor, and language. But these are never anything more than tendencies, immediately opposed and as it were undermined from within.[7]

The new approaches to natural history, economic studies, and language analysis at the end of the eighteenth century each delimit the observable purview of their disciplines by making visible previously unseen relations within them; at the same time, these newly observed relations constitute transcendental patterns, beyond the objects of study, luring us toward metaphysics.[8]

So in the analysis of wealth, the study of the representations of need and desire that in the eighteenth century set the rate of exchange between one commodity and another is diverted toward study of a more basic and uniform element that determines commodities while remaining radically distinct from them: labor. Exchange is no longer a circulation of "objects of need representing one another" but one of "time and toil, transformed, concealed, forgotten" as noumenal forces behind commodities.[9]

In natural history, meanwhile, classification shifts its sights from the ordering and arranging of visible structures to the analysis of underlying relations that constitute an organic whole and allow it to function. Visible forms are henceforth seen as revelatory of this deeper organicism. "To classify, therefore, will no longer mean to refer the visible back to itself . . . ; it will mean . . . to relate the visible to the invisible, to its deeper cause, as it were, then to rise upwards once more from that hidden architecture towards the more obvious signs displayed on the surfaces of bodies."[10]

In the comparison of languages, finally, attention moves away from the collecting of cognate roots, equivalent in what they represent, that point backwards to a single, original tongue from which modern languages are descended. Instead languages come to be characterized by the systems of inflection through which they alter their roots. A new formal, grammatical analysis emerges that is not reducible to the representative values of words; a phonetics appears that "is no longer an investigation of primary expressive values" that echo the representations of primal cries, but instead is an examination of sounds and their relations and transformations. These grammatical and phonetic systems grant to languages individual histories that reveal their relatedness without tying languages to a single representative origin. (The great period of investigation into the origins of language, the eighteenth century, which had sought these origins in a uniform tonal expression of passions, gives way to a time when the Linguistic Society of Paris will ban any speculation on that topic.)[11]

In each of these cases, the newly discerned, previously invisible relations within an area of thought—labor, organic structure, systems of inflection—are not themselves the forms of knowledge of their respective disciplines. Instead they stand behind and beyond the kinds of knowledge they determine, invisibly ordering them and defining their limits. In their position relative to knowledge they reproduce, within specific areas of thought, the structure of Kant's transcendentalism. They are, so to speak, specific disciplinary noumena.

This disciplinary transcendentalism makes possible an analysis of representation—now the mind's representation of objects to itself in the form of phenomena—that had not been feasible in the Cartesian period. Then representation had revealed an ineffable order above and beyond the soul; now it would broach the soul's own mysteries to itself. Also, disciplinary transcendentalism solidifies in specific areas a characteristic gesture of modern Western thought: the noumenal analysis of its own conditions of possibility. Through the nineteenth century the intellectual choices, in the wake of Kantian transcendentalism, most often moved in one of two directions. On the one hand, they responded to the range of Kant's critique by exploring the impossible objectification of the noumenon in one or another new, postcritical metaphysics (as did Hegel with his phenomenology of *Geist* and Schopenhauer, in a different way, with his noumenal will); on the other hand, they questioned the usefulness of metaphysics and limited investigation strictly to the phenomenal world (the positivist position). In the form of either an objectification of metaphysics—a materialization of the invisible, as it were—or a limitation of knowledge, the noumenon had its due.[12]

The noumenal analysis of representation could only, however, move as far as the Kantian limits of knowledge. The noumenon itself could not be objectified except as a kind of quickly fading after-image of analyzed phenomena. For this reason noumenal analyses needed to fall back, at a certain liminal point, on the indication of a mystery or a mysticism at their heart.

So it is, for example, with Marx's analysis of the capitalist commodity. The exchange-value that is fundamental in defining this commodity relates to use-value as form to substance. But it is a mysterious kind of form. Because it arises only in the circulation of commodities, as a fact of their social movement, exchange-value is expressed only in the equivalence struck up between the commodity it defines and the use-value of another commodity equivalent in exchange. That is, the formal value of one commodity is manifested only in the substantial value of another. In a relation that mirrors the relation of noumenon and phenomenon, "use-value becomes the form of manifestation, the phenomenal form of its opposite," exchange-value, while exchange-value itself remains elusive.[13]

Moreover, as Marx's analysis continues, exchange-value itself takes on a phenomenal relation to even deeper noumenal forces within the commodity: the forces of labor. The social reality of labor is disguised and hidden in exchange-value: the fact of a commodity's value in exchange expresses the abstract equality of human labor; the quantity of its value in exchange represents the duration of labor necessary to produce it; and its exchange with other commodities reproduces the social relations of laborers. In these ways the relation among laborers takes on "the phantasmagoric form of a relation between things." The commodity becomes a fetish, but one of a unique sort: an object endowed, not in itself but in its potential for exchange, with mysterious noumenal forces.[14]

Other characteristic themes of modern thought waver similarly between the attempt to materialize the noumenon and the admission of supersensible mysteries. Romantic and postromantic ideologies of poetry as image or symbol communicating "to the sense some truth from the intelligible world" provide an obvious case in point. The broaching of something beyond full verbal expression that these views discover in poetry converts noumenal mysticism into the mark of privilege of poem and poet alike.[15] The doctrines of organic form in the arts that are bound up with such notions of poetry offer another instance, one particularly familiar to music historians, since outgrowths of organicism led to a formalism that could celebrate the nonsemantic nature of instrumental music and, along the way, offer a new approach to musical exegesis and analysis.[16] Indeed, the antisemanticism of instrumental music is precisely the feature that allows it to prefigure the noumenon, as Nietzsche and others would maintain. This suggests that the analysis of music emerges in the nineteenth century as a manifestation of the post-Kantian urge to objectify the noumenon. The conundrums of such analysis express the predicament of a transcendentalism striving to be a positivism, a postcritical metaphysics striving to deny metaphysics, a noumenon seeking an impossible but full objectification.

One of the most influential figurations of the noumenon in modern thought—perhaps *the* most influential, alongside Marx's commodity form—is Freud's unconscious.[17] Here, as in Marx's analysis, noumenal notions resolve themselves in the invocation of a superseded animism that returns to haunt the subject. But now, instead of sponsoring an economic order (capitalism), resurgent animism takes the form of a psychic state: the experience of the uncanny. Viewed from the broader perspective of a modern subject defined by its transcendentalism, uncanniness might be defined as the peculiar sensation aroused by confronting the noumenon.

The two causes of this sensation that Freud discerns both face, in the manner of other noumenal analyses, fundamental mysteries. The first cause is animism per se. In an ontogeny that recapitulates a cultural phylogeny—Freud does not elaborate how this happens—the individual psyche in its early development retraces the path of civilization through a putative "animistic stage." The individual grows beyond and "surmounts" this animism, but it leaves traces within the psyche capable of being tapped by everyday experience: "Everything which now strikes us as 'uncanny' fulfils the condition of touching . . . residues of animistic mental activity within us and bringing them to expression."[18] The first source of uncanny sensations, then, amounts to the shadowy resurgence of a whole "primitive" worldview.

The second source is, instead, the return of specific thoughts repressed in the form of infantile complexes: the Oedipal complex and so forth.[19] But in the Freudian development of the psyche such repression—in the most general terms, of the "pleasure principle" in favor of the "reality principle"—formed the unconscious mind in the first place. And, moreover, the emergence of repressed thoughts must be seen as the primary action of this unconscious in later life. In other words, Freud's second cause of the experience of uncanniness stems from the individual history of repression that divided the psyche into conscious and unconscious minds in the first place, and it manifests the characteristic workings of the unconscious.

Now, given the proximate location in the early development of the psyche of both the animistic stage (the first cause of uncanniness) and the formation of the unconscious (the second cause), it is not surprising that the two causes cannot be reliably distinguished. Thus while Freud tries to separate conceptually a "surmounted" animistic worldview from the "repressed" thoughts of the individual, he quickly admits their close kinship: "When we consider that primitive beliefs are most intimately connected with infantile complexes, and are, in fact, based on them, we shall not be greatly astonished to find that the distinction is often a hazy one."[20] It is almost as if the whole analysis of uncanniness tends toward the broaching of the identity of the unconscious in the form of a resurgent animism. But this is, we might say, only what the post-Kantian subject should expect when it moves to objectify the noumenon. Freud's explanation of uncanniness is a prime instance of a noumenal analysis that must eventually confront a mystery at its heart.

Because it is a product of transcendentalism and the noumenon that arises with it, the uncanny may rightly be said to be an experience peculiar to the modern subject. An analysis of the passions of the soul since Kant—were such a neo-Cartesian project feasible—might even find uncanniness to be the single most characteristic state of the modern subject, something analogous to the baseline passion of wonder that Descartes had discovered in his own analysis. Perhaps, indeed, we might indulge further this schematism, aligning it with the general evolution of subjectivity in the West. Thus the participatory subject of the Renaissance might be characterized by an experience of familiarity, boundedness, and community; the transcended subject of the early modern era by wonder; and the modern subject by the experience of uncanniness—an experience folding into itself both familiarity and wonderment. And we might correlate this progression with the effects on the Western psyche of its "discovery" of other cultures, languages, and worldviews, a movement at once toward estrangement and wonderment and toward assimilation, domestication, and familiarizing domination.

Whatever the value of such speculation, it seems clear that the condition of modern Western subjectivity involves, at root, a dualism of appearances and things in themselves that fixes a familiar but unknowable supersensible noumenon as the inevitable aspiration of knowledge. A characteristic experience of this dualism is the sensation of the uncanny.

· · · · ·

Early in the modern period, this new kind of dualism and its features came to pervade the operatic voice. Unlike the voice of the Cartesian subject, which in its representation pointed beyond itself to a transhuman harmony, the modern voice is altogether human. Its revelation of mystery points not out but inward, toward the center of human knowledge that now encompasses its own supersensible realm. This voice consists, like the modern subject it describes, in a doubling over on itself of empirical and transcendental fields. It is a place where the phenomenal world extends itself to a noumenal margin, so it holds out the hope of embodying before our ears, finally, a transcendental object. Its most congenial space of operation is at the borders marking off phenomena from noumena, conditioned from unconditioned thought. Its operations in this space summon a sense of the uncanny.[21]

In this, the operatic voice is only a synecdoche for the voices of modern music in all. The conception of music that took shape from the mid-eighteenth century on, that marked its high water in the Wagnerian age, and that we still live with in modified form today evolved together with the emergence of Kantian subjectivity. The puzzles of musical representation, once understood as a matter of mimesis or, more deeply, of the outcome of variously interpreted correspondences between musical and psychic motions, came to be seen in a new light. Music was heard now not as representing a semantics of the soul, which might be reduced to and described in words, but instead as adumbrating a non- or supersemantic realm beyond the reach of words. This view builds on—and outlines post-Kantian inversions of—two related developments mentioned earlier: the separation of sonorous vocality from verbal meaning (evident in Lullian recitative and early modern aria and in theories of the origins of language such as Rousseau's) and the emergence of representational powers of instrumental music after the Renaissance.

But whatever its prehistory, the new, supersemantic musical object would, by the period of Wagner, take on the featureless face of the noumenon. When Nietzsche wrote, before his break with Wagner, that "Language can never adequately render the cosmic symbolism of music, because music . . . symbolizes a sphere which is beyond and prior to all phenomena," his terminology was Kantian and his allusion, to the noumenon.[22] Music, as it came to be understood early on in the era of the Kantian subject, marked out a transcendental place and seemed to provide a language to go there. This seemed true of vocal music, which could overcome the specificity of the words joined to it, departing from them toward transcendental realms; of programmatic music, which likewise was heard to transport the listener beyond mundane, descriptive particulars to a general and ideal configuration of its themes and topoi; and of absolute music, whose advocates repeatedly rescued the forceful, affective play of its pure forms from the doubts Kant and others from the eighteenth century on had mooted concerning them.[23]

In opera studies, the history of this noumenalism has not yet been fully described. The explanation for this lacuna probably reaches beyond innocent scholarly inattention to suggest that we work within a powerfully naturalized ideology of music's transcendental autonomy. It suggests, in other words, that a noumenal reach has come to seem so pervasive a feature of music, so familiar a capability of musical voices, that we tend to characterize with it musical experience all told. If we have indeed naturalized musical noumenalism in this way, we could not have helped in the process but render it almost transparent, invisible to our scrutiny and analysis.[24]

If the noumenalism of the modern operatic voice has not been much analyzed, it has in recent years at least been adumbrated from two perspectives in particular: from the vantage point of narrative theory, in the work of Carolyn Abbate, and from the post-Freudian matrix of Lacanian psychoanalysis, in the works especially of Guy Rosolato and Michel Poizat.[25]

Lacanian approaches scrutinize the response of modern audiences to the operatic voice. They attempt to analyze, in a manner directly descended from Freudian thought, the sensations opera arouses in us. They rely on a hypothesis of a deep-seated, ontogenic division of the psyche, a division rooted in Freud's duality of conscious and unconscious. These Lacanian accounts take their place, as Freudian psychology had taken its place, in modern attempts to theorize the emergence in the psyche of the Kantian dualism of phenomenal and noumenal knowledge. But in contrast to Freud, they reserve for voice a central role in the psychological development of the individual. They locate the functions of voice at the heart of the forces that divide the self in the first place; hence they can offer a hypothesis as to the extraordinary and dividing effect the operatic voice can exert. Their key element, the Lacanian "cry," is another figuration of Kant's noumenon.

This cry (as described, for example, by Poizat) is a pure, non-signifying form of sonorous materiality that marks for the infant a mythical moment in its psychic history when it was not yet distinct from its mother. The inevitable separation from the mother, the distinguishing of mother as other, takes the form of a move away from this non-signifying sonorousness toward meaningful utterance. It takes the form, in other words, of a movement toward language, a movement set in motion already in the first maternal responses to an infant's cry, which assign to it a specific significance ("The baby is hungry," and so forth). But this language is shot through with difference—the Saussurean difference of one signifier from another that allows meaning in the first place—and is marked by the desire for the absent objects it calls for. The signifying voice, then, embodies this difference and absence in the form of desire. Its displacing of the primal, non-signifying cry represents an inexorable slide away from a longed-for wholeness. The materiality of that mythical cry comes to form

an unattainable but always desired vocal object, hidden somewhere behind and beyond the signifying voice. For writers like Poizat and Rosolato, it is this lost object that operatic song occasionally manifests in ecstatic moments of vocal *jouissance*. At such rare moments opera evokes
the primal cry.

It is not difficult to discern the noumenal nature of this vocal object.
Just as the noumenon transcends objective understanding, and so poses a
limit to it, the cry stands beyond linguistic meaningfulness and forms its
far boundary. The cry is a transcendental object in that it adumbrates
conditions for voice that, in their inaccessibility and primal status within
the development of the psyche, take on a character somewhat like Kant's
a priori. And, like the subject in the phenomenal world, pushed toward
noumenalism, the Lacanian psyche within earshot of voice is impelled by
an internal imperative to move beyond the voice's phenomenal presence
toward the cry. The lost, pure phonic materiality of the vocal object poses
to the subject a necessary (and necessarily futile) quest that is involved in
all reception of voice and that takes the form of the (necessary and necessarily futile) attempt to objectify the noumenon.[26]

To be sure, this assimilation of a primal cry to the noumenon is not
new with Lacan-derived conceptions. It is anticipated in a passage of
Wagner's essay "Beethoven," cited by Poizat for other purposes. And, as
we shall see, it is described also by Nietzsche in terms close to Wagner's
but with a different historiographical agenda. For Wagner—at least the
later Wagner, after his encounter with Schopenhauer's philosophy—the
cry can envoice the music that forms a direct representation of the all-
pervading will. The cry is the "immediate expression of the anguished
will" that puts us in touch with an alternative to phenomenal reality, a
"sound-world." This alternative reality, parallel to the "light-world" of
dreams, is "an Essence of things that eludes the forms of outer knowledge, Time and Space," the forms, in other words, that were for Kant the
a priori conditions of sensible intuition and hence of phenomenal knowledge. It is a realm in which we come close to knowing "the nature of the
Thing-in-itself," which is to say that it allows an approach to Kant's noumenon. Wagner's cry, in granting access to a realm that escapes phenomenal knowledge, is the most immediate avatar of the noumenon. His music is an art that arises from this noumenal cry even while its artifice and
consciously constructed nature distance it from its wellspring: "If we take
the Scream in all the diminutions of its vehemence, down to the gentler
cry of longing, as the root-element of every human message to the ear;
and if we cannot but find in it the most immediate utterance of the will,
. . . then we have less cause to wonder at its immediate intelligibility than
at an *art* arising from this element: for it is evident . . . that neither artistic
beholding nor artistic fashioning can result from aught but a diversion of

the consciousness from the agitations of the will." Music both listens for and drowns out the noumenal cry.[27]

To relate the Lacanian cry to the broader phenomenal-noumenal dynamic of the modern subject requires making two qualifications to approaches to opera such as Poizat's. First, the range of modern operatic styles and voices gravitating toward the noumenal cry might be a good deal wider than Lacanians tend to suspect. Poizat distinguishes the "*pure or sheer cry*," which is "beyond the range of music and out of reach of the word," from other, less pure cries or non-cries,[28] a distinction that might seem merely a naive attempt to mark points along a spectrum of vocal uses that must (according to its own theorization) be continuous and pervasive. But its perniciousness becomes evident when Poizat employs it to exalt certain operatic traditions—especially Wagnerian ones—and marginalize others. The modern operatic voice needs to be understood in all its manners of broaching the Kantian subject, not theorized with an eye to bolstering by-now tired exclusionary evaluations.

Second, the Lacanian cry, in its noumenal affiliation, stands behind not any and all voices but only the voice that is peculiar to the modern Western subject. Lacanian theories, like the Freudian theories they spring from, provide no grounds for their universal extension through history. They are the creation of a culture in which the noumenon has emerged as a defining feature of subjectivity. The noumenal operatic voice revealed by these theories will be circumscribed within the same cultural territory, while other voices approach invisible realms along other paths.

If Lacanian approaches ultimately might describe the psychic ontogeny that leads us to perceive the modern operatic voice as noumenal and uncanny, Carolyn Abbate instead analyzes the conditions under which this voice is presented. She is concerned primarily with the phenomenology (and "noumenology," we should add) of the vocal presence onstage in opera, and she pursues its conditions through close scrutiny of specific musico-dramatic situations from the nineteenth-century repertory. She traces in opera the creation of what Freud called the "literary uncanny": an imaginative context that embodies uncanniness and yields to us a true experience of the uncanny without being "submitted to reality-testing."[29]

In *Unsung Voices* Abbate starts from a strong conviction that the usual approach to musical narration since the nineteenth century, though purportedly describing in words the events traced by the music, actually obscures music's true narrative capacities. This customary "miming model" grants to music only the ability to reproduce the gestures of a nonmusical narrative. It does not isolate any intrinsically musical narrativity. To discern music's specific potential for narrative, Abbate starts from Gérard Genette's idea that a diegetical distance, introduced by the presence of a voice that controls and orders (and reorders) the events related, is fundamental to the creation of narrative. For Abbate, music only superficially traces events. But in profound ways it replicates Genette's distanced, controlling voice. In doing so, music sets up its own, antimimetic narrative.[30]

This musical narration is evident especially in certain moments of disruption and disjunction of the musical fabric. Abbate's unlikely example is the reemergence of the main bassoon theme at the center of Dukas's *Sorcerer's Apprentice*. Here the theme itself, once reestablished, does not narrate; rather, the bassoon's repeated attempts to restart the theme mark the presence of the discursive voice fundamental to the *condition* of narration. It is not the events of the story that are important but instead the bassoon's "act of enunciating itself," which functions as "the sound of *speaking one's art into being.*" This voice gives us momentary access to a kind of displaced hearing, a "second hearing" akin to second sight, that Abbate links in general with "what is uncanny in music."[31]

Abbate associates the uncanniness of such irruptions of a musical narrating voice with features of nineteenth-century opera. It is reproduced, at the level of plot, by the introduction of mysterious, otherworldly, or supernatural characters (such as Wotan the Wanderer in *Die Walküre* or *Siegfried*), an oft-repeated romantic gesture that Abbate calls "the myth of the numinous intruder." More deeply, uncanny irruptions also cluster around the fault lines between two different musico-dramatic modes: phenomenal music—stage songs and the like portrayed within the drama as song which, as a result, the characters onstage are meant to hear as music—and all the other music of opera, which the characters hear problematically if at all. At times Abbate calls all this latter music "noumenal."[32]

The "deafness" of the characters onstage to the noumenal music heard by the audience, then, is breached by moments of phenomenal song. The spectral intruder, often enough associated with such moments, becomes a reflection of "Romantic concerns with the notion of 'unheard music,' and a view of music (alone among the arts) as a higher form that originates in a transcendental and inaccessible space." The intruder also betrays "nineteenth-century fears (and obsessions) with the notion of otherness." More generally, at moments of disjunction between noumenal and phenomenal music the narrating voice assuages the deafness of the characters by crossing the border between these two kinds of music, thus "bringing 'unheard' sound into the human world onstage."[33] For Abbate the uncanniness of nineteenth-century opera resides especially in these extraordinary moments when the characters onstage hear what they normally cannot hear.

Richard Taruskin, in one of the few reviews of Abbate's *Unsung Voices* that has done justice to the book's depth and prescience, has taken issue with this conception of operatic deafness and its assuaging. For him,

Abbate's noumenal music amounts not simply to the music unheard by the characters onstage; it is the very environment they live in. For this reason it is, in the form it assumes in Abbate's argument, a nonissue: "If we are operatically literate we do not wonder whether the characters are 'aware' of the music they inhabit." In a more general form, on the other hand, it is essential and pervasive; it represents for Taruskin an inhabiting of a sonorous ambience that is inherent in all our musical experience. In opera it takes the stage as a transference of this ambience to a dramatic context, as "a metaphor for what the characters are experiencing."[34]

Abbate tends at times, perhaps indulgently, to call "noumenal" all the music of operas outside their occasional phenomenal songs; still, her argument as a whole warrants a different, more restrictive view. This view reasserts the importance of her insight in the face of Taruskin's sweeping generalization. It also ties her argument to the emergence of Kantian transcendentalism, localizing it in the historical flux of Western subjectivity. The non-phenomenal music of operas, in this view, indeed embodies the psychological experience of the characters onstage, as Taruskin suggests. But the undifferentiated totality of this experience cannot properly be called "noumenal." The notion of noumenal music needs to be reserved for something at once more specific and less accessible. It is not merely the ever-present, sonorous environment, heard or unheard. Instead it is the form this environment takes at those moments when a character attains a special self-consciousness of the musical nature of his or her experience. It is the musical expression of a character's approach to the limit of phenomenal knowledge.

Abbate calls such moments the "uncovering" of narration. She hears an exemplary instance near the end of Tannhäuser's Rome Narrative,[35] where orchestral ostinatos that had appeared earlier in a "semantically neutral" accompaniment are transformed into a halting motion that the singer employs self-reflexively to signify his spiritual "progress" toward the Pope (see example 6). Here Tannhäuser also breaks down the strophic outlines apparent earlier in the narrative in favor of a free-formed, associative musical progress that he creates and controls. He stops "singing a narrative song, and yet he still *sings;* the sounding world of the opera comes from him, he hears the music that he creates." We might quibble with particulars of Abbate's interpretation. The key transformation here is, perhaps, not precisely from a nonsemantic to a signifying figure, since the ostinato even in its first occurrences probably should be heard as something of a stock gesture embodying a sense of journey, in its iconicity not unlike the ostinatos of the storm that begins *Die Walküre.* But Abbate's main point, concerning the alteration of Tannhäuser himself, is well taken: he becomes, as she asserts, a "character who *hears.*" What he hears—and can thereby participate in and exploit—is a musical dimension inaccessible to the characters around him. He hears an *a priori* condition that is the noumenal limit, cast as music, of all the envoiced understanding he might gain. Tannhäuser, in short, is rendered musically transcendent.

At liminal moments, such as this one, nineteenth-century opera explicitly reveals the post-Kantian subject. Characters are portrayed as capable of glimpsing the noumenal limits of knowledge. This capacity brings them to the verge of envoicing a realm that is normally unperceived—a

Example 6a. From Wagner, *Tannhäuser*

Example 6b. From Wagner, *Tannhäuser*

supersensible world, in other words. But this world answers to the name and features of that particular supersensible dispersed through European elite culture after Kant. It takes the form of an encompassing noumenalism at the far horizon of phenomenal experience. Modern opera portrays this realm as musical; hence it can seem to be objectified in moments of Abbate's second hearing. The unheard catadupe suddenly rendered audible at these junctures, the momentarily deafening pervasion of the character's experience with music, is opera's sonorous approach to the realization of a transcendental object. It is song in the sketchy and paradoxical form of noumenon.

Another feature of romantic opera highlighted in *Unsung Voices* also embodies the new transcendentalism. From the late eighteenth century on, the prominence of stage songs in opera—Abbate's phenomenal music—poses a dualism that had not been an issue in early modern operatic expression. This is not to say, of course, that stage songs had not occurred earlier, but only that the expressive and representational problems they raised were of a different nature then. In seventeenth-century opera a lullaby functioned as a code that might carry the reassurance of a stable if arcane representational connection. A narrative ballad in romantic opera instead invokes the specter of a split between two kinds of music, one transcendent to the sensibilities of the characters onstage and one immanent to them. The association of ghostly intruders with such phenomenal songs might be considered the reversed reflection of this dualism, the inevitable impulse to materialize in the phenomenal world the noumenal realm beyond it. The diegetic distance established by the irruption of the phenomenal voice forces the issue of the distinction between the two realms.

It should not be thought, however, that the noumenon is a fixed form constantly assumed by this voice. Instead the noumenon functions as limit. The voice, embodying the Kantian subject, tends toward this limit as the end point of the subject's always incomplete self-realization. In singing, it traces the path of Foucault's journey without end but not without hope. The modern voice carries the same sort of transcendentalism as the subject it embodies. Just as the thought of this subject will approach the noumenon as the limit-case of the phenomena that are its enduring preoccupation, so the operatic voice will look toward its own limit in a fashion that only occasionally comes close to making it explicit. This voice cannot be conceived or heard outside the conditions of phenomena, but the noumenon exerts on it an ineluctable and uncanny gravitation. Nineteenth-century listeners and twentieth-century listeners as well—we who are still the problematic products of Kantian constructions of subjectivity—hear the modern operatic voice in the context of this noumenal temptation. This voice, like the modern subject it represents, is impelled toward the borderline that separates the phenomenal and the noumenal, even though it only occasionally moves so far as to seem to adumbrate the noumenon.

·   ·   ·   ·   ·

Abbate's disjunctions that mark narrative moments—the launching into a stage song or, as in *Tannhäuser*, the breakdown of such a song that leaves behind a novel musical consciousness—are only the clearest indices of a modern voice much more widely experienced as gesturing toward the noumenon. Abbate is correct, no doubt, in locating the most self-conscious presentation of this voice in Wagner: witness his remarks on the noumenal cry quoted above. But what she describes in *Tannhäuser* as a fateful moment in the Wagnerian corpus, when the singers could begin to make their own music in a "discursive and leitmotivically active voice" (when, as I have said, the noumenal limit is approached), needs to be set against a broader backdrop.[36] What Wagner could not resist turning into a theoretical project was elsewhere being unself-consciously proffered onstage as a fundamental condition of modern voice. Opera in the age of Kantian subjectivity was susceptible to a hearing that made of it a tissue of more or less veiled noumenalism.

This is true even for Italian melodrama of the early and mid-nineteenth century, the romantic repertory usually placed at a far extreme from Wagnerian music drama. Here, too, at many moments and in many manners, the singer shadows forth noumenal realms. At some of these moments the music reveals a psyche that can be divided within and from itself in a way inconceivable with the Cartesian subject. It offers a hazy representation of aspects of a protagonist's soul previously (and normally) invisible, of psychological forces at once graspable and yet uncannily out of reach and control. At other moments the music functions, more generally, to reveal the presence of hidden dimensions of the psyche or to project these dimensions out as audible features of the external stage world. All these approaches to the limits of phenomenal experience amount to envoicings of the transcendental subject I have described in Kantian terms.

In *primo ottocento* melodrama the Kantian subject and its noumenalism are most evident in climactic mad scenes and in closely cognate scenes of sleepwalking, dreaming, and entranced vision. Indeed this repertory supports an extraordinary proliferation of portrayals of these altered psychic states. In these portrayals the psyche assumes a form unprecedented in early modern opera, a form that reflects the substrate of transcendental subjectivity on which they build. The misfortunes visited (or seemingly visited) upon a Griselda are no less wrenching than those suffered by a Lucia, but their effects in the early modern era cannot be depicted as a madness that fragments the mind and doubles it over upon itself in a revelation of the invisible realms that condition its knowledge. This must await a modern view of the self. Rather than so inward-turning a convolution, madness before the modern era is conceived as externalization, as a movement of the mind outside itself toward supersensible forces there— a movement nicely preserved in such Italian archaisms as "fuor di sè" and "forsennato."[37]

Recitative and aria function in early nineteenth-century mad scenes in a different way than elsewhere in the repertory. The normal pacing, still Metastasian in essence, caps a forward-moving recitative with a lyric number that affectively marks the progress of the drama up to that moment. In mad scenes this pacing stalls. Here the singer speaks only of a past—her mind moves forward only in memory—and of a past that exists as a reality refracted by arcane forces in her psyche. The reflexivity here draws us toward those obscure forces and away from the active, objective surface of the plot and the conscious emotional responses of the protagonists to its events. The singer's compulsion to remember congeals the plot around an obsession that is, finally, uncanny in its escape from conscious or rational control.

The means that these post-Kantian, romantic depictions of madness exploit quickly developed a great degree of consistency and conventionalism. They include a lengthy recitative *scena* with greater lyric interest than in most recitatives; the recollection in this *scena*, primarily by the orchestra, of themes from earlier in the opera; certain orchestration, especially the emphasis of woodwinds deemed to sound ethereal (such as flute and clarinet); and glittering vocal acrobatics. All these features join together in the *locus classicus* for this sort of portrayal, the penultimate scene of Donizetti's *Lucia di Lammermoor*. But they are found also in other scenes that portray versions of psychic introjection distinct from madness as such. Amina's sleepwalking in Bellini's *La sonnambula*, for example, is not synonymous with Lucia's tragic dementia. It is a milder pathology, suitable, we might say, to the countrified, semiseria context in which it appears. But her sleepwalking scene at the climax of the opera anticipates by four years all the techniques that Donizetti employed in *Lucia*. The repetition of this congeries of technical means suggests that the two states of psychological introjection were allied in the minds of the creators of the repertory.

These techniques adduce, clearly enough, the internal otherworldliness that marks the Kantian subject. The recalling of themes heard earlier in the opera, almost always presented now in less-than-complete form and by the orchestra, portrays a surfacing of memories from hidden realms within the psyche. The willy-nilly, fragmentary appearance of these themes captures the disordered and uncontrolled confrontation of consciousness with its mysterious other. Their instrumental presentation assigns the voice of this other especially to the orchestra, widening in dramatic fashion its expressive independence from voice that we have followed from Scarlatti through Gluck. Now the orchestra does not expand slightly the feelings expressed by the voice (Scarlatti) or expose feelings unknown to or purposefully denied by the voice (Gluck). Instead it *sings to* the singer, divulging secrets to her from deep within her own soul. The orchestra here portrays itself as a true voice from an internal noumenal realm.

Meanwhile the emphasis on the recitative *scena*, with its characteristic formal freedom, likewise betokens the psyche's loss of conscious control in its broaching of noumenal forces. The unpredictable irruptions of lyricism within the recitative increase its musical variety, emphasize its shifts of mood, and thereby contribute to its portrayal of psychological waywardness. The ethereal woodwind timbres—especially the flutes—imbue the psychological otherworldliness of the scene with overtones of a heavenly, Christian supersensible. The proliferating vocal virtuosity came quickly to signify not only the trancelike state in which noumenal forces could be rendered sensible but also the unpredictable flights of fancy of the maddened mind.

The Kantian force, so to speak, of such techniques is considerable. But it by no means comprises the full impact these noumenal scenes can have in the operas where they occur. A case in point is Lady Macbeth's sleepwalking scene. Here Verdi avoided some of the earlier mad-scene conventions, which must have seemed tired by 1847, and transformed others. There is no sign of vocal acrobatics—Verdi chose instead a path of relative realism and employed a hushed *canto declamato* punctuated by more sustained lyricism (see example 7)—or of woodwind quintessence. (Verdi had not foregone such techniques, of course; in *Rigoletto*, for example, they join in a different sort of representation that has its own noumenal aspects, Gilda's entranced response to the advent of "Gualtier Maldè.") Neither is there any lengthy or elaborate *scena* with the reprise of earlier melodies. Instead Verdi transferred the formal freedoms that had tended in earlier noumenal scenes to inhabit such *scene* into a single, huge lyric movement, and he reduced the recitative to a minimal exchange in which Lady Macbeth *sings not a word*. Stunningly, in the light of the tradition out of which this scene came, the lyric movement "Una macchia è qui tutt'ora" bears the full burden of the depiction of Lady Macbeth's pathology.[38] In "Una macchia" Verdi's orchestra does not recall full-fledged themes heard earlier in the opera. Instead it concentrates its thematic connection to earlier music in just a tiny motivic gesture.

The effect of these technical transformations is both to deepen the sense of noumenalism in the sleepwalking scene itself and to broaden its impact across *Macbeth* as a whole. Within the scene they deepen it by rendering it, paradoxically, at once more striking and more subliminal. Abrupt tonal detours and freedom of form are far more telling in the context of a lyric movement such as "Una macchia" than in a passage of recitative, where loose and discursive organization is the norm. Lady

Macbeth's ceding of control to invisible forces in her psyche is plainly enacted by means of three jolting harmonic shifts that underpin, but also undermine, an otherwise conventional tonal plan.[39] Meanwhile, since the orchestra's recollection of earlier materials functions at a motivic level that, unlike the thematic recurrences in *Lucia* and *La sonnambula*, can defy easy definition, the orchestral voice is not heard to speak in the overt, objectifying manner of its counterpart in *Lucia*. Instead it comes to represent a psychic force that is less tractable because it is less easily isolated, a force that limns the noumenon all the more accurately in resisting objectification.

This motivic reminiscence encompasses not only Lady Macbeth's obsession but Macbeth's related anguish as well, in this way exploring the invisible psychic force central to the whole drama. The reminiscence is elemental: the rocking figure from ♭VI–V heard in the English horn as part of the accompaniment. In his *Studio sulle opere di Giuseppe Verdi* of 1859, Abramo Basevi recognized this figure as "a type of lament . . . that repeats, in a certain fashion, the internal cries of the conscience."[40] This conscience is noumenal in that it inhabits depths of Macbeth's and Lady Macbeth's psyches: it can undermine their conscious motivations and actions, it can breach the surface in moments of introspection or altered awareness, but it cannot come into full and unimpeded visibility.

Verdi portrays in music, as explicitly as we could wish, the submerging of this force in Macbeth's psyche, a repression that results in a separation of his singing voice from his orchestral voice. As he returns from murdering Duncan—and just after the hallucinatory dagger scene that signals his own altered, noumenal awareness—he gasps, to a ♭VI rocking motive (see example 8) like the one that will later haunt Lady Macbeth's dreams, that the deed is done: "Tutto è finito!" Immediately the orchestra appropriates the motive and spins it, before our ears, into the obsessive accompanimental figure of the *primo tempo* of his duet with Lady Macbeth.

The motive returns at important junctures through the opera: in a literal reprise (along with the first phrases of the duet movement), to open act 2; a short time later at the moment of Macbeth's decision to murder Banquo;[41] and just before "Pietà, rispetto, amore," as Macbeth ponders his life stripped of consolation (". . . inaridita"). It takes on its most tumultuous, public, and objective form as the theme of the finale to act 1, where the assembled protagonists and chorus call on heaven and hell to avenge Duncan's murder ("Schiudi, inferno, la bocca ed inghiotti").

Against this background the rocking figure in the sleepwalking scene can only link Lady Macbeth's noumenal awareness to her husband's. In doing so it connects out to the play of mysterious forces (that especially

Example 7. From Verdi, *Macbeth*

preoccupy Macbeth) across the opera as a whole. The crudely objective forms that these forces assume—the witches, ghosts, and apparitions—certainly need some noumenal reaffirmation. It is just this rehabilitation of uncanniness that Lady Macbeth's scene effects. It comes to function as the noumenal limit toward which the whole opera—Macbeth, apparitions, and all—tends.

Not surprisingly, Verdi chose to use the orchestral introduction to the sleepwalking scene as the primary material of the Prelude opening the opera. Neither is it surprising that as Lady Macbeth dreams her crimes across "Una macchia," as she compulsively repeats what her internal de-

Example 8. From Verdi, *Macbeth*

Example 9. From Verdi, *Macbeth*

mons will not relinquish, the rocking motive, at first an incomplete version of Macbeth's V-♭VI-V (see examples 7 and 8), comes to approximate
more closely its archetype (see example 9).

. . . . .

Just as Wagnerian music drama found its spokesman and the propagan-
dist for its noumenalism in Wagner himself, *primo ottocento* opera had a
shrewd observer in Giuseppe Mazzini, who in his own fashion signaled
the noumenalism there. To be sure, the sources of Mazzini's *Filosofia
della musica* of 1835 are not those of Wagner's "Beethoven" essay of
1870. In place of Schopenhauer are influences from closer to the heyday
of romanticism (and indeed closer in some cases to the sources that ani-
mated Wagner in his own early writings): the politically engaged drama-
turgy of Victor Hugo in the years around 1830, the Christian liberalism
of Félicité Robert de Lamennais, and ideas of music's sociality and of
distinctions between melodic and harmonic expression that reach back
into the eighteenth century. Through such sources, and through Mazzini's carefully worded agenda for a reformed melodrama, we glimpse the
outlines of the Kantian subject. From the *Filosofia della musica* we take

marching orders, so to speak, for the operatic "genius" of the future who "will draw from art heretofore unsuspected secrets, disseminating, with Raphaelesque melodies over uninterrupted harmonies, a shadow of that infinite our souls yearn for." Reading this manifesto we acclimate our ears to the pervasive noumenal undertones of the new operatic repertory that was taking shape as Mazzini wrote.[42]

For Mazzini the state of opera at the time of his writing represents at worst a shallow individualism, at best a cultural movement on the verge of an inchoate future. The opera of the past is exhausted. Romanticism, in the figure of Rossini, has cast off the rules and strictures of an earlier art and set in motion an essential transition, but it is a movement of liberation, not consolidation, and can provide no "organic conception" for "the musical drama of the future." (*Filosofia*, pp. 38, 53, 55n) Most followers of Rossini, custodians of a musical art that should be "a harmony of creation, an echo of the invisible world," satisfy themselves with superficial and objectifying displays of emotion, devoid of any grounding or unifying "idea." (pp. 41–43) With the exception of some extraordinary passages in works by Rossini himself, operas in this style neglect the infinite, which music alone can touch in its expressive generality and indefiniteness. (p. 60)

Mazzini seems at first to describe this infinite in conventional Christian terms, as a God and a sacred order outside and above humankind. In this guise it is opposed to the individualism that forms the central feature of the Rossinian style. This individualism makes Rossinian music materialistic, allowing it to depict specific things but denying it access to more general forms, ideas, and invisible realities. The style renders only actions and sharply etched appearances; lacking are "the indefinite, the shadowy, the airy, which would seem to belong most specially to the nature of music. . . . It is music without shades, without mysteries, without twilight," Mazzini goes on; ". . . middling or mixed gradations of affect are absent or rare; breeze of the invisible world that surrounds us: none." (pp. 53–56)

Set aside the recurring, telling references to mystery, indefiniteness, twilight, and so forth, and we would seem to be faced here with something close to a characteristic early modern view, in which a conventional Platonic idealism combines with Christian transcendence to delimit hidden realms outside and above the subject. Of noumenal places within the psyche there is little sign.

All this changes, however, when Mazzini comes to delineate his program for the opera of the future. He envisages a union of German musical idealism in the form of harmony with the individualism and materialism of Italian melody. This new, pan-European style will enable "musical expression [to] encompass the two fundamental terms: individuality and the idea [*il pensiero*] of the universe—God and man." (*Filosofia*, p. 58) In this formulation God is carried into the psyche as thought, as a universal conception of the mind given expression, along with individuality, in music. The "spiritualizing" of music that Mazzini calls for (p. 60) assumes the form of endowing the individualistic subject of romantic opera with the limitless, universal a priori of thought, of locating a metaphysics within Rossinian materialism—of, finally, asserting the individual itself as metaphysical material. The transcendental subject with its noumenal background appears.

This subject grows clearer still as Mazzini lists specific desiderata of the new opera. "Individuality is sacred," he asserts twice in this discussion, confirming the introjection into the subject of the invisible world that music can touch. (pp. 61, 64) This sacral and mysterious subject must sing in various forms in the opera of the future—not as a function of the character of individual melodies, which are restricted, as in the Rossinian mold, to the expression of singular and isolated emotions, but in other guises: as a historical individualization of operas to the epoch and locale where they occur (Hugo's *couleur locale*); as the consistent and deep musical characterization of the individual protagonists of the drama, for which Mazzini adduces the exemplary cases of Don Giovanni and Meyerbeer's Bertram in *Robert le diable*; and even as the varied portrayal, specific to the situation, of the "collective individuality" that speaks the conscience of the people in the chorus. (pp. 61–67)

This sort of thinking begins to reveal the full range of noumenal apperceptions in Italian romantic opera. It projects noumenalism far beyond mad scenes, in which it most evidently appears, to reach potentially every corner of the work. Mazzini envisages an opera whose whole musical character—the tint of its localization in nature and history, the personalities of its protagonists, the distinctive musical colors that unify and also vary it—could be heard as a vast externalization of the sacred, universal mysteries at the heart of the individual subject. For him noumenalism could seep out from the subject onstage to color even the landscape around.

Heard in this context, the enigmatic orchestral figure in example 10 from the last act of *Rigoletto* comes to epitomize the proliferation of noumenal forces in the Italian repertory. A Mazzinian hearing would not understand this as a simple, objectified fate motive, although it certainly gathers a fateful momentum as it punctuates at accelerating intervals the large-scale circle of fifths that drives the action forward here. Neither would this hearing reduce it to a straightforward pictorialism, along the lines of the flute's lightning and the offstage, humming chorus's wind in this scene, though it might be thought to carry some iconic charge too as a depiction of the hush before a violent thunderstorm in a Po valley op-

Example 10. From Verdi, *Rigoletto*

pressed by summer heat. Instead it would hear in this motive the external-ization of invisible, implacable psychic forces that *will* bring about the tragic denouement. It would hear an intractable destiny congealed in Monterone's curse and in the complex musical means Verdi used to con-vey its force: the recurring juxtaposition of the tonalities of D♭ and D in acts 1 (at the moment of the curse) and 3 (across almost the whole of the act), and the augmented-sixth "curse" sonority (see act 1, scene 2, at "Quel vecchio maledivami!") introduced as the first harmony of the op-era and recalled, as Gilda expires, to pivot momentarily once more be-tween D♭ and D. But this Mazzinian hearing would recognize always that the fateful power of the curse originated in Rigoletto's own divided soul, where the opposed forces Verdi made so much of in conceiving his pro-tagonist reach down to hidden sources.

In the light of such pervasive noumenalism it is clear why Mazzini thought he caught glimpses of the opera of the future in some few pas-sages by Rossini: in the historical hues of *Semiramide* and the patriotic *communitas* of *Guillaume Tell*; in the supernatural force of *Mosè*; espe-cially in the last act of *Otello*, with its distant, hovering gondolier's mel-ody and its "Willow Song" and prayer, so poignantly revealing and so different from the more neutral ("materialistic," Mazzini would say) note-spinning elsewhere in Desdemona's role. (*Filosofia*, pp. 54n, 63n) It is evident also why Mazzini took Donizetti to be the genius to bring forth the new opera—Donizetti who, at the time of Mazzini's writing in the mid-1830s, loomed as the composer most vividly coloring his settings and deeply exploring his protagonists' souls; Donizetti whose *Marino Faliero* seemed, with its tormented Doge, its indomitable man-of-the-peo-ple Israele Bertucci, its choral populace rising up against tyranny, its dark Venetian shadows, even its own gondola song, to realize in some part Mazzini's fondest hopes. (*Filosofia*, pp. 70–76) And, when we look ahead to the resonance of *Marino Faliero* through the later Italian repertory—through works as diverse as *Il bravo, I due Foscari, Simon Boccanegra,* and *La Gioconda*—it is evident also, finally, that the echo of Mazzini's opera of the future sounds across almost the whole of the nineteenth cen-tury as the musical calling of a noumenal mystery.

Wagner too heard this call. His noumenalism ultimately would draw on different sources than Mazzini's and move in different directions. But when in his "Beethoven" essay, Schopenhauer in hand, Wagner described hearing the noumenal cry of the will in a dialogue of gondoliers' songs over dark Venetian canals, he moved along imaginative pathways known well to his contemporaries.[43]

Excursus 3

NOUMENAL THEMES

The ghostly intruder—the mysterious stranger embodied in protagonists such as Bertram in Meyerbeer's *Robert le diable* and Wotan in *Die Walküre* and *Siegfried*—was not the only topos through which the creators of nineteenth-century opera sought to objectify noumenal realms. Several other possibilities frequent the repertory.

Figure 7: Weber, *Der Freischütz*, the Wolf's Glen scene. Lithograph after Carl Wilhelm Holdermann's staging in Weimar, 1822. Credit: Kunstsammlungen zu Weimar. Photo: Eberhard Renno.

Untamed nature, first, was transformed in the years around 1800 into a dark and menacing landscape, familiar from the painting and poetry of the period. Such natural surroundings took also to the operatic stage, signally in the Wolf's Glen Scene of magic conjuration from Weber's *Der Freischütz*, pictured here. Here landscape itself assumes the diabolical noumenalism of Abbate's otherworldly visitors. It is commonly supposed that such novel landscapes betoken a new identification of the human psyche with nature, and so much is true in the superficial sense that they are viewed as projections outward of the psyche. ("Orrida è questa notte," says Edgardo at the tempestuous beginning of act 3 of *Lucia*, "come il destino mio!") At a deeper level, however, these landscapes reveal the opposite: a new distance between humanity and nature that arises from the post-Kantian breakdown of confidence in the transparency of empirical reality to our knowledge. Now nature, insofar as we can know it, is only what human cognitive capacities are able to make of it. Its objective, empirical presence stands beyond the limits of our knowledge. It reflects back the structuring of the psyche that conceives it, but this structure is Kant's internal dualism, where all forms of phenomenal knowledge beckon toward a mysterious, noumenal horizon. It is no surprise that representations of the external landscape easily took on the shadowy trappings of this liminal realm.

Closely related to Abbate's spectral intruder is the theme of forbidden knowledge. This might, as in Gounod's and Boito's *Faust* operas (not to mention Liszt's and Berlioz's symphonic versions), involve the general implication of limits to knowledge beyond which mortals can move only with overweening hubris or through Mephistophelean bargains. More suggestively, it might take the form of the unknowable identity itself of a mysterious visitor from spiritual or supersensible realms. *Lohengrin* is the most famous example, one foreshadowed in Wagner's first opera *Die Feen*, Conradin Kreutzer's *Melusine*, Heinrich Marschner's *Hans Heiling*, and other works. (The type resonates also, if less clearly, in *The Flying Dutchman*.) To be sure, opera had a long tradition of disguised characters and unknown or mistaken identities. But in the late-seventeenth and the eighteenth centuries concealed identities, whether in comic or in serious opera, usually took the form of a puzzle to be solved in order to bring the plot to its denouement, a puzzle involving no spectral characters or realms but mortals alone. In the post-Kantian era, on the other hand, the identity concealed typically was posed not as a puzzle to be solved but as a knowledge of supersensible, divine, or spirit realms inaccessible to mortals—a knowledge whose revelation, or even attempted revelation, brings climactic and even fatal consequences. Concealed identity was posed, in other words, as a noumenal limit beyond which human, phenomenal knowledge might not range.

The tantalizing suggestion of knowledge beyond its Kantian limits took on intersocietal dimensions in the vogue of exotic subjects—of orientalist opera—in the later nineteenth century. Again the novelty of the post-Kantian treatment of such subjects is revealed by comparison with the Turkish and other exoticisms of eighteenth-century opera. From the noble savages or ultimately enlightened monarchs they had once been, for instance in Carl Heinrich Graun's *Montezuma* or Mozart's *Entführung aus dem Serail*, exotic characters increasingly became the locus of secret knowledge or forbidden, mysterious sensuality. Such treatment is evident in operas such as Delibes's *Lakmé*, and it culminates in Strauss's *Salome*. A subtler but more radical example is the character of Carmen, whose differences from the other protagonists of Bizet's opera cut so very deep that her actions are misconstrued throughout the work as the utterly familiar language of romantic passion (see chapter 5).

Excursus 4

COMPOSING SCHOPENHAUER

The great idealist philosophies of the modern West have all had their distinctive puzzles at heart: Descartes's mysteriously traversed chasm between mind and body, Kant's unknowable noumenon conditioning our knowledge, Hegel's *Geist*—spirit or mind—and its phenomenology that aims to abolish Kant's noumenon but seems unable to succeed. The paradox of Schopenhauer's thought also arises from the noumenal-phenomenal distinction, but poses it in a more accessible, dynamic fashion than Kant had done. Schopenhauer's metaphysical will is equivalent to Kant's thing in itself; it is the world in itself, all that there is behind phenomenal appearances. In objectifying itself, the will moves as a force to create a phenomenal world whose existence is at once intimately connected to and alienated from it. Individuals are aware of the force of will in the natural strivings and actions of the body—in the movement of digestion, for example, or the arousal of the sexual organs. But they can only fully experience will by ceasing to be individuals, by a self-annihilation that amounts to a collapse of time and space, along with the causality operative in them, into a realm where no individuation exists. Thus Schopenhauer's will can be said to intersect with individuals both at the bodily locus of their most private experience of self and in some cosmic surmounting of individuality.

In human expression music constitutes, for Schopenhauer, a kind of limit case of this paradox. It alone among the arts yields direct representation of the will, free from any constraining concepts or ideas. It offers, as Schopenhauer put it in lines quoted by Nietzsche (see chapter 5), "an immediate copy of the will itself." It can even be equated to the will: "We could just as well call the world embodied music as embodied will." Yet the manner in which music achieves this unmediated expression follows the double pattern of our experience of the will. The language of music is "exceedingly universal" while being of "the most precise distinctness." It intimates will to us, Schopenhauer explains, because its motions of dissonance and resolution are minutely analogous to those bodily motions of striving and satisfaction that are our surest experience of will. But in those tiny analogies, at the same moment, music provides the clearest glimpse art can give of the all-encompassing world-will.

In this light we might consider a famous question concerning Wagner's *Tristan und Isolde*: to what degree is it the translation of Schopenhauer's philosophy into music drama? It is evident enough that the question is not idle. The conception of *Tristan* took shape simultaneously with and under the influence of Wagner's discovery of Schopenhauer in the mid-1850s, and the central imagery of Wagner's text, which separates the illusory appearances of the day-world from the transcendent truth of the night-world, was inspired by the philosopher. But a more precise reflection of Schopenhauerian doctrine in the plot is difficult to find. Indeed the final *Liebestod* of both protagonists amounts to their escape through death into the night-world, where their love can find unconstrained, transcendent fulfillment. To many this has seemed more a celebration than a renunciation of their individuality. It has seemed closer, that is, to an ultimate apotheosis of romantic love, with its foundation of unabashed selfhood, than to Schopenhauer's brooding renunciation of self.

In a broader view, however, it is less the plot or the poem than the general functioning of music here that may be considered Schopenhauerian. The particular musical idiom Wagner created for *Tristan*—and it must be acknowledged that no opera composer before him had forged so distinctive a style for each of his mature works—can be heard, at the level of local gesture, as the composer's self-conscious attempt to feature *as the primary element of style* the flux of tension and release Schopenhauer had likened to will. This is evident from the very first, famous measures of the Prelude, and evident also in Wagner's overwrought characterization of the whole work: "yearning, yearning, insatiable desire, ever reborn—languishing and thirsting; the sole release—death, dying, extinction, never more to wake!" At the same time, however, the cumulative effect of these local gestures, abetted by a large-scale, ebb-and-flow pacing that Wagner sets out with almost miraculous skill, is to portray larger-than-life forces that somehow transcend the phenomenal world onstage. (These forces are particularly apparent in the Prelude and at all the major articulations of the drama: the drinking of the potion in Act 1, with the reprise of the music of the Prelude; the love duet of act 2; and Tristan's delirium and Isolde's *Liebestod* from act 3.) The most general condition of Wagner's music here expresses the dualism characteristic of Schopenhauer's will. Much more than the dramatic actions depicted or the poetic imagery of the libretto, the music captures a phenomenon-transcending experience at once intimate and all-encompassing.

V

NIETZSCHE: OVERCOMING

OPERATIC METAPHYSICS

NIETZSCHE'S DIONYSUS sang, at first, with noumenal operatic voice; but this same Dionysus, hardly a moment later, ridiculed noumenalism as a farce of romantic culture. The opposition reflects two roles Dionysus plays in Nietzsche's thought. He serves as agonistic counterpart to Apollo, as the personification of the deep-seated, ecstatic forces in Greek culture that were controlled, counterbalanced, and rationalized through Apollo. Meanwhile, in another role whose significance deepens across Nietzsche's career, he stands in a complex relation to Christ, at once prefiguring Christ's sacrificial religion and representing all that was stifled through two millennia of Christian moralizing.

In the first role Dionysus sponsors Nietzsche's earlier, exuberant celebration of noumenal opera, his historico-philosophical meditation on the emergence of the forces behind it in ancient Greek tragedy and their resuscitation in Wagner: *The Birth of Tragedy out of the Spirit of Music*. In the second role Dionysus is emblematic of a provocative and problematic repudiation of Wagner and a surmounting of Kantian and post-Kantian metaphysics. In this later Dionysus we discern, darkly, the possibility of a fourth era of opera: "What," Nietzsche asks, "would a music have to be like that would no longer be of romantic origin, like German music—but *Dionysian?*"[1]

That this fourth kind of opera, post-Wagnerian and, more generally, postmetaphysical, has never come to pass suggests the depth and tenacity of our need to hear in song a voice that conjurs the supersensible—to render song, in a word, metaphysical. It suggests the persistence of Kantian modes of subjectivity, in revised or distorted form, down to our own day, a persistence traceable to the end even in Nietzsche's own writings. And it suggests also why it might be claimed that, if opera did not end with Wagner, it at least has not moved beyond the problematic of Wagnerism broadly conceived.

Before this dilemma of modernism, however, there was culmination, marked by Nietzsche's joyous pronouncement of the revival of Dionysian tragedy in the music drama of Wagner. *The Birth of Tragedy* writes the prehistory of this music drama and, by extension, of all opera, as a ritual of possession drawing power from invisible realms. It is specifically and centrally concerned to describe the noumenal powers of song: their devel-

opment in the Dionysian festivals, satyr plays, and Aeschylean and Soph-
oclean tragedy; their suppression in the Socratic and Euripidean age; and
their resurgence in Wagner. Whatever else he would become, Nietzsche
was first a rhapsode of the musical supersensible.

The Birth of Tragedy attests its noumenalism obviously enough. Its
whole Schopenhauerian apparatus (which remains crucial, however
much recent investigations have detailed Nietzsche's ambivalence toward
and divergence from it already at this early date) builds on Kant's distinction between empirical appearances and things in themselves. Schopenhauer's will, a universal and indifferent drive constituting nature and objectified in individual beings, corresponds, as I have signaled above, to
reality in itself. It is Kant's noumenal realm, newly conceived. In
Nietzsche's adaptation, its metaphysical status is complicated, perhaps
attenuated, but not discarded. Nietzsche takes over other Schopenhauerian topoi as well: Schopenhauer's *principium individuationis* posits
Kant's a priori conditions of sensibility, time and space, as the matrix in
which subjects come into separate and distinct consciousness; his "veil of
mâyâ," borrowed from the Hindu *Upanishads,* represents the illusion of
material reality to be torn aside as we come to see the in-itself beyond our
individuality and the objective world of phenomena. All this bespeaks a
metaphysics still in touch with Kant-derived noumenalism.[2]

In *The Birth of Tragedy,* as in Schopenhauer's *World as Will and Representation*, music derives its force from its special relation to the will. It
is, like the other arts, a phenomenon, an appearance—not some impossible objectified noumenon. Unlike them, however, music is as direct a
representation of the will as human perception can find. Other arts are
copies of copies of the will, twice removed from it by virtue of representing the Platonic Ideas that are, as the most general objectifications of will,
already once removed. Music alone bypasses these Ideas to achieve a direct objectification of will. Music is not a mimesis of other phenomena
but rather connected to the noumenal realm as directly as are the Ideas
themselves. Twice Nietzsche quotes a passage from Schopenhauer on this
point: "Music is distinguished from all the other arts by the fact that it is
not a copy of the phenomenon, or, more accurately, of the adequate objectivity of the will, but an immediate copy of the will itself, and therefore
complements everything physical in the world and every phenomenon by
representing what is metaphysical, the thing in itself."[3] Music, Nietzsche
says at another point, is not will itself, which is in its moving, passionate
nature opposed to the contemplation and passivity that Nietzsche links,
here, to the aesthetic. But it *appears as* will, rather than as a copy of some
phenomenal objectification of will.[4]

The appearance of music therefore has nothing to do with the mimesis
of extramusical phenomena, that is, with tone painting. Nietzsche's early

views on this subject again follow Schopenhauer's and mark the culmination of the romantic turn away from the mimetic understanding of musical expression, which had characterized early modern thinking.[5] Such
pictorialism was, in Nietzsche's argument, just the feature that signaled
the degradation of the New Attic Dithyramb, where Dionysian force was
replaced by musical "counterfeit" of phenomena such as battles or
storms. (*The Birth of Tragedy*, section 17) The older, Dionysian dithyramb brought "the essence of nature" into symbolic expression through
the movements of tone, melody, and harmony, and also through a complete bodily involvement in pantomime and dance. (section 2) The New
Attic Dithyramb expressed not this movement of will manifested in the
body but rather a reasoned analogy between phenomena and "certain
rhythmical figures and characteristic sounds" such as marches, fanfares,
and the like. (section 17) In doing so it subjugated music to phenomena
and sacrificed for the sake of trivial particulars the general connection of
Dionysian music to universal will.

Neither has music's appearance anything to do with the balance and
proportion of form found in the plastic arts, and so the aesthetic criterion
transferred by formalists from those arts to music, "the arousing of *de-
light in beautiful forms*," is in Nietzsche's view utterly inapplicable. (section 16) We will see that this is not to deem music formless, for formless-
ness is precisely one of the sins Nietzsche will later lay at the door of
Wagner. Rather it is to insist that music's form cannot be dissociated
from metaphysics (in the manner attempted by Hanslick) but must be
recognized as a direct objectification of will.

For Nietzsche the criterion of beautiful form pertains to the Apollinian,
plastic arts and to music made subservient to them but not to truly Dionysian music. Apollo is the god of artistic appearance, of objectified and
controlled form, and—since this objective world is not essential, not the
primordial unity of nature itself—of illusion. Through reconciliation
with Dionysus he allows for a likeness of truth to be captured in individual phenomena; he is "the transfiguring genius of the *principium individuationis* through which alone the redemption in illusion is truly to be
obtained." (section 16; also section 21)

Dionysus instead sponsors a rapturous, "will-full" melody that resists
its inevitable bodily individuation and even moves to abrogate all individuality in the great flow of will. In Dionysian song the *principium individuationis* collapses. (*The Birth of Tragedy*, section 1) In Dionysian festivals—not the orgies of non-Greek barbarians, but the rituals in which
Dionysus and Apollo were carefully reconciled—"the destruction of the
principium individuationis for the first time becomes an artistic phenomenon." (section 2) Music has the particular capability, derived from its
intimate relation to will, to enable us to "understand the joy involved in

the annihilation of the individual." (section 16) We can see that we are not far, here, from a Schopenhauerian reading of *Tristan*, and of course Nietzsche will invoke this work as his primary example of Wagner's revived balance of Dionysian and Apollinian powers.

From a broader, more distant vantage, however, we perceive here a turning of the Kantian noumenon, and of the whole subjectivity based on it, back toward older and more widely dispersed cultural practices. The collapse of individuation leads toward Schopenhauer's will, to be sure, but it also recalls an ancient permeability of one subject by others. It leads toward the habitation of one's body by another's voice, or whatever that voice conveys. It proposes, then, an understanding of operatic song as a matter of *possession* and *mediumship*: mediumship and possession visited on the singer, whose voice is not hers but some other, more universal voice that seizes, inhabits, and sings through her. And it is possession of the listeners, too, whose individualities are besieged and ultimately dissolved by the great sweep of primordial vocal will. Almost three hundred years into the history of opera, almost a hundred into the era of the Kantian subject, the Greeks and their irrational have led a young Wagnerian classicist to voice a venerable, spectral formula: "Let anyone have the ability to behold continually a vivid play and to live surrounded by hosts of spirits, and he will be a poet; let anyone feel the urge to transform himself and to speak out of other bodies and souls, and he will be a dramatist." (*The Birth of Tragedy*, section 8)

For Nietzsche the perfect poetic medium is the much-misunderstood lyric poet, whose original and archetypal figure is Archilocus. The puzzle of the nature of music's phenomenal appearance is resolved in the proper interpretation of the lyrist. (section 5) The lyrist is not, as earlier aesthetics would have it, the quintessentially "subjective" artist—for the notion of pure subjectivity, individuality distanced from will, is incompatible with the Dionysian art of song, which militates against the *principium individuationis*. Neither does the lyrist's song embody, as Schopenhauer had maintained, the tension of a struggle between the individualized will and a "pure, will-less knowing" somehow stimulated by the beauties of surrounding nature. Nietzsche's Dionysian lyrist, instead, has from the first unmade himself, "surrendering" his subjectivity and identifying with the broader, primordial oneness of nature, "with the primal unity, its pain and contradiction." His music is a copy of this unity, an objectification as cry of this pain.

But then Apollo intervenes, counterbalancing generalized Dionysian primordiality with specific objectivity and re-presenting the poet's music to him in the likeness of a "dream image." Since the poet has already merged with the collective "I" at the heart of the world, the first-person voice in which he sings of this image is not the subjective poet as "non-genius," but rather the universal "world-genius" expressing itself through him. The Dionysian poet's images, in contrast to the more superficial Apollinian images of the plastic artist, "are nothing but *his very self*," a self that "is not the same as that of the waking, empirically real man, but the only truly existent and eternal self resting at the basis of things." (section 5) The lyrist has "been released from his individual will, and has become, as it were, the medium through which the one truly existent subject celebrates his release in appearance." It is in this celebration achieved through the mediumship of genius, as Nietzsche famously asserted, that the essence of the world is justified as aesthetic phenomenon.

The overwhelming, invasive, compelling power of this song (much later in his brief career Nietzsche names "the inability *not* to react" as symptomatic of the Dionysian frenzy) resides in its Dionysian rapture, not its Apollinian control and discharge as image. This rapture, as Henry Staten says, is not a matter of representation but a "communication of force."[6] It manifests a possession, and in its throes, Nietzsche writes, "the enraptured servant of Dionysus senses the nearness of the god." (section 8) It takes the shape of the irrepressible cry that Wagner had described in his "Beethoven" essay, written at about the same time as *The Birth of Tragedy* and lauded by Nietzsche in his dedication to the composer. In an early draft of *The Birth of Tragedy* Nietzsche had connected this cry to Schopenhauer's will, using terms close to Wagner's (though without any of Wagner's prudency in the face of artistic artifice): "When does Tone become Music? Above all in the will's states of the most extreme pleasure and displeasure, . . . in the transport of feeling: in the cry."[7] In *The Birth of Tragedy* Nietzsche notes that Archilocus, compared to the Apollinian Homer, "appalls us by his cries of hatred and scorn, by his drunken outbursts of desire." (section 5) Or, more generally, he speaks of the "cry of horror" at the climax of Dionysian revelry (section 2) and conjures up its outbreak in Apollinian Greece:

> Let us imagine how into this world, built on mere appearance and moderation and artificially dammed up, there penetrated, in tones ever more bewitching and alluring, the ecstatic sound of Dionysian festival; how in these strains all of nature's *excess* in pleasure, grief, and knowledge became audible, even in piercing shrieks; and let us ask ourselves what the psalmodizing artist of Apollo, with his phantom harp-sound, could mean in the face of this demonic folk-song! (*The Birth of Tragedy*, section 4)

For Nietzsche the triumph of Greek tragedy came in Aeschylus and Sophocles, when this Dionysian song was ordered and objectified in the illusory dream-images of Apollo but not silenced by them. The decline of tragedy, instead, followed when Euripides embraced the anti-Dionysian, individualistic rationality of Socrates. Then the Dionysian musical cries, those "reconciling tones from another world," ceased. Dionysian possession disappeared, and Apollinian dream-contemplation and imagism was debased. (section 12) In Euripides, he says, "What still remains of music is either excitatory or reminiscent music, that is, either a stimulant for dull and faded nerves, or tone-painting." The "metaphysical comfort" that tragedy had offered in its Dionysian mode is lost—the joyous and painful affirmation of the self-negating, eternal unity of nature expressed in the satyr chorus from which tragedy originated, and the mark, by virtue of its affirmation, of Nietzsche's break with Schopenhauerian resignation. In its place is the superficial spectacle of the *deus ex machina*, the hero artificially rewarded after his sufferings. (section 17; for the satyr chorus see section 7.) But this solace, to repeat, had been in the era of its Dionysian preeminence the solace of possession abetted by the shamanistic medium, the poet.

   The metaphysical solace lost in late Greek tragedy was recovered not in conventional opera but only in Wagner's music drama. Nietzsche made this case, famously, in the last ten sections of *The Birth of Tragedy*, excoriating earlier opera for its superficial phenomenalism and championing Wagner for touching, in *Tristan*, Dionysian reality. Opinions on these last chapters have been as varied as opinions on Wagnerism itself, with many these days sharing in the embarrassment of Nietzsche's comprehensive editor and exegete Walter Kaufmann.[8] But the value of these pages does not lie in the accuracy of their view of operatic history and of its recent, Wagnerian apotheosis. It is not found in their strength of argument, since for long stretches argument as such is submerged in a torrent of effusive eloquence. Neither, finally, does it reside in Nietzsche's concluding remarks on musical dissonance (sections 24–25), for these remarks, if suggestive, remain undeveloped and are cut from the same cloth as Schopenhauer's schematic attempts to discuss musical specifics in *The World as Will and Representation*.[9]

   What makes these pages significant is instead the straightforwardness with which they link the history of opera back to a prehistory of musical ritual, musico-dramatic contact with invisible realms, and sung possession. *The Birth of Tragedy*, whatever else it might or might not be, stands out from three centuries of debate and discussion as the clarion affirmation of opera as a rite of possession. In turning from ancient tragedy to "analogous phenomena of our own time" (section 16) Nietzsche binds the development of opera to the Dionysian-Apollinian dualism at the heart of his conception. He locates the origin of the powers of sung drama in the same metaphysics that was envoiced in pre-Socratic tragedy.

   This view spills over beyond Wagnerian music drama to the pre-Wagnerian opera that Nietzsche condemns. It cannot help but do so.

Nietzsche's very condemnation of opera, after all, marks it as a genre that *ought* to have approached more nearly the Dionysian limit finally reached by Wagner. His rhetoric does not avoid this categorical slippage from music drama to opera. He is scathing in treating the "extra-artistic," purely "theoretical" origins of the "*stilo* (sic) *rappresentativo*," the "idyllic seductions and Alexandrian flatteries" of number opera, its reliance on tone painting, its making of music the servant of the text, "the slave of phenomena," and its destroying of music's "Dionysian-cosmic mission."[10] And Nietzsche is ingenious in interpreting the function of myth in Wagnerian music drama: its ability to intervene as a generalized Apollinian scrim between the listener and the Dionysian music, offering the illusion of a reversal of roles, in which music serves only to enhance dramatic image. "What can the healing magic of Apollo not accomplish," Nietzsche asks, "when it can even create the illusion that the Dionysian is really in the service of the Apollinian and capable of enhancing its effects—as if music were essentially the art of presenting an Apollinian content?" (*The Birth of Tragedy*, section 21)

But if Apollinian magic is so potent, what grounds are we afforded for distinguishing between Dionysian music drama and nonmetaphysical opera? How can we know that we are *not* under its spell? How can we discern, in the presence of such powerful illusions, which appearances lack Dionysian force and which, instead, lead to "a spasmodic unharnessing of all the wings of the soul"? Only, it would seem, through the spasm. Only through the *a priori* definition of "genuine musicians" as those who feel that Wagner succeeds in balancing Apollinian appearance and Dionysian reality and those who judge that composers of conventional opera fail. (section 21) Only, in other words, through Nietzsche's personal *parti pris*, his own preferences and the force of his Wagnerian effusion. Just as in the cases of Poizat's Lacanian Wagnerism and Abbate's noumenal Wagnerism, so in *The Birth of Tragedy* there is no categorical boundary between metaphysical music drama and sublunary opera, no bounded space within the culture of opera for a metaphysics that does not also escape into its other reaches. There is only the idea, elaborated by Nietzsche with a self-consciousness and confidence unprecedented in operatic discourse, of a musico-dramatic history shot through with metaphysical forces and its own conceptions and uses of them.

· · · · ·

However mighty the boundary Nietzsche proposed in *The Birth of Tragedy* between Wagner and the rest, it could not withstand his own later turn away from Wagner. By 1888 Bizet's *Carmen* would stand in for *Tristan* in realizing a revised Dionysian rapture. Now Nietzsche would don gloves to read Wagner's score.[11] Now earlier ambivalences, taking root perhaps already at the moment of Nietzsche's championing of Wagner, would well up as an almost obsessive force driving him again and again to articulate an anti-Wagnerian and non-metaphysical conception of art. "An anti-metaphysical view of the world," he exclaims in an unpublished note, "—yes, but an artistic one."[12] At the very moment when he proclaimed opera's heritage and triumph as a rite of possession still linked to a grand metaphysics (and what rite of possession has not been grandly founded on the invisible realm and its soul?), Nietzsche was moving toward this different stance: toward a model of subjectivity that repudiated the age-old division of body and soul, a model that suggested a view of the force of music granting possession (in its conventional guises) no place.

Fundamental to this model is the powerful opposition Nietzsche mounted to metaphysical presuppositions of all sorts. The will has now shed the Schopenhauerian baggage it still carried in *The Birth of Tragedy* and emerged as a resolutely sensate "will to power." This is no longer Schopenhauer's universal noumenal force from which the subject emerges and back to which it disappears as it transcends the *principium individuationis*, but instead a multiple array of forces that plays itself out in sensible appearances. The material world, including the body, is nothing other than the flux of these appearances, "force throughout, . . . a play of forces and waves of forces, at the same time one and many." It is sustained by no invisible "other world," but instead *"is the will to power—and nothing besides!"* Subjectivity appears out of the same flux ("And you yourselves are also this will to power—and nothing besides!"), but now it is a kind of *inter*subjectivity, a play of bodily permeabilities and a communication through impulse and force, gesture and movement.[13] The subject, as a fragmented interpreter whose grounds for interpretation are always unstable, faces the infinite regress of both appearances and the forces that circulate through them.

The soul is absorbed into this world of flux and appearances. In *Thus Spoke Zarathustra* it is made into body and deprived of its transcendence: "the awakened and knowing" speak against "the despisers of the body," saying "body am I entirely, and nothing else; and soul is only a word for something about the body."[14] In the *Genealogy of Morals* soul comes to be understood as a necessary bane brought about by human socialization. It is demoted from its Kantian identity as the place within the subject where phenomenality brushes up against transcendence, reduced to no more than "bad conscience," the unhealthy internalizing of all the vital instinctive drives thwarted by society.[15] The introjection of invisible, transcendent realms, fundamental to views of the subject after Kant, is superseded by an attempt to repudiate invisibility altogether.

No more than an attempt, perhaps,[16] but the attempt itself is extraordinarily significant. The "aesthetic phenomenon" Nietzsche had earlier pronounced a "simple" matter of possession has been vastly complicated by the undermining of the metaphysics that, in one fashion or another, had always provided its foundation. Aesthetics has been returned to the bodily, sensory issues that Adolf Baumgartner had meant to connote in coining the term more than a century before Nietzsche. But the soul that Baumgartner took for granted as the metaphysical backdrop against which to define bodily sensibilities is now folded into the will to power, the product of the same forces that create body. Nietzsche asks us now—and it is the first time the challenge has been posed—to imagine an aesthetics without metaphysics. In *Nietzsche contra Wagner* he pronounces aesthetics to be "nothing but a kind of applied physiology."[17]

In Nietzsche's later writings the impulse of Dionysian music takes the form of a heightening of the body and its interplay in the world's flux of forces. It is a ripple of muscles and a turning of senses that manifests the will to power, and in so doing it creates world and body—and soul only as "something about the body," if at all. In this new Dionysian rhythm we sense the formation of a musical aesthetic distinct from that of *The Birth of Tragedy*, one arising as a play of sensible powers and denying all supersensible realities.[18] In moving away from metaphysics Nietzsche limns musical force as a play of the will to power that creates corporeal and sensory movement and, through this, determines bodily interaction with other bodies. He offers an image of *aesthesis* in the guise of *kinesis*.

Dionysian art in Nietzsche's later writings stands opposed to the turning away from life, sense, and sensuality that is for Nietzsche the foundation and constant urging of Christianity. Just so, Dionysus and Christ, however similar in their martyrdom and their cults, look nevertheless in opposite directions, the first toward "a *promise* of life," the second toward negation of life and redemption from it.[19] The new Dionysus can still be juxtaposed with Apollo, but now the juxtaposition becomes something more like a triangulation, in which however the importance of Apollo is much diminished. Christ figures, explicitly or implicitly, as the denial of body and the negation of life, to which Dionysian art, not Apollinian, is the effective rejoinder. Dionysian art is an "affirmation of the world as it is, without subtraction, exception, or selection." It is an embracing of the full array of forces that comprises the world, a *love* of these forces that conceives them as the joyous, fateful being of the world and does not pit itself against some otherwise determined, inevitable, hateful destiny. "To stand in a Dionysian relationship to existence—" Nietzsche muses, "my formula for this is *amor fati*."[20] This relationship eliminates, as Michel Haar has pointed out, the Christian opposition between love, as an act of will, and destiny, as a predetermined course beyond the reach of will. The Dionysian relationship transforms will, so that it "no longer searches for what is not yet."[21]

Music remains the fundamental medium in this new Dionysian art. Nietzsche described both the art and music's place in it in a long, crucial passage from the *Twilight of the Idols*:

> What is the meaning of the conceptual opposites which I have introduced into aesthetics, *Apollinian* and *Dionysian*, both conceived as kinds of frenzy? The Apollinian frenzy excites the eye above all, so that it gains the power of vision. The painter, the sculptor, the epic poet are visionaries par excellence. In the Dionysian state, on the other hand, the whole affective system is excited and enhanced: so that it discharges all its means of expression at once and drives forth simultaneously the power of representation, imitation, transfiguration, transformation, and every kind of mimicking and acting. The essential feature here remains the ease of metamorphosis, the inability *not* to react (similar to certain hysterical types who also, upon any suggestion, enter into *any* role). It is impossible for the Dionysian type not to understand any suggestion; he does not overlook any sign of an affect; he possesses the instinct of understanding and guessing in the highest degree, just as he commands the art of communication in the highest degree. He enters into any skin, into any affect: he constantly transforms himself.
>
>   Music, as we understand it today, is also a total excitement and a total discharge of the affects, but even so only the remnant of a much fuller world of expression of the affects, a mere residue of the Dionysian histrionicism. To make music possible as a separate art, a number of senses, especially the muscle sense, have been immobilized (at least relatively, for to a certain degree all rhythm still appeals to our muscles); so that a man no longer bodily imitates and represents everything he feels. Nevertheless, that is really the normal Dionysian state, at least the original state. Music is the specialization of this state attained slowly at the expense of those faculties which are most closely related to it.[22]

Here Nietzsche tries to describe the fullness of Dionysian art in terms of the will to power. This art is a force that drives the whole body into motion—indeed transforms and even *creates* the whole body in motion. It enables in the body a special sensory receptivity, causing an emotional overload that releases itself in an irresistible rhythm, mimicry, and "histrionicism." This "total discharge of the affects" gives the Dionysiac a power of imitation and representation unknown in Apollinian frenzy, restricted as it is to visual excitation. The Apollinian discharge-of-dream image Nietzsche had described in *The Birth of Tragedy* is no longer broached as a countermeasure, moderating and channeling the Dionysian force of the lyric poet, but only as a pale, distilled alternative. It is Dionysian frenzy, alone and unqualified, that fully affirms life, body, and the senses in the face of Christian negativity.

This affirmation is brought about by music, but not fully by modern music. For the modern musician is the product of the crystallization of the category "music" that we discerned in the early modern period. The musician of Nietzsche's day springs from a specialization that had gradually separated him from other Dionysian artists-of-motion that Nietzsche names in the next section of *Twilight of the Idols*: the actor, the mime, the dancer, and the lyric poet. Through this specialization modern music has limited its kinetic fullness, "immobilized . . . a number of senses," especially the musculature set in motion by some fuller Dionysian art.[23] Nietzsche now reconceives as purely sensate the "metaphysical solace" he had discovered at the time of *The Birth of Tragedy*. The *Gesamtkunstwerk* he now envisages is an enacted, danced poetry, conveyed in song, that forms the body in motion, *informs* other bodies *with* motion, but speaks to no soul.[24]

Compare the passage from *Twilight of the Idols* to the ostensibly similar excerpt quoted earlier from the seventeenth-century theorist Teodato Osio (see p. 16 above). Osio, too, esteems the effects of music (the poet's music) over those of visual arts (in his case, painting and acting). He too attributes music's greater power to its motion. But Osio continues the venerable tradition—which reaches back before Plato and which will reach forward to Nietzsche's own time—that traces music's power, one way or another, beyond its motions to their correspondences with those of the soul. Nietzsche instead breaks with this tradition and attempts to relate music's powers only to the movements of the body. Osio *internalizes* music's effects, in other words, and thus moves immediately to the realm of the invisible—to the soul and its affiliations—to explain them. Nietzsche tries to *externalize* music's effects, to conceptualize them exclusively as a force of will driving muscles and senses.[25]

In relation to this new, kinetic aesthetics, this applied physiology, Wagner's music does not measure up. Its motion, first and foremost, displays "the complete degeneration of rhythmic feeling, *chaos* in place of rhythm." To experience the attenuated momentum of Wagner's ongoing orchestral fabric is akin, Nietzsche avers in a famous image, to wading into the sea until we lose our footing and must swim. The "physiological presupposition of previous music," which Wagner has overthrown, was dance; now instead we tread water.[26] Most likely because of this rhythmic indirection (though he ascribes no specific cause), Wagner's music, Nietzsche says (recalling a phrase he had used in *The Birth of Tragedy* to characterize the degenerate song of the Euripidean age; see p. 114 above), is no more than "a means to excite weary nerves." It does not set the body in motion: *we are able not to react to this music.*

Wagner's music recalls the Euripidean age in another regard as well: its gesturism. Wagner "begins from a hallucination—not of sounds but of gestures," Nietzsche says, alluding to the composer's leitmotivic technique; "Then he seeks a sign language of sounds for them."[27] He subordinates music to images in a way that is un-Dionysian and that harkens back to that failing of the New Dithyramb, tone painting. (The subordination, however, accords well with Wagner's stated goal, in *Opera and Drama*, of restoring music to its proper place as the means, rather than the end, of music drama.)[28] Wagner is for Nietzsche the supreme musical miniaturist; "his real masterpieces," are all "very short, often only one measure long."[29] He supports these miniatures with "the mud of the most contrary harmonies," which for Wagner comprises the definition of passion.[30] And he strings them together in a formless, undeveloped melange that is acceptable only because of the undiscriminating tolerance of "theater taste."[31] In pandering to and celebrating the lowest common denominator that determines this taste, this "right of theater to *lord it* over the other arts," Plato's *theatrocracy*, Wagner can be compared only to the other arch-romantic dramatist, Victor Hugo.[32]

What is worst, all this is in the service of a redemptive metaphysics that trucks in a melange of Schopenhauerian pessimism and Christian negation of life, body, and sensibility.[33] To explain his disgust with this Wagnerian stance Nietzsche returns, in the Epilogue of *The Case of Wagner*, to the duality of "master" and "Christian" moralities he first delineated in the *Genealogy of Morals*. Christian morality offers denial, want, and escape from the self in some redemption beyond life. It breeds an aesthetics of decadence that relies on idealism and the "counterfeiting of transcendence and [the] beyond," of which Wagner was the greatest advocate.[34] Master morality, rooted in the ancient, pre-Christian and non-Judaic world, is instead an affirmation, a celebration of the powerful movement of self that spills over into aesthetics, into "sublime symbols and practices," out of fullness of heart.[35] Modern man is the legatee of both these moralities, and so he is peculiarly prone to the falsification that denies their abiding opposition. An archetypal instance of such falsification is the achievement of Wagner in taking Icelandic sagas, prime exemplars of master morality, and infusing them with Christian denial and otherworldly redemption. Hence, for Nietzsche, Wagner and his whole enterprise sum up modernity itself.[36]

·   ·   ·   ·   ·

Against all this, Nietzsche yearned for an art that could be an apotheosis of Dionysian movement, an art that would yield what he found lacking in Wagner: "*la gaya scienza;* light feet, wit, fire, grace; the great logic; the dance of the stars; the exuberant spirituality; the southern shivers of light; the *smooth* sea—perfection—."[37] It is going too far to say, simply, that he found it in *Carmen*. After all, Nietzsche's remark in opening *The Case of Wagner*, that "It is not merely pure malice when I praise Bizet . . . at the expense of Wagner," leaves plenty of room for malice and is hardly a gesture of unmixed enthusiasm toward the French composer. And later in the same work Nietzsche is categorical: "When in *this* essay I declare war upon Wagner . . . the last thing I want to do is start a celebration of any *other* musicians. *Other* musicians don't count compared to Wagner."[38] We must not posit *Carmen* as the unqualified fulfillment of Nietzsche's longing for a postmetaphysical Dionysian art.

But by the same token we should not discount altogether his admiration for "Bizet's masterpiece," or, for that matter, even his attraction mentioned elsewhere to the "divine frivolity" of Offenbach's music.[39] It is clear from Nietzsche's enthusiasm alone—enough enthusiasm to support twenty viewings, by his count—that *Carmen* counted for something significant. In his late Dionysian relish for the work, we sense Nietzsche's vision of an utterly *worldly* opera and, hence, a true surmounting of Wagnerism. We gain the impression that *Carmen* touched, at least, on all the great antimetaphysical themes of his later writings. It is clear that these themes brush up against more trivial attractions that drew Nietzsche to the opera. But often enough even these attractions, on closer inspection, open out on Nietzsche's repudiation of otherworldliness. In *Carmen*, unexpectedly and with Nietzsche's enigmatic guidance, we draw near to postmetaphysical opera.

To Nietzsche *Carmen* offers, first, a rhythm unlike Wagner's. "This music . . . approaches lightly, supply, politely. . . . 'What is good is light, whatever is divine moves on tender feet': first principle of my aesthetics."[40] This is music that steps boldly, marches, *dances*—no treading water here. And if Nietzsche needs to traffic in orientalizing images to convey this kinesis ("And how soothingly the Moorish dance speaks to us? How even our insatiability for once gets to know satiety in this lascivious melancholy!"),[41] this circum-Mediterranean exoticism makes it all the more evident that *Carmen's* irresistible motion represents for him the possibility of a midday Dionysianism, a southern rhythm of life to be embraced, a movement that will sweep the feet with it and remake the body in its force of will.[42]

Moreover, if the rhythmic efficacy of *Carmen* operates plainly enough at the local level of its musical style, in dance-like or march-like music, it is also, for Nietzsche, a function of the opera's longer spans and larger formal outlines. Bizet's music "is rich. It is precise. It builds, organizes, finishes: thus it constitutes the opposite of the polyp in music, the 'infinite melody'," Nietzsche writes, with a jab at the handiest catchphrase for

Wagner's formal iconoclasm. In this organization Bizet's music substitutes variety and change for the stasis and especially the tautologies of Wagner, whose insistence and disrespect for the listener reduce Nietzsche to an eloquent stammer: "Wagner treats us as if—he says something so often—till one despairs—till one believes it."[43]

The potentially Dionysian rhythms Nietzsche heard in *Carmen* arise as much from this variety, I think, from the conciseness and vitalizing juxtaposition of its numbers, as from any individual kinetic energies. As number opera, in other words, *Carmen* is imbued with a broad rhythmic dynamism that Nietzsche missed in Wagner's music. Indeed, in the same months when he was writing of *Carmen*, Nietzsche seems to have reconsidered the Wagnerian condemnation of number opera he had acquiesced to in *The Birth of Tragedy*. "Convention," he asserts in a note of this period, "is a condition of great art, *not* an obstacle." Conventions manifest the "superabundance of means of communication" that marks the "aesthetic state." They are themselves rhythms, "movements," and "mimic signs" of the sort that embody the will to power and permit the communication of one body with another.[44] Just so, the abrupt, high-level rhythmic shifts across Bizet's score—from the Seguidilla to the finale of act 1, from the Gypsies' song to the entrance chorus for Escamillo to his *couplets* in act 2, and so forth—function as kinetic emblems, musical forces enlivening the bodies they bring into interaction onstage.

Carmen offers Nietzsche also a postromantic depiction of love: "Love translated back to nature. Not the love of a 'higher virgin'! No Senta-sentimentality! But love as *fatum*, as fatality, cynical, innocent, cruel—and precisely in this a piece of nature." This love refutes the romantic and Wagnerian notion, with all its metaphysical baggage, that "one becomes selfless in love because one desires the advantage of another human being."[45] But if we are tempted, in turning away from such romance, to read love in *Carmen* as some Pavlovian response or Darwinian struggle to get one's own, we need to move cautiously: Nietzsche evidently has something rather more nuanced in mind. His love is a "tragic joke" (whose expression, he says, raises *Carmen* above thousands of other works)[46]—a joke that itself is implicated in the central and idiosyncratic Nietzschean conception of fate.

The tragedy is that love is essentially selfish, a fundamental assertion of self. The joke is that it is an enactment of will to power through which the organism enters into the movement of becoming and breaks down the notion of a stable, bounded self; love's selfishness is precisely self-defeating. The Dionysian choice is to embrace this tragedy, love this love as all the world there is, and own up to the illusory nature of its conventional façade of selflessness. Bizet succeeds (where, for Nietzsche, Wagner fails repeatedly) in depicting this choice without the flinch of metaphysical obfuscation: "Have more painful tragic accents ever been heard on the stage? How are they achieved? Without grimaces. Without counterfeit. Without the *lie* of the great style."[47]

In this the music of *Carmen* is redemptive, but in an entirely different way than Wagner's music. Bizet does not stage the sham redemptions by love of protagonists who love. Instead he redeems music itself from the foggy metaphysics of northern Europe. He discovers, as Nietzsche memorably put it in *Beyond Good and Evil*, "a piece of *the south of music*," and moves toward "a supra-German music that does not fade away at the sight of the voluptuous blue sea and the brightness of the Mediterranean sky."[48] He begins to answer the question Nietzsche had posed as to the nature of a music "that would no longer be of romantic origin, like German music—but *Dionysian*."

Here again Nietzsche has recourse to ethnic and geographic exoticism—indeed, to a typically Teutonic orientalizing of the south of Europe itself. The tried-and-true gypsyisms and hispanisms of *Carmen's* music obviously provided the stimulus for the outpouring of Mediterranean imagery in his discussion of the opera. But these exoticisms also marked for Nietzsche *Carmen's* turn away from the cultural regions of Europe where metaphysics showed no sign of burning off as the day wore on. They functioned as musical codes, pulling the listener away from the haunts of Christian or metaphysical negation and toward a place where a Dionysian affirmation might be feasible. ("You begin to see how much this music improves me?" Nietzsche asks; "*Il faut méditerraniser la musique.*")[49]

The question of fate in *Carmen*, so closely intertwined with that of love, also evokes from Nietzsche the language of orientalism: "Another sensuality, another sensibility speaks here, another cheerfulness," he writes. "This music is cheerful, but not in a French or German way. Its cheerfulness is African; fate hangs over it; its happiness is brief, sudden, without pardon."[50] To understand the fate Nietzsche heard here as identical to the metaphysical force so basic to romantic opera is to misunderstand, however, all the most important tendencies in his later thought. What Nietzsche perceives is not the "evil destiny" that Tchaikovsky and countless later commentators have heard in *Carmen*.[51] It is neither the counterbalancing vengeance that tracks the protagonists across decades and two countries in *La forza del destino* nor the cosmic order trodding through heroic epochs in the *Ring*. It has lost all the otherworldly backing of those conceptions and has not a whiff of the mystical, the metaphysical, or the Christian about it.

Instead Nietzsche's "happiness . . . without pardon" takes the form of the play of forces that unfolds the world as will to power. It is what the Dionysian artist or actor in the world must embrace, the object of love in

the maxim *amor fati*.[52] Of all operatic protagonists, Carmen herself
seems most able to embrace this sort of fate. Nietzsche says nothing specific about her, but she is the implicit subject of all his talk of love as fate,
and it is impossible not to cast her as the protagonist of his postmetaphysical hearing of the opera. She stands entirely clear of the immaculate,
maternal metaphysics (not to mention the "higher virginity") of Micaela.
In the face of Don José, and indeed of Escamillo and Zuniga and all the
men she encounters, she seems almost to play a role like that of the
woman in the "Dancing Song" sections of *Thus Spoke Zarathustra*—she
is "life" to their (pitifully inadequate reflections of) Zarathustra. Except
that to call those men, even in severely qualified terms, Zarathustrian is to
speak nonsense: none of them has even an inkling of the sidestepping of
Christian morality and its metaphysics that Carmen lays before them.
What to them seems effrontery, impertinence, sorcery, finally unforgive-
able faithlessness to a romantic ideal is her Dionysian movement with and
in the rhythms of life. She embraces these rhythms in a different way than
they do, as a participant in them, in part determining rather than help-
lessly determined by them. They are for her a Nietzschean, rather than a
Christian, *fatum*.

   She seems well aware of this difference. She warns those around her,
incapable of her embrace of fate, to keep clear ("Mais si je t'aime, prends
garde à toi!"). She befuddles them with songs that are better heard as the
irresistible flow of the will, connecting her out into the world, than as
resistance to her captors or as conscious efforts at seduction. (We must
take very seriously her "Je ne te parle pas, je chante pour moi-même" in
her Seguidilla.) She predicts Don José's murder of her, long before such a
thought could have entered his head ("Tu me tuerais, peut-être. . . . Que
m'importe? Après tout, le destin est le maître!"), and she accepts the murder when it comes ("Je sais bien que c'est l'heure. . . ."). Catherine
Clément is right to say that Carmen ("very pure, very free. . . . My best
friend, my favorite") acts like a man. But it is a *Nietzschean*, Dionysian
man her actions portray, a man of a sort none of the male characters in
the opera can recognize.[53]

   Dionysian also, most deeply, is Carmen's voice. Susan McClary has
justly called attention to the variety of stylistic registers encompassed in
Carmen's singing, which sets her apart from the other, one-string voices
in the opera. In addition to her gypsy exoticisms, she can share the passionate romantic idiom of Don José (in their exchange in the Seguidilla
and their duet in act 2). She can enter into idle banter with her compan-
ions and the smugglers or, in act 4, take on the self-important earnestness
that characterizes Escamillo throughout. McClary views this chameleonic
presence as Carmen's ultimately defensive ability to adapt herself to the

languages in use around her: she "can slip easily in and out of them without revealing 'herself'."[54]

Nietzsche would have heard this variety differently, I believe, not as a veil that Carmen draws in front of her essential subjectivity but as that subjectivity itself, in its truest form. We have witnessed Nietzsche describing the "Dionysian type," in the *Twilight of the Idols*, as uniquely impressionable, interactive in the highest degree with the communicative gestures roundabout: "He enters into any skin, into any affect: he constantly transforms himself," Nietzsche wrote. In denying the Kantian subject its metaphysical underpinnings, Nietzsche's late Dionysianism fragments it across the horizon of forces that play out the will to power. Subjectivity is not island-like, monadic, and comforted in an internal sovereignty. Instead it is opened out to the bodily movements around it that are the fullest—the only—expressions of other subjectivities. As Michel Haar explains, Nietzsche's individual "does not have . . . a substantial original reserve to bring to the light of day, an In-itself that calls for objective expression. The individual is not a substance, but exists and constitutes itself by entering various roles." Haar goes on to quote Nietzsche's description of a "role": an "effect of the external world upon us, a world with respect to which we attune our 'person' in the same way as one tunes the strings of an instrument before playing it."[55]

Music, song, and voice remain, as always, basic media for conveying these roles; they offer the most compelling communicative movements and gestures. Nietzsche's shift from metaphysics to antimetaphysics does not affect the power of these gestures but only explains it on different grounds. "The substructure to the metaphysics of 'music' which could persist after this metaphysics has been stripped away," in Henry Staten's words, was for Nietzsche "a concern with the possibility of transcending the boundaries of individuality by some sort of sympathetic sharing of subjectivity."[56]

Nietzsche must have heard in Carmen's voice (we may try to hear) almost an archetype of this postmetaphysical subject. Her voice is no purveyor of invisible wares. Her embrace of fate is not a submission to metaphysics but an empowering of her song to inform the world around her, an empowering experienced as a shaping and reshaping of herself in interaction with that world and its other voices. In her ease in singing many languages, Carmen maximizes her engagement in a *this-worldly* flux of powers. Her special vocal prowess makes of her a Don Giovanni without the ghost. She sings as the gesturing of one body in interaction with others. She defines herself, in her varied music, not by reference to hidden realms, whether within or outside herself, not by tapping a secret heart she may veil or reveal, but by the array of intersubjective roles she takes on. With only a little effort she can be heard to epitomize Nietzsche's postmetaphysical opera. This is an opera in which the interaction of souls brought about by voice is replaced by interactions (brought about by voice) within a flux of forces that determine and dissolve bodies. It is an opera that stages not the invisible soul and its myths, but the subject's embodiment of its most basic, forceful drives.

VI

GHOSTS IN THE MACHINE

*C*ARMEN HAS RARELY been heard as Nietzsche heard it. This fact says much about our persisting metaphysical needs, about the older kinds of solace we continue to seek in opera—we "solid citizens," as Adorno once put it, "for whom art can never be irrational enough."[1] But while we seem still to long for contact with supersensible realms, and while many of us still seem to find it in opera, we do so in altered circumstances that have reshaped the significance such contact carries, as Adorno recognized. The operatic voice labors, after Wagner and Nietzsche, in new, unanticipated surroundings. It sings still of a noumenalism defined in the era of Kant, but it sings to a subject no longer confidently Kantian, a subject listening, in part, for other things. This subject is divided, pulled by large forces in the late modern world away from the post-Enlightenment autonomy and self-sufficiency that it comes to regard, in a turnabout of basic import, with nostalgic desire.

In operatic culture such a divided, nostalgic subjectivity helps to explain the crystallization, just at the high-water mark of artistic modernism, of a historical canon of opera with its heart in the romantic repertory. For this repertory seemed (and still seems) best to depict a free, autonomous definition of self that appealed all the more as it grew increasingly elusive. The same subjectivity, aspired to by the middle class that by the early twentieth century found itself more and more the group chiefly consuming opera, assured the international triumph of Puccini and the later Strauss—whose operatic visions were similarly bourgeois in their avoidance of moves toward self-critique. And, as we shall see, this subjectivity found early, compelling expression in Wagner's achievement and determined the fascination it continues to exert.

The history of opera in the twentieth century has sometimes been understood as a simple trajectory of *Entzauberung*, of decline in the midst of a demystified West. But operatic magic does not simply fade away in our time. Instead it persists in new, disguised, and enigmatic forms. In this regard, at least, the twentieth century stands in much the same relation to the nineteenth as did the mid-seventeenth century to the late Renaissance: in each case a reshaped metaphysics emerged that seems almost imponderable because it is cloaked in ostensive rationalism. The cloak that hides metaphysical intuitions in the modern world, operatic or otherwise, is however no longer the two-sided mantle of irreconcilable fabrics that pertained in the heyday of Cartesian dualism. Now it is the humble linen coat from Marx's *Capital*.

With its ever-increasing pervasiveness across the later nineteenth and twentieth centuries as a dominant structure of bourgeois culture, the capitalist commodity shifted the foundations of Western metaphysics. Once, in the era of Marx himself, it had appeared (as we saw in chapter 4) as one among so many mysteries of Kantian noumenalism. At that time the paradigm of noumenalism could provide a basis for the first thorough-going analysis of the capitalist commodity. Now, in the course of the commodity's huge proliferation, the tables were turned. The commodity form grew to subsume the paradigm, to be the encompassing determinant of noumenalism. It became the definitive meeting point of material and immaterial realms and hence the framework on which contact with the supersensible formed its meaning. In overtaking noumenalism, however, this commodity form also altered the material products it was comprised of and the human subjects that exchanged them.

Discussion of operatic culture in the light of such topics should start from Adorno—but not just any Adorno. It is an unfortunate fact that many readers of this grim genie of the Frankfurt school (and most English-language ones), first encounter his views on opera by reading his late set of lectures, the *Introduction to the Sociology of Music*. It is not an ingratiating introduction, to say the least. Instead, as Adorno holds forth on the irrelevance and obsolescence of opera, the overtone of "patrician grousing" that Terry Eagleton has heard elsewhere in his work swells to deafening levels. Deafening also, it seems, to Adorno himself: at certain moments the views on opera here threaten to devolve into a heedless rant that overwhelms the finer perceptions elsewhere in his writings. Two such lost perceptions, both redolent of opera's peculiar metaphysics in the twentieth century and the late modern subjectivity that responds to it, need to be retrieved here.

First, in the *Sociology* Adorno argues that opera is simply too irrational and unrealistic for audiences "trained to watch at the movies for the authenticity of each uniform and telephone set," later adding "The antagonism between the disenchanted world and a form that is illusionary to the core, . . . seems too great ever to grow fruitful."[2] The bald assertion here that the march toward scientific rationality and cinematic realism precludes opera is at odds with a much subtler analysis in a number of Adorno's earlier writings. Far from minimizing the role of the irrational, Adorno in his earlier view identified it as an important strand connecting aspects of modern society ranging from totalitarianism through popular occultism to, precisely, Wagnerian and post-Wagnerian opera. Opera provides an arena for the dialectical interaction of a rationality and an irrationality both distinctly modern. It "strives paradoxically,"

Adorno wrote, "to preserve the magical elements of art within and with recourse to the disenchanted world."[3] This view led Adorno not to oppose opera and film but instead to link them together, indeed to describe Wagnerian music drama as the very source of Hollywood's magic, "the artwork of the future in which we witness the birth of film out of the spirit of music."[4] These are deeply felt, characteristic Adornian gestures: not separating off modernist art from mass culture, or post-Enlightenment "aesthetic magic" from modern rationality, but instead asserting the productive dialectical tension extending between them.

Second, in the *Sociology* Adorno attributes opera's decline also to the inability of modern listeners, who have "forsworn individuality," to identify with the individuals depicted on the operatic stage: "There is no chance any more of identifying with the ostracized 'kept woman' whose type has long since died out, nor with the opera gypsies who keep vegetating as costume party outfits . . . a kind of chasm has opened between opera itself and present-day society."[5] Even if we set aside Adorno's very dubious assumptions concerning the identification of earlier listeners with a Violetta or a Carmen and if we recognize that the loss of individuality Adorno alludes to rehearses an *idée fixe* across much of his work, the theme of the ego weakness of the modern self, the viewpoint here seems simplistic. It appears to rely on an almost pop-psychological notion of identification as a straightforward, empathic bond entered into by an integral subject on the basis of perceived affinities with some object.

This does not accord with Adorno's own, more careful thoughts elsewhere on modern subjectivity. In one of the longest and most telling of his *Minima moralia*, for instance, he assailed the notion of a genuine, authentic, self-identical subject that the *Sociology* would later seem to presume. He described a different subject, almost Nietzschean in outline, that forms the stuff of which it is made in social, that is, intersubjective relations. This subject is defined not in identification with itself (and, by extension, in its identification with objects) but in the traces of nonidentity that comprise it.[6]

These traces of the subject's social constitution are, however, invisible. The reasons for this form the crux of Adorno's analysis of late capitalist subjectivity and its relation to the commodity. In its self-conception, the subject attempts to escape the swelling, alienating control of commodification, of a society defined by exchange. To do so it borrows from Enlightenment ideology a model of its own incorruptible genuineness, authenticity, and truth-to-itself—its own *un*exchangeability, so to speak. The subject is consumed in and constituted by a nostalgic hankering after this older-style vision of autonomy.

But this retrospective move is antithetical to an intersubjective view of the self. The appeal to autonomy hides the social relations of language and practice that make up the subject in the first place. In its nostalgia, the subject thus retraces the life-history that Marx had discovered in the commodity, which came to be a fetish by just such an occultation of social relations (the social relations, that is, of labor). The escape from commodification is futile, inasmuch as the subject's claim of authenticity, by which it would make good its escape, only draws it nearer to the processes it would avoid. Just as the social forces of labor are outshone by the unlimited exchangeability of the commodity they produce, so the alluring sheen of the authentic, self-sufficient subject obscures the secret of its social creation.

The mechanism of commodity fetishism thus invades the whole formation of the late-modern subject. In the self, as in the commodity, it renders noumenal a social realm (a constitutive intersubjectivity, or forces of labor) by concealing it behind ostensibly asocial forms (the monadic self, or products).

The effect of this concealment of social relations is far-reaching. It is the assertion of a powerful leveling relation, the pervasive relation of exchange value, among subjects and objects alike. In commodification the material product is emptied of its materialism and comes to be defined fundamentally by its equivalency in exchange with other products. At the very historical moment of the greatest worldwide circulation of material things, the tangible individuality of these things comes to seem somehow spectral, unreal, nothing more than the shadowy reflection of their defining potential to be displaced and replaced by other things.

Just so, the autonomous self undergoes a leveling in the era of commodification that works against its imagined uniqueness and self-sufficiency, and this in two ways. First, the social relations of human, subjective labor are, as we have seen, concealed within the objective presence of the commodity.[7] Second, since the subject's assertions of a retrospective autonomy over and against this objectification, while seeming to assure it distinctness and individuality, in fact take the form of another concealment of social relations, they obscure the individuality of the social formation of the subject. Hence, they liken one subject to another in island-like, monadic isolation. They evacuate meaning from gestures toward distinctive autonomy in the same way that exchange overshadows the palpable distinctness of things. Objects and subjects alike come to seem false—precisely in the qualities on which they stake their claims to be true: the "thingishness" of material objects and the individualistic self-definition of selves. As Adorno gloomily puts it, "The ungenuineness of the genuine stems from its need to claim, in a society dominated by exchange, to be what it stands for yet is never able to be."[8]

We might generalize thus: the broaching of metaphysics in the late-modern West takes the form of the subject's attempt to recuperate in some manner the social forces hidden by its own immersion in exchange and its nostalgia for autonomy. This is, from the first, a metaphysics that circulates within the horizon of the commodity form that defines it. It cannot, given the subject's complicity with this form by virtue of its claim to self-sufficiency, escape to reassert some putative earlier, as yet uncommodified, noumenon. Seeming reassertions of this sort are the alienated subject's vain attempt from within the commodity culture to recapture an imagined, earlier metaphysics outside it.

Adorno saw such a regression in modern-day occultism, whether expressed in Victorian and post-Victorian spiritualism or in astrology columns in the daily papers. Such trends functioned to replace the social forces rendered invisible in commodification with the manifestations of other, supersensible (and social, in their otherworldly way) forces. This attempt was allied in Adorno's view with more sinister efforts to forge pseudo-transcendental *communitas* in the modern era, especially those relying on anti-Semitism. Modern-day occultism remains distinct from earlier occultisms because its context—the culture of nostalgic monadism, unlimited exchange, and fetishized commodities—channels the expression of the supersensible into the creation of additional, undifferentiated monads. The specters it attempts to summon (for example that ultimate *reductio* of Hegel's *Geist*, the prosaic and domestic ghosts of the séance), ring false exactly in proportion to the solidity it assigns to them. Even ghosts have become impossible except in the form of a debased autonomy.[9]

.   .   .   .   .

It is this sort of metaphysics that early on had so troubled Adorno in his experience of Wagner. Wagner's music dramas, like other gestures of late modernism that would follow them, were captured in the gravitational field of the commodity form. Their effect was a false, overcompensating objectification of the noumenal, reflecting, for the Adorno of *In Search of Wagner*, the most general features of commodity culture. For this reason he described it with the adjective Marx had applied to the fetishized commodity, *phantasmagoric*.

These music dramas stand in a relation to the capitalist commodity analogous to that of the late-modern subject itself. They work strenuously to hide the labor that goes into producing them, in this both duplicating the operation of the commodity and reaching nostalgically toward an earlier, Kantian artistic autonomy. "A contradiction of all autonomous art is the concealment of the labour that went into it," Adorno writes. But now this concealment is captured within the logic of the commodity form: "In high capitalism, with the complete hegemony of exchange-value and with the contradictions arising out of that hegemony, autonomous art becomes both problematic and programmatic at the same time."[10] It is programmatic because it conceals as a noumenon the social relations that produce the effect of subjectivity, problematic because this concealment appears to sustain the illusory possibility of a not-yet-commodified autonomy.

Wagner deployed, paradigmatically but through no self-conscious agenda of his own, the dialectic of the artwork in the era of late capitalism—which is to say the dialectic of both the commodity and the subject. His works proclaimed their autonomy, as stridently as have any before or since in the Western tradition, but in the same act they marked their affinity to the commodity form, placing themselves alongside so many other mass-culture claims of self-sufficiency and distinction. More clearly than any other artist, Wagner revealed that in high capitalism it is only through a dialectical absorption into commodity mass culture that the artwork stakes its claim to noumenalism.

In a number of ways, some more convincing than others, Adorno located this commodity dialectic in the leveling, objectifying force he heard in Wagner's orchestra. The orchestra carries the all-important leitmotivs, repeating them as so many atomized advertising slogans that defeat any true (which is to say, for Adorno, Beethovenian) thematic development (see *In Search of Wagner*, chaps. 2–3 passim). Moreover, the orchestra, as a unified body controlled by an overpowering conductor, objectifies the audience too, bludgeoning it with repeated, calculated effects (pp. 30–31). In this orchestral body even the individual players are the fragmented, isolated victims of the sonorous division of labor Wagner forced on them (pp. 78–84). And the singers onstage are distanced from the poetic and dramatic effects they produce by the "emancipation" of the orchestra and by their exclusion, in large part, from its language of associative leitmotivs (pp. 98, 103).[11]

All these objectifying tendencies are ostensibly opposed, Adorno recognized, by Wagner's recourse to myth (chapter 8). Wagnerian myth functions by asserting a "universal humanism" that answers to the late modern subject's felt need to rediscover some generalized community of feeling in the face of the occultation of specific social relations. But in the vicious circularity of commodity culture, the relation the subject discovers is the leveling commonality of exchange value. Wagner's myths cast individual human interactions as nothing more than a contingent "residue" of "an unvarying human nature"; they exclude political and historical specificity from the music dramas (pp. 114–15). They militate against subjective individuality and so anticipate other, later mass movements toward mythic forms: toward the mist-shrouded heritages of ethnic purity that sponsor fascism and toward modern brands of occultism.[12] The seeming opposition of myth to orchestral objectification, then, operates as part of the machinery of the commodity form, rather than offering true resistance to it. Its leveling force haunts the plots of Wagner's music dramas, manifesting itself in their tangle of tautologies and symmetries, which has appeared to many exegetes to be precisely their riches. With good reason it sometimes seems that most all the protagonists in the *Ring* are, by facile twists of interpretation, interchangeable with one another in their complicity and moral taint.

This leveling force eventually draws Wagnerian music drama near the structure of an encompassing, static, and repeatable ritual: the *Bühnenweihfestspiel* at Bayreuth. For Adorno, the logical outcome of Wagnerian myth was the Christian consecration of *Parsifal*: "Nowhere is Wagner more mythical and heathen than in this very consecration, a vain attempt to recapture the essence of the mystery play." (p. 125) Adorno, in other words, offered *Parsifal* as the ultimate expression of the commodification increasingly apparent throughout Wagner's oeuvre.

. . . . .

Parsifal as phantasmagoria—there is much to be said for such a hearing. It helps to situate in broader context features in the work that have figured largely in its interpretation almost since its premiere. It points up, too, as Bernard Shaw remarked, how *Parsifal*, along with the political events of its time, "demonstrated practically that the passing away of the . . . capitalistic order was going to be a much more complicated business" than Wagner had portrayed in the *Ring*.[13] More to the operatic point, it illuminates *Parsifal's* legacy to later opera composers, sharply outlining their struggles both to further its consecrative, almost liturgical tone and at the same time to recast it as a rite that could somehow resist, rather than capitulate to, the culture of the commodity. This, in general terms, is the expressive dilemma *Parsifal*—and so the rest of Wagner's output that led up to it—bequeathed to the twentieth century.

This is not to say that *Parsifal* was the first opera configured as ritual. My assertion throughout this book has been, to the contrary, that operatic history is ritual through and through. Opera from 1600 on has taken the form of a repeatable enactment of relations between its creators and audience on the one hand and the metaphysical realms they conceive on the other. But the logic of these rituals has changed according to the changing cultural circumstances. While late-Renaissance opera presented a ritual of participation, extending the subject through song out into the cosmos of which it formed the centerpiece, opera seria staged the unbridgeable distance between subject and divinity as the ritual affirmation of the ineffable, absolute king. Don Giovanni leaped across the distance, or attempted to do so, offering the spectacle of a subject whose hubris, materialized as vocal prowess, might once more make metaphysics a tangible prospect. Romantic opera ritualized this Mozartian subject as the locus of a metaphysical space at once internal and unattainable—a ritual that Nietzsche at first championed, only to repudiate it in his vision of a somatic, and perhaps unrealizable, ritual-without-metaphysics.

In this historical line *Parsifal* presents the operatic rite under the aegis of the commodity form. The novelty of *Parsifal's* ritual consists in its superimposing on an earlier, Romantic metaphysics a more recent one that emerges as a mystery of commodities. The archetypal force of the work stems from its prescient formulation of the dilemma of late modern opera: *Parsifal* adumbrates noumenalism, but only in the guise of an unlimited exchange that empties the mystical significance out of the tangible objects, musical and material, it presents. In configuring noumenalism as exchange, the work offers an operatic case-in-point of the workings of Marxian fetishism.

In this feature, moreover, *Parsifal* forms a culminating microcosm of Wagner's whole output. Across his oeuvre Wagner had gradually slid toward an ever-more precarious perch, one between a yearning invocation of the post-Kantian subject (arguably his overarching, self-conscious project, even if he might never have put it quite this way) and an expression of the particular metasubjective forces that were beginning to overwhelm this subject and position it as a telos of nostalgia. Wagner is the opera composer who more powerfully than any other championed the transcendental, post-Enlightenment subject. But in this very act he became the first composer to stage its predicament in the age of late capitalism. Against its will, so to speak, *Parsifal* offers a subjective magic whose modernity consists in its submission to the commodity form.[14]

Parsifal as phantasmagoria—the musical machinery of the work, mirroring the commodity form, configures encompassing noumenal powers as a function of an objectification that is, in turn, the obverse face of exchange. The key to this dialectical complex is Wagner's success in joining sharply etched motives and an unprecedented flexibility of motivic transformation and interrelation. In this *Parsifal* represents a ne plus ultra of leitmotiv technique. Motivic transformation acts as a leveling force that allows any motive to be related to or indeed transformed into any other one, no matter how distant and unconnected they might seem elsewhere in the work. It constitutes a musical exchange pervasive enough to prefigure the exchange-value equivalencies of all motives. *Parsifal* merges the bald, objectifying tendencies of motivic usage in parts of the *Ring*—the advertising-slogan style Adorno had condemned—with the seamless "art of transition" that Wagner vaunted as the breakthrough of *Tristan*—in which motivic differentiation is less important than the definition (from the first notes of the Prelude) of what Robin Holloway has termed a "sonorous image-cluster" that suffuses and characterizes the entire work. *Parsifal* represents Wagner's last, most radical striking of the unique balance that is basic to his mature aesthetic: the balance between a putatively autonomous musical continuity and a musical articulation determined by extramusical forces. The composer himself conceived this balance as the contrast of symphonic structure on the one hand and subordination of music to poetic and dramatic ideas on the other.[15]

Wagner's special achievement in *Parsifal* consists in the almost incredible ease with which he follows both these paths simultaneously. Motives take on an individuality that is at once heightened and undermined. They are caught in a dialectic by which they attain a crystalline, objective self-sufficiency—nothing plainer in Wagner's music dramas than the faith or prophecy motives, for example—that turns out to be predicated on their unheard-of exchangeability. Thus Adorno and Dahlhaus can both speak rightly, from opposite poles of this dialectic, while seeming to contradict one another. Adorno perceives in *Parsifal* a juxtaposition of "fragmentary motifs ... arranged one after another like little pictures," while Dahlhaus extols here a perfected "art of ambiguous expression and paradoxical intermingling," furthering *Tristan's* transition technique. The technique of the work sustains and rewards both hearings, which is to affirm with John Daverio that it embodies its "art of transition" only in a "rhetorical dialectics" that is, in its turn, saved from fragmentation by the continuity of transitions.[16]

Parsifal creates, in this way, a musical exchange that at once enables and thwarts motivic objectification. But the creation is ideologically marked. In enabling, it seems to hold out the hope of embodying, in the form of material (musical) objects, the noumenal powers that are the work's true subject matter. In thwarting, it moves toward a plastic musical exchange that reveals its noumenon only as it falsifies the mystical force of its objects. In *Parsifal* the element that mediates between Wagner's poles of transitional fluidity and rhetorical juxtaposition may be, as Daverio has it, the mystic chord. From a broader societal perspective, however, the mediator is the commodity form itself.

In the *Ring*, motives tended to be introduced in clear outline and only later combined with other motives and transformed in relation to them. In *Parsifal*, on the other hand, motives usually emerge gradually and, from the first, in flexible interaction with other motives. Already in their genesis, in other words, *Parsifal's* motives are marked by an exchangeability they never leave behind. A famous instance is the melody that opens the work, not a leitmotiv in itself but rather a congeries of germinal motives that supply the raw material for many—by some analyses most—of the leitmotivs in the music that follows, even ones as far afield in dra-

matic association as those of Klingsor's realm. Because of this compositional method, this chameleonic art of transformation Wagner had
attained, the dramatic associations of musical motives tend to be much
less definite and more fluid in *Parsifal* than in the *Ring*.[17] In *Parsifal*, more

Example 11. From Wagner, *Parsifal*

than in any other of Wagner's works, motives are born of a musical and dramatic parentage that is promiscuous, so to speak, and hence in some measure indeterminate.

Take, for example, the plangent chromatic descent with suspensions over circle-of-fifths harmonic motion associated with Amfortas's suffering—a crucial musical gesture in any hearing of *Parsifal*.[18] This gesture is first heard, three times, in the overpowering scene-change music of act 1 that accompanies Gurnemanz's and Parsifal's walk from the forest to the grail castle (see example 11).

At this point the associations of this music are rich but unsettling. It evokes in its forte dynamics and its granitic harmonic motion a sense of

architectural solidity in keeping with the crags the protagonists pass
through and the hall they approach, but at the same time its chromaticism
and dissonance connote a grail domain overshadowed by the dark forces
whose history Gurnemanz has already narrated. These dark associations
are confirmed when, some minutes later, the motive returns as Amfortas
breaks out in despair at his father's request that he uncover the grail
("Wehe! Wehe mir der Qual!").

But from the first the motive has emerged also in another, very different
shadow, a musical one: the shadow of the prophecy of redemption that
will ultimately restore the grail domain (see example 12).

The three-note chromatic descent at the top of the suffering motive is
nothing other than a climactic magnification of the chromatic descent
twice stated in an inner voice of the prophecy motive. Wagner had fea-
tured this descent in the gradual emergence of the prophecy motive itself.[19] He reinforces in a number of ways the connection it creates between the prophecy and the suffering music. In its initial statement the
suffering music gravitates toward the D minor that is the fixed tonality of
the full prophecy motive; the core of its exposition, and particularly the
second statement of the suffering motive, then, are in D minor (with a
seven-measure chromatic ellipsis, which itself begins with the chromatic

Example 12. From Wagner, *Parsifal*

descent; see music example 11, mm. 4–14). At measure 4 (example 11), moreover, to first assert D minor, Wagner lingers for a whole measure over its dominant-minor-ninth with suspension—the distinctive opening harmony of the prophecy motive. Finally, when Amfortas bursts forth in pain and dispair, his "Wehe!" is sung to the falling diminished fifth that opens the melody of the prophecy. *Leid* emerges in constant interplay with *Mitleid*.

Lest this last relation seem no more than coincidence—there are certainly other, unrelated descending tritones in Wagner's vocal declamation—Wagner recalls it again at the dramatic crux of the whole work: at the moment in act 2 when Parsifal turns away from Kundry's kiss and assumes the full burden of Amfortas's pain ("Die Wunde! Die Wunde!"). Here Parsifal takes over the suffering motive also, and we discover what Wagner had planned all along for us eventually to know: it is not Amfortas's motive, but rather, crucially, Parsifal's, just as much as the prophecy motive related to it is his. The falling diminished fifth, moreover, is only one half of the relations that extend out from the melody of Parsifal's prophecy motive: the half that connects Amfortas and Parsifal in, again, the bond of *Leid* and *Mitleid*. The other distinctive turn of the prophecy melody, its descending fifth and rising minor third on "reine Thor," relates Parsifal instead to Kundry. This is the naming (rather than pitying) portion of the melody, so to speak, and Kundry invokes it, as she enters Klingsor's Magic Garden, to name Parsifal for the first time in the work ("Parsifal! Weile! Parsifal?"). But she names him with a twist aimed at furthering her seduction: he is not so much the Pure Fool as "Falparsi," the Foolish (and presumably vulnerable) Pure One.

Much more could be said about these two motives, of course. The suffering music is especially fecund in its connections with other thematic complexes. In Parsifal's monologue in act 2, for example, it is superimposed on the so-called spear motive, derived from the end of the opening melody of the Prelude (see, e.g., at "Des Heiland's Klage da vernehm'ich"). This ties it into a much broader complex of themes. The ascending eighth-notes that begin the spear motive are an inversion of the faith motive, a connection made explicit both at the beginning of act 1 and, through cadential similarities, in the Prelude. These eighth-notes come to be assimilated with those at the end of the grail motive, whose development in act 1 had introduced the suffering music in the first place. And so forth.

An example such as this one may suggest the extraordinary richness of thematic interrelation in *Parsifal*. This richness is carried so far, again, that all things in the work seem relatable to all other things. This was, I think, a conscious strategy on Wagner's part, one that he deemed appropriate to the dramatic subject he wished to portray. With it he asserted in

music the encompassing nature of the particular noumenal force that
needed ultimately to subsume all other forces in the work: the healing,
redemptive power of the grail. The world suffused in Christian redemption is a world where evil and good may be clearly enough defined, but
only temporarily. No evil can be categorically and eternally sealed off
from good. This is one reason why *Parsifal's* seemingly opposed characters turn out to merge, as the motives of the work do. The wounded
Amfortas and self-wounded Klingsor, the seduced Amfortas and tempted
Parsifal, the resistant Klingsor and Parsifal, the black-magical Klingsor
and white-magical Titurel all are refracted images of one another.[20]

Parsifal resembles *Tristan* in that each work needed to embody in its
musical processes a diversity that could ultimately be captured within the
unity of a comprehensive force (in this both works signal the general
influence of Schopenhauer). Wagner's mastering the art of transition
made this possible in *Tristan*. But the situation of *Parsifal* was different
and pressed him further. Its manichaean vision of a world rent down the
middle between good and evil called for broader musical contrasts than
had *Tristan*. But at the same time, its triumphant Christian eschatology
required an expressive means that could demonstrate the ultimate unity
of these contrasting materials.

In *Parsifal*, then, the force of Christian redemption comes to be configured as *the very plasticity of the musical materials*, their potential for
interrelation, mutual dissolution, and exchange. At the same time, however, the work labors to convince us that this force lodges in the autonomy and expressive self-sufficiency of individual leitmotivs. Motivic self-
identity, as much as motivic transformation, seems to point toward the
broaching of a pervasive noumenalism. But the momentary coalescings of
motives in objective form are overwhelmed by their transformations.
They are swept into a universal, unlimited exchange that itself becomes
the final province of the noumenal. Religious mystery assumes the form
of an objectification that strives to recall an earlier autonomy even as it
disappears into the play of exchange. Like the formation of the late modern subject itself, the musico-dramatic configuration that Wagner
achieved in *Parsifal* reaches out toward a noumenon manifested as ostensive autonomy—but determined by the commodity form. Like that subject, it replicates the broader flux of exchange value in the era of late
capitalism.

Wagner did not, of course, set out to compose an allegory of the commodity form. This was the effect on his work of a broader set of societal
forces than even his megalomaniacal mind could comprehend or control.
Wagner's own aim was to present the grail as a nonobjective symbol of an
ideal religious truth. He made this clear in the famous opening words of
his essay "Religion and Art," in part a kind of programmatic statement of

the aims of *Parsifal*: "One might say that where Religion becomes artificial, it is reserved for Art to save the spirit of religion by recognizing the figurative value of the mythic symbols which [religion] would have us believe in their literal sense, and revealing their deep and hidden truth through an ideal presentation."[21] Here Wagner suggested his hope for the *Bühnenweihfestspiel*. It was not to be a furthering of what he saw as religion's movement toward objectivity and away from the ideal but the opposite: a merging of the subject and Christian belief in a state of unmediated religious affect, a dissolving of all "abstract dogma" in a spiritual exercise of pure emotion.

Wagner's effort depended crucially on music. This was true because, as he specified in "Religion and Art," only music among the arts could disperse completely the palpable objectifications of Christianity's dogma and reveal its spiritual ideals with an immediacy that is Schopenhauerian (though Schopenhauer would never have turned it to Christian ends). "As pure Form of a divine Content freed from all abstractions," Wagner wrote, "we may regard [music] as a world-redeeming incarnation of the divine dogma of the nullity of the phenomenal world itself."[22]

The musical force Wagner deployed to express this transcendent divinity, however, gravitated toward the commodity form exactly insofar as it configured the noumenon as a dialectic of objectification and pervasive exchange. The gestures of this music toward the noumenal only assimilated it more closely to the forces of commodification, and in doing so they showed Wagner's ideal to be nothing other than the point where the objective disappears into exchange. From the first, Wagner's aims in *Parsifal* were subject to this predicament, destined to enter into the commodity's dialectic, rather than advocating, as he had hoped, one side of a simple dualism of literal (objective) and figurative (ideal) revelation of hidden truth. His efforts to separate further the substance and the ideal of Christianity were like the late modern subject's attempts to reassert an earlier autonomy in the face of rampant exchange: they only made them more proximate. His spiritual symbols were captured in the prevailing circulation of commodities.

This dilemma appears most straightforward in the objects themselves at the heart of *Parsifal*: the grail, its surrogate spear, and the dove. These stolid materials resist circulation and try to insist, like the modern subject, that a noumenal force might reside in their autonomy alone. They seem to become more, rather than less, tangible as they are bathed in Wagner's music, refusing to relinquish their sinking heaviness even in the purple glow of his final scene. From this refusal emerges the falsity of their manifestation of the divine. Their unerodible presence has troubled the whole history of *Parsifal*'s reception, catching the attention of even its earliest viewers.[23] It threatens to overwhelm the work's spirituality, shifting it

somewhere near to the position of the beliefs of Adorno's modern occult-
ists. Indeed Adorno implied this connection at the end of his brief essay
on *Parsifal*. For him the consecrative tone of the work aimed "to conjure
a metaphysical meaning, the substance of which is lacking in the disenchanted world." The final truth the work recouped from this futile and
false attempt was the impossibility, in the modern world, "of conjuring
lost meaning from spirit alone."[24]

In this sense *Parsifal* directs our attention to magical objects at the
same time as it undermines their magical capacities. The work thus helps
define the latest stage of the history in the West of the relations between
magic and material things. Materials were endowed with magic in the
Renaissance by virtue of their adjacency to immaterial regions, and in the
early modern period through the mystery of their representative congruence with those regions. The noumenal qualities of materials at the beginning of the modern world arose from an in-itself beyond our knowledge
and were formed by the nature of our capacities to know. By the time of
Parsifal, however, this variety of noumenalism was growing ever less ten-
able. Now the claims of material objects to magical qualities were weakened to the same degree as the objects themselves emptied out their material identities in exchange.

The materiality of the stage-props of *Parsifal*, we need to remember, is
only the extreme case of the illusion of noumenal objectivity that went
hand-in-hand with exchange and transformation in the work. The grail
and the spear are, in their relation to the noumenal, nothing other than
leitmotivs congealed to the utmost, frozen in the objective form the musical materials themselves strive to attain. In this connection their taint of
religious falsity or vulgarity cuts to the heart of Wagner's project as a
whole. This taint is the mark of Wagner's own self-defining nostalgia,
anticipating the divided, late modern subject. It inhabits the noumenal
subject matter, finally Christian, he longed throughout his career to portray but could not dissociate from materialism; and it resounds in the
musical language he forged, which came to reproduce more and more
faithfully the machinery of a commodified culture. It is all well and good
to argue, as Lucy Beckett has, that the richness of *Parsifal* lies in the binding of "the sacred and the secular in a knot we find hard to untie";[25] the
statement is, in itself, unimpeachable. But the tangles of the knot are the
crux of the matter, for *Parsifal* poses the predicament of all sacred
noumena, and finally all magic *tout court*, in the late modern West. It
brings to light an objectification that broaches the spiritual only as it
evanesces in exchange and simultaneously claims not to do so. It comes,
in this sense, to consecrate magic as a commodity. Truth this may be, as
Adorno has it, a truth rescued from falsehood. But it is hardly the truth
Wagner intended.[26]

Excursus 5

MECHANICAL REPRODUCTION OF OPERA

"Empathy with the commodity is probably empathy with exchange value itself," Walter Benjamin once wrote to his colleague Adorno. Benjamin's famous, complex, shifting notion of "aura" may be seen from one vantage point as his attempt to elucidate the effects of commodification on the work of art, a project Adorno pushed him to pursue. This aura is the specific history and immersion in tradition conveyed by an artwork such as a painting or sculpture. It is a mark of uniqueness that reaches back to the work's use value in some original ritual for which it was created, an embeddedness in ceremony that was blurred and altered but not effaced by the secularization of art from the Renaissance on. Aura is the history we invest in an artwork. Benjamin described it as the work's ability to gaze back at us as we view it.

Modern technologies that limitlessly reproduce plastic or pictorial artworks sever them from their roots in ritual and disrupt their gaze on us. Such reproduction replaces use value with a pervasive exchangeability; numberless copies of artworks—so many plastic replicas of Michelangelo's *David* sold in the portico of the Uffizi—can come into the grasp of numberless individual consumers. Benjamin wavered in his feelings about the political value of this mass dispersion of art (more so than Adorno, who consistently condemned it). He lamented its objectification of the artwork and its closing of the ritual distance between work and viewer, but at the same time he upheld it as a socialist counterforce to fascist attempts to co-opt aesthetics into politics.

Film provided Benjamin with a prime instance of a modern artistic medium created under the condition of limitless reproduction and mass distribution. In film, he argued, artist and audience alike experience the alienation of commodification. The actress in front of the camera reaches through her labors toward an audience that is utterly out of her reach. The camera, while recording her likeness, does not return her gaze as would an audience at a live performance or, indeed, as earlier artworks had done. The ritualistic aura of her performance cannot survive this technological estrangement. So the audience fills the affective void left by the decline of aura with the artificial cult of the movie star, external to the studio scene of film production.

Something of the effects Benjamin describes of estrangement and pervasive exchange have been created also by the overwhelming predominance of recordings in operatic culture across the last half century. These have proliferated to the point that attendance at live performances now amounts to only a tiny portion of operatic experience. The distant forebears of these recordings reach back at least to the nineteenth-century, taking the form of publications, then issued by the hundreds, of the music of favorite arias and overtures in arrangements for piano, voice and piano, and various combinations of instruments. Unlike those print ancestors, however, modern recordings hold out the promise of a complete and faithful reproduction of operatic voices. They offer an experience that pretends fully to replace the live performance, and with it the auratic self-fashioning of performers and audience alike, formerly restricted mainly to the opera house. This claim itself defines a new realm of operatic metaphysics, one located within the confines of a CD box or VHS cassette.

But the replacement of the earlier self-fashioning fails on two counts to evade commodification. First, the social distinction it aims to proffer, which formerly relied on attendance at the opera house with all its complex but clear paraphernalia of class distinction and privilege, is now devalued to the cost of a mass-produced, three-CD set. Subjective differentiation, attempting to assert itself through consumption of highbrow art, sinks in a sea of undifferentiated exchange. Second, the psychological investment of the opera fan is now shunted away from a public relation with the performers and other audience members and instead directed toward a private interaction with material things: the CDs, the gratifyingly hefty libretto booklet, the audio equipment, the videotape, the TV screen. These grant access to the distant, resonating bodies they represent in an estranged form, equivalent to the film viewer's relation to movie stars. So it is no surprise that cults of voice of a qualitatively new sort have taken root alongside the supremacy of recordings. These cults have, at least since the heyday of Callas, replicated the adulation of disembodied movie stars. Today they cross a broad spectrum of operatic microcultures, extending from the specialized desires and knowledges of opera buffs or opera queens to the consumption, by reassured public-television subscribers, of the prepackaged bonhomie of "Three Tenors" concerts.

Excursus 6

FILM FANTASY, ENDGAME OF WAGNERISM

When Adorno pronounced film to be the telos of Wagnerian music drama, it is improbable that he had anything quite like George Lucas's *Star Wars* series in mind. Nevertheless the films—"space operas," as Lucas himself has called them—show enough points of contact with the *Ring* to amount to something of a late-twentieth-century *reductio* of it under the aegis of full-blown mass-commodification (toy tie-ins included; might Siegfried action figures be soon to follow?). Like the *Ring*, the *Star Wars* films rely on leveling myth—in this case, a generalized but heavy-handed and immensely approachable mythical ethos—to portray their struggle of titanic forces of good and evil. The films, like the music dramas, play out across a cosmic scale where little less than the fate of the universe hangs in the balance. The corrosive evils they portray are such that even the noblest of characters may be twisted by them: like the ever-more-deeply implicated Wotan, Darth Vader (once a Jedi knight with a less menacing name and wardrobe) can be "seduced by the dark side of the Force."

The films are accompanied by a score that trucks in the straightforward leitmotivism and brassily heroic orchestration that were always lurking in Wagner's style. These features became, largely by force of John Williams's *Star Wars* scores, the coin of the musical realm for the epic film fantasies that conveyed the simplified moralism and U.S. self-confidence of the Reagan era: *E.T.* (though this enduring children's fable shines with an innocence, musical also, lacking in the rest), the *Raiders of the Lost Ark* series, the *Superman* series, and so forth. Indeed a climactic scene of *Superman II* cinches the Wagnerian connection. It echoes exactly the musico-dramatic techniques of Siegmund's discovery of the sword in the tree in Hunding's house: to the accompaniment of a fanfare motive the superhero spies, shining in the gloom, the lone surviving shard from which he will rebuild his crystal palace at the North Pole and reacquire his powers. Here the film closes a circle, unsettlingly: to portray a superhero invented in the 1930s as an American answer to the Fascist *Übermensch*, it returns to Wagnerian gestures that had defined the *Übermensch* in the first place.

The *Star Wars* films also have involved their creator Lucas in a back-and-fill maneuver that eerily reproduces the genesis of the *Ring*. Just as Wagner started with a drama concerning Siegfried's death and gradually expanded his conception to tell the story of heroic and divine generations before Siegfried, so Lucas now promises three *Star Wars* "prequels," across the turn of the millennium, that will trace the prehistory of Luke Skywalker's adventures in the youths of Obi-Wan Kenobi and Darth Vader. The forward progress of each narrative seems to call for deeper and deeper immersion in mythic prehistory.

The most significant resemblance of all, however, is also the most general: *Star Wars* continues the tradition inaugurated by the *Ring* of an unchallenging packaging of mysticism, myth, and religion whose very ease or digestibility, as Adorno saw in related varieties of modern occultism, encourages its alliance with the commodity form. Indeed such pablum-mysticism in recent film not only resembles Wagnerian myth but is derived from it. It looks back to Wagnerian fantasy along a straight path that includes fiction as well as film: the religio-mystical epics of such writers as J.R. Tolkien and C.S. Lewis, distant sources for *Star Wars* alongside more direct influences such as Edgar Rice Burroughs's Martian series and Frank Herbert's *Dune* novels, sprang from the Wagneromania that seized Britain already in the 1890s. The coordinator of the rerelease of the *Star Wars* trilogy in 1997 (expected to gross more than $600 million in worldwide ticket sales alone) was referring to the movies' original release when he remarked, grandly, "It's like we're . . . part of a cultural phenomenon that after all these years has never lost its impact on mankind." But he could just as well have been thinking back all the way to the *Ring*.

In case the example of *Star Wars* might suggest that Hollywood missed one stock-in-trade of Wagnerian myth, redemption from purgatory by love of woman, *Groundhog Day* steps forward to fill the void. Here the fate of the Flying Dutchman is neatly reenacted in contemporary Punxsutawney, Pennsylvania. The comic genre draws out elements that are, after all, not far beneath the surface of Wagner's opera. A cynical, shallow news anchor (Bill Murray), sent from Pittsburgh to cover annual Groundhog Day observances, is magically condemned to relive the day until his shriveled soul is enlivened by the love of his producer (Andie MacDowell). He wakes, every morning, to the ultimate claptrap version of the Wagnerian topos: Sonny and Cher's "I Got You, Babe." ("So put your little hand in mine, / there ain't no mountain, baby, we can't climb"; we are as relieved as he when, on the umpteenth morning, he smashes his clock radio.) Before *Groundhog Day* was released, real-life Punxsutawney could expect a few hundred visitors for the yearly prognostication by its groundhog Phil; in 1997 some 40,000 gathered.

VII

THE SUM OF MODERNITY

*P*ARSIFAL was a heavy burden for modernist opera composers to bear. Usually they were in some degree suspicious of it, sensing and resisting its falsity. Yet they also were lured to its consecrational solemnity, which came more and more to seem the gravity required of modernist "high art," the quasi-liturgical seriousness by which it could distinguish itself from commodified kitsch. This ambivalence sums up the untenable position Wagner carved out for opera in the age of late capitalism: it evades the culture of the commodity by invoking an operatic legacy and presence that were produced by and productive of that culture.

Modernist opera of the early twentieth century and its outgrowths even to our day seem snagged in this Wagnerian dilemma. They seem, that is, unable to materialize noumenal magic without relying on forces that, all told, falsify material presence. The ghosts of Versailles have the feel of a séance room to them; they are, like Wagner's grail, too quick to deny their exchangability for their materiality to be convincing. (As for the ghosts of Bly, they will have their say later.) Perhaps, at the last, this is the self-defeating form that the Orphic legend, which had marked opera's beginnings, would need in order to be recast as a myth for the twentieth century: a fable in which the powers of song operate under different conditions than in earlier periods, conditions in which looking at ghosts destroys them not by dissipation but by rendering them tangibly real. The fragility of our modern operatic fantasies originates in a commodification that inspires the hope of an impossible, too-solid presentation of the noumenon.

This dilemma is the subject matter of *Moses und Aron*, a fact that makes Schoenberg's work the most intense and thoughtful coming-to-grips with the legacy of *Parsifal*. Not that it was alone in the effort. A diverting musicological parlor game might consist of describing the ways modernist operas of various stripes reveal their backward glances at Wagner's last work. Adorno set the tone with his likening of *Pelléas et Mélisande* to *Parsifal* in their shared ornamentalism, the one anticipating and the other reflecting *Jugendstil*. "The aura of the pure fool," he wrote, "corresponds to that of the word 'youth' around 1900, the 'casually dropped' flower maidens to the first *Jugendstil* ornaments; in Mélisande such an ornament became a heroine."[1] Another player in the game might follow with *Salome*: even if we grant Deathridge's hearing of Salome's death as "alien to" Brünnhilde's and Isolde's redemptive perorations (and we should do so only if his notion of alienness is not too categorical to take account of the distorted but loud resonance of the *Liebestod* in Salome's final monologue),[2] *Salome* otherwise trades heavily on Parsifalian themes: attempted seduction of sacred purity; the living entombment and, later, death of a holy man, and a morbid sensuality associated with wounded bodies. The head of Jochanaan even functions as a sort of perverted and gruesome countergrail—a grail for the Kundry of Klingsor's garden.

Yet another player would invoke *Wozzeck*: the spectacle of a subject yearning for a Wagnerian, nostalgic autonomy who can, however, perceive no glimmer of its redemption in modern culture. (And isn't the grand D-minor orchestral climax before the final scene, the distanced apotheosis of Wozzeck's suffering, also a bow, characteristically Bergian, to the music of Amfortas's agony?) One more participant might hear in *Oedipus Rex* by Stravinsky, who had walked out on *Parsifal* in disgust some years before, the representation of a purging world order self-consciously cleansed of Wagnerian redemption but also, finally, without much humanity—might hear in *Oedipus Rex*, in other words, an attempt to reestablish under the aegis of mass culture the unfathomable abyss between the subject and metaphysics. Such a strategy, at any rate, would signal Stravinsky's affinity with early modern expression more meaningfully than all his recycling of pre-Classical music.

From the far corner of the parlor an Italophile would pipe up, unexpectedly, to remind us that Puccini had *Parsifal* in mind as he wrestled with dramatic problems in the libretto of *Turandot*. Indeed Puccini's mature operas, too, labor under the dilemma presented by Wagner. We savor these operas still, but with a troubled conscience. The reasons for this malaise cannot be fully described by recourse to the operas' internal features or even to the putative failings of their composer—not, in other words, by enumerating dramatic weaknesses (found easily enough in other, less chastened operas, after all); or by detailing the ethical lapses that caused Puccini, according to Kerman's infamous rant, to traffic in "sensationalism" rather than aspire to "art"; or by lamenting some supposedly Italianate overemphasis of lyricism at the expense of Teutonic motivic development. The taint of bad faith in our enjoyment of Puccini instead has to do with the broadest interaction between his works and the context in which they circulate. Puccini proffers, more directly than any other twentieth-century opera composer, climactic, overwhelming moments of vocal force (especially, but not exclusively, in the showstoppers regularly extracted and performed in concert: "E lucevan le stelle," "Nessun dorma," and so forth). These brief, culminating melodic distillations, distantly descended from the intense vocalism of the *primo ottocento* cabaletta, harken back to an era when the noumenal cry seemed plausible. They bring us face to face with a force we can believe only through a willfully nostalgic engagement. Puccini impels us toward this engagement, toward the attempt to ignore commodification by reveling in autonomous expression. In recent operatic history he is the most aggressive purveyor of longing for a song-before-commodification. But a part of us knows better, however swayed we might be, than to trust pushy salesmen.

Whatever these other connections, it is *Moses und Aron* that is, from start to (unfinished) finish, a musico-dramatic elaboration of the aporia posed by *Parsifal*. Philippe Lacoue-Labarthe is justified in calling it an anti-*Parsifal*, a photographic negative of the earlier work that shows, as negatives will, all the contents of its counterpart in converse form.[3] It constructs this negative by taking as its subject matter the Mosaic prohibition of graven images: the antipode of Wagner's all-too-confident materialization of the sacred.[4] This prohibition brings intractable questions of representation to the center of *Moses und Aron*. On such questions the work forms a sustained and for the most part self-conscious meditation that can offer, however, no solutions. (As various commentators have suggested, the opera's subject matter no doubt determined in advance that it would remain incomplete.) The work becomes a meta-opera, an opera about the nature of opera—but a far more profound one than Strauss's several ventures in this direction, from *Ariadne auf Naxos* on, and a more melancholy one, too, since its outcome only affirms the untenability of what it puts to the test.

Schoenberg's meditation ramifies along at least three intersecting axes. The first is internal to the plot of the work. Its defining feature is Moses' dilemma at having to convey to the people an uncompromisingly inexpressible conception of God. This sets in motion the agon between Moses and Aron (employed, by injunction of the burning bush, as Moses' mouthpiece) and dictates the famous distinction in the score between Moses' *Sprechstimme* and Aron's full song. But the dilemma is hardly resolvable. Aron's assigned task is to represent the unrepresentable, and the inevitable failure of his melodic suavity leaves Moses tormented at the end of act 2, where Schoenberg's music breaks off ("O Wort, du Wort, das mir fehlt!"), by the unutterability of his God.

This breaking off of the music betokens a second axis that reaches out from the plot to connect Moses to Schoenberg himself, for the composer shares Moses' dilemma of representing the unrepresentable. Schoenberg set himself the compositional task of expressing in his opera something that not only his protagonist but also his Judaeo-Christian religious convictions and Schopenhauerian philosophical leanings affirmed as inexpressible. As Adorno saw, his project put into question the possibility of a sacred work of art in the modern era. It brought into direct conflict the immense, but not limitless, expressive powers of the Hegelian great man or genius, that "metaphysical transfiguration of bourgeois individualism" that Schoenberg aspired to embody, and the still greater divinity somehow to be put across. It thus led directly enough to the contradiction Adorno perceived as inescapable in the opera: "By conjuring up the Absolute and hence making it dependent on the conjuror, Schoenberg ensured that the work could not make it real." By virtue of the attempt to represent it, the divine is brought under the aegis of the post-Enlightenment subject and thereby rendered mundane. In the same motion, the composer arrogates to himself the greatest possible subjective powers: "The desire to outdo every form of subjectivity meant that [Schoenberg] had subjectively to create a powerful, dominant self amidst all the feeble ones." The whole endeavor demands at one and the same time the utter submersion and the greatest emergence of the subject. But since it is Schoenberg's endeavor (and not God's), emergence triumphs. *Moses und Aron* reveals with crystalline clarity Schoenberg's unabated longing to assert the kind of creative autonomy and self-identity that had defined Wagner's nostalgic subjectivity.[5]

Schoenberg's arrogation of subjective powers to himself depended on music's own special capabilities. It was bound up in the definition and manipulation of musical technique and style. From the point of intersection of the first two axes, then, extends a third, the axis of musical expression itself. Here, too, unresolvable dilemmas arise. In Adorno's reading, the success of *Moses und Aron*, such as was possible, was illusory through and through. (His distress in saying so is palpable: after almost twenty pages on the cultural conundrums and historical antinomies embedded in the work, he throws himself on the mercy of a purely musical jury, pleading, "The crucial question . . . is what Schoenberg made of the work despite everything.") The opera's fulfillment of its theological task of providing "an image of the nonpictorial" depended on a musical construction that could seem self-engendering, free of the composer's intent, and expressionless, thereby fostering a sense of superhuman monumentality and the negation of any subjectivity behind it.[6] It depended on a technique whose integration could endow it with the appearance of utter self-determination and whose "rounded totality" could seem to deny "the existence of anything outside its own cosmos."[7]

Schoenberg sought such a construction in his use of a single tone row for the entire work. It seems likely that his own Schopenhauerian idealism led him to think of this row as an infinite musical idea whose specific realizations in the work adumbrated its limitless totality.[8] Moreover, Schoenberg framed these realizations as a polyphonic web of interrelated themes that enhances the work's illusion of freedom from subjective con-

trol. For Adorno, such developing variation harkens back to the polyphony of Bach and to a period before the modern, autonomous subject;
at the same time it captures the situation of the late modern subject whose
realization "depends on society as a whole." Thus it suggests a supersubjective, cultic, and theological totality.[9] Pamela White, along parallel
lines, discovers in this thematic working a web of leitmotivs (with musical
distinctions of more-than-Wagnerian subtlety). This hearing, too, points
toward the orchestral fabric of *Moses und Aron* as an objectifying force
striving toward supersubjective expression.[10]

But, as Adorno himself recognized, the theological illusion of the music
of *Moses und Aron* is undermined in various ways. It is weakened by the
integrated homogeneity itself of the music, which does not permit "what
the subject matter requires above all: the strict separation of Moses's
monotheism from . . . the regression to the tribal gods."[11] The very musical means by which the opera approaches an objectivizing cultic expression, twelve-tone organization and organic thematic working, undo what
it approaches. In the process of representing metaphysics through an integrated musical totality, in other words, Schoenberg loses *the possibility of
representing the impossibility of representing metaphysics*—the most
basic premise on which the whole endeavor of *Moses und Aron* was
predicated.

What is involved here, as Lacoue-Labarthe has pointed out, is the attempt to capture in music Hegel's sublime, the "incommensurability of
the finite and the infinite."[12] The specific musical-historical tradition behind Schoenberg, of which he saw himself as a culmination, offered him
no access to an unintegrated musical language—a musical language of
difference—that could have captured and represented this inadequation
within the sublime. Such a Word (style, technique) *was* truly lacking to
him, and there was little else for him to do, beyond a certain point, but
admit the uncompletable nature of his project. Schoenberg was caught in
the bind of a musical language that could approach metaphysics only
when it concealed the possibility that the failure to broach metaphysics is
built-in to itself. This is akin to the condition of *Parsifal's* musical language, which materializes sacred metaphysics only through an integration that, in its commodity-like exchange, conceals metaphysics and dissi-
pates its materialization.

But whereas this conundrum was marked in *Parsifal* by a dialectic of
smooth transition and piecemeal leitmotivic construction, it is signaled
most strongly through different means in *Moses und Aron*. Here it takes
the musical form of the contrast between the objectivizing orchestral and
choral polyphony and the individual, pathos-ridden voices of the two
protagonists. Adorno recognized both the primacy of declamatory solo
voice in the opera and also its expressive force. He attributed the latter,

justly enough, to the unbroken expressive traditions extending between Schoenberg's and earlier music. But at the same time as he owned up to this older subjectivism of Schoenberg's approach, he insisted also that the vocal pathos of *Moses and Aron* did not arise from it. He heard their expressive force instead only as an outgrowth of the metaphysical totality, beyond expressiveness, of the work. He refused to hear in it the assertion of the composer's subjectivity itself.[13]

The vocalism of *Moses und Aron* certainly calls out for an interpretation less labored than this, one that opposes it to the objectivizing forces in the opera rather than trying to absorb it into them. The voices of Moses and Aron both seem to achieve the same thing in the opera: they assert individual subjectivity in the face both of the rampant social disarray of the tribes—culminating in the orgy around the Golden Calf—and of infinite divinity and its figuration in the thematic workings of the musical fabric. They are a part of this fabric, of course—a fact given theological weight by the encompassing of both their vocal techniques, *Sprechstimme* and full song, in the voice from the burning bush in the first scene. But they also stand apart from the rest of the texture, proffering an almost incantatory force that is, for all its intended theological resonance, stubbornly individual. This force is present throughout the opera but felt most movingly, perhaps, in the meeting of Moses and Aron in act 1, scene 2.

The distinction between Moses' and Aron's approaches to God and the technical difference in their modes of utterance are relatively superficial when heard against this deeper expressive affinity. Paradoxically, though, it is only from the difference of their vocal presence—the Michelangesque *terribiltá* of Moses' speech-song as contrasted with the elegant virtuosity of Aron's full-fledged melodies—that this likeness in their subjective presence emerges. Their kinship consists, in other words, in their difference, in their respective abilities to utter not the identity of God but their own, distinctive identities. In this ability they distance themselves from the theological totality of the opera.

It is here that Schoenberg's unwillingness to relinquish post-Enlightenment or, more specifically, Hegelian subjective powers of expression declares itself most loudly. The individualization of the voices of Moses and Aron is the clearest outcome of Schoenberg's own subjective concerns, of his wary skirting of the potential of twelve-tone technique to objectify *him*. His remarks on the composition of the opera reveal his relief at the discovery that he was able not merely not to submerge his individuality in the working out of the row, but positively to assert it in the face of what he feared might be a homogenizing, totalizing force:

> In the first works in which I employed this [twelve-tone] method, I was not yet convinced that the exclusive use of one set would not result in monotony. Would it allow the creation of a sufficient number of characteristically dif-

ferentiated themes, phrases, motives, sentences, and other forms? . . . Soon I discovered that my fear was unfounded; I could even base a whole opera, *Moses und Aron*, solely on one set; and I found that, on the contrary, the more familiar I became with this set the more easily I could draw themes from it. . . . One has to follow the basic set; but, nevertheless, one composes as freely as before.[14]

In this intent preservation of his own expressive powers in the musical variety of *Moses und Aron*, Schoenberg reveals the significance for him of the individualization of his protagonists' voices: it offers the composer's view of his own autonomous powers. Schoenberg's words refute Adorno's attempt to salvage the sacred work of art by absorbing the pathos of Moses and Aron back into the theological totality of the opera. If theological infinitude is glimpsed, insofar as it can be, in the composing out of the row, Schoenberg's most basic compositional impulses pitted his own claims to subjective power and autonomy against the mechanism he had set in motion.

In his self-consciousness of this opposition Schoenberg stands apart from Wagner. He expresses a moment further along in a generalized, growing awareness of the internal dilemmas of late modernism. But his ultimate inability to extricate himself from the opposition again draws him near to the earlier composer. It marks the inevitability that individual subjectivity would have to struggle for definition in his opera against the totalizing forces that at once objectify and devalue it.

.   .   .   .   .

The allure of Moses' and Aron's vocalism, whatever it says about Schoenberg, persists for us, forming, as I have suggested, the affective heart of his opera. This durable power arises in some good measure from our own continuing need to grasp after the individualist selves Moses and Aron each portray. Their vocalism is the primary marker in the opera of their subjective autonomy; as such it resonates with our own nostalgic desire for a subjectivity extricated from exchange. And, if we respond with a clearer conscience to this appeal to nostalgia than we do to ostensibly similar appeals in Puccini (or, for that matter, in Strauss), this is in good measure because we believe Schoenberg issued his appeal after exacting and self-conscious struggles with modernist dilemmas these other composers tried to evade.

Nevertheless, this force of vocalism, as I noted in chapter 6, operates to conceal, behind the desired appearance of a clearly bounded self, the intersubjective exchange that constitutes the self in the first place. The dilemma of *Moses und Aron* is, once again, the dilemma of modern subjectivity all told, which strives to escape the commodity's erasing of social forces by virtue of a self-concept that fosters the same erasure. The voices at our horizons, though they make us what we are, are overwhelmed, dissipated, and rendered ghostly by our assertions of autonomy.

To put the matter somewhat differently: ghosts in the modern world consist of the constitutive social forces and presences at the boundaries of the psyche. These are rendered spectral by the claim of the self to autonomy, unequivocal boundedness, and subjective (rather than intersubjective) formation. Ghosts arise from the very means the self employs to elude commodification and exchange; but at the same time they are the lingering traces of social exchange itself. To give these ghosts solid, palpable form, then, is to risk upsetting a carefully gauged dialectic. It is to risk portraying them as so many additional autonomous selves, thwarting the depiction of intersubjectivity. Like the mirroring of commodity fetishism in modern subjectivity, materialized ghosts once again conceal formative social relations toward the end of asserting their own stable, stolid self-identities. But the incongruity of these with the exchange-ridden rhythms of modern life renders them, from the first, unconvincing and false.

This paradox is nowhere clearer in modern opera than where the ghosts themselves must sing: in Benjamin Britten's *Turn of the Screw*. Here the presences at the borders of the psyche, specters of the ideology of autonomy, move center stage to assert a bodily fullness through the power of song. Britten's work is an unintended exemplary tale of the implausibility, in the modern age, of ghosts made too solid. In this it is (like *Parsifal* and *Moses und Aron* if with different emphases), paradigmatic of late modern opera, enacting the effacement of self-making social exchange that occurs in the attempt to escape commodification.

Henry James's novella is a different matter altogether. Unencumbered by audible vocalism, James could narrate ghostly presence through his governess without ever answering—indeed without enabling the reader to answer—the question of the material reality of the ghosts she sees. He was free, in other words, to structure his narrative in the form of an encompassing and unfathomable ambiguity. This ambiguity might not admit of resolution one way or the other, a fact that literary critics have recently begun to celebrate, after decades of back-and-forth interpretive debate. Instead, *The Turn of the Screw* may be seen to present narrative itself, in Shoshana Felman's words, as an "incessant *sliding* of signification." In this view James's story takes the form neither of a study of psychopathology nor of a tale of real specters, but rather of a "mounting crisis of distinctions" between the two.[15]

In this, *The Turn of the Screw* is ideally suited to portray the constitutive presences that crowd in at the blurred borders of the subject. James's ghosts, eminently Victorian though they may be, are not the nostalgic harbingers of autonomy that Adorno deplored in the spirits of the séance.

Instead they demonstrate the intersubjective construction of the narrator's own psyche. Quint and Miss Jessel are the noumenal, asymptotic limit-case of all the others who shape the governess throughout the story: the children, their uncle who hires her, Mrs. Grose. Hence one deep fascination of James's story arises from the inability it depicts to distinguish between the otherworldly and mundane forces shaping the self. James plays on this ambiguity even in his works involving no ghosts, in the uncanny sense of occult forces that he summons at moments of epiphanic awareness from *The Portrait of a Lady* on. More generally, he portrayed the intersubjective shaping of selves in the flow and flux of his late dialogue style, already apparent in *The Turn of the Screw*: a style laden with preternatural sensitivities and empathies of one speaker for another which, working especially through intercepted thoughts and incomplete sentences, melds individuals at times almost to the point of obscuring who is speaking.[16]

Britten could not sustain James's systematic ambiguity. This was in part a simple by-product of dramatic representation. The way he chose to present the ghosts, with direct interactions between them, and between them and the children, threatened already to render them too solid. To present them in the theater in a radically different, unmaterialized fashion would have led Britten down dramatic pathways uncongenial to him. (One could imagine, for instance—if without much enthusiasm—an ambiguity-preserving operatic *Turn of the Screw* presented as the governess's internal monologue, in the fashion of Schoenberg's *Erwartung*.)

But there is a more palpable materialization of the ghosts than this, a more bracing dissipation of James's ambiguity. It stems from their singing. From the moment early on in the conceiving of the opera when Britten resolved that the ghosts would have to sing, he linked them to a tradition of operatic vocalization anything but disembodied. The ghostliness of Quint and Miss Jessel is congealed in their audible presence—moreso even than in their visual one, for while the possibility of immaterial visual apparitions has been explored often enough in opera of the modern age, the idea of singing without any bodily source is far rarer.[17]

As Quint is far the more prominent of the ghosts, so his vocalized body is the more solid. His seductive cantilena to Miles in act 1, scene 8—the first singing we have heard from him—varies a theme the governess had earlier sung to express her worried premonitions (I, 1) and her resolve to protect the children (I, 5); it will revert to that theme, in unsettling culmination, at the ghosts' "The ceremony of innocence is drowned" (II, 1). But its frequent circling back to the tenor's high E flat lodges this pitch in our ears as the sonic body, so to speak, of the ghost. Thereafter Britten does his utmost to solidify this body. He makes E flat the center of Quint's singing throughout the remainder of act 1, scene 8 and in all his subsequent appearances (act 2, scenes 1, 4–5, and 8). He dwells on the pitch to the point of obsession. Indeed, so prominent is the pitch that its final shift up a half step to E natural, marking the governess's triumph and Quint's farewell to Miles in the final scene, carries no power to efface it.

This vocal presentation of Quint, above all else, portrays him as an autonomous subject equivalent to, and locked in a struggle with, the governess. In an operatic tradition of solidly embodied voices the tenor's vocal powers are too potent and too compelling not to stake this claim for the ghost. But by virtue of these powers they strain the listener's ability to sustain the illusion of ghostliness. And in this, in turn, they solidify all the subjects in the opera in a manner inimical to James's narrative. Quint's voice, in short, militates against the uncanniness his portrayal must aim for.

It is, of course, not news that Britten's insistence that the ghosts should sing undermined the signal mystery of James's story. More than one of the first reviewers of the opera objected to the stagey solidity of Quint and Miss Jessel. And the materiality of the ghosts—or at least their material equivalence to all the other characters—has stimulated readings of the opera, from Joseph Kerman's soon after the premiere to Philip Brett's of recent years, that have pointed up differences between Britten's presentation and James's.[18]

What seems worthy of note is that Britten's singing ghosts place his work in the mainstream of operatic modernism reaching back to *Parsifal*. Just as the overweening solidity of Wagner's objects—of the spear and the grail—made claptrap of their claims to divine powers, so the uncanniness of Britten's ghosts does not survive their vocal assertion of subjective autonomy. On the one hand are objects whose materiality obscures the exchange that defines their sole, lingering noumenalism; on the other, subjects whose rich and mysterious social constitution is lost in a vision of monadism. In objects, commodification narrowly limits the sources of magical power; in subjects, it inspires a flight from intersubjective magic. As a result, for the first time in long epochs of operatic song, doubt arises whether the voice can sustain metaphysics anymore at all.

NOTES

CHAPTER I
VOICES OF THE INVISIBLE

1. Carl Dahlhaus, *Foundations of Music History*, trans. J. B. Robinson (Cambridge: Cambridge University Press, 1983), p. 5.

2. Theodor W. Adorno, "Bourgeois Opera," trans. David J. Levin, in *Opera through Other Eyes*, ed. David J. Levin (Stanford: Stanford University Press, 1993), pp. 25–43; see p. 34. To be sure, Adorno qualified his affirmation of multiple metaphysics in ways that answer to his overriding interest in the modern period and that will need to be left opaque here until chapter 7: his glimmer of metaphysics is "powerless" except insofar as it embeds itself in history, and its recent history renders it "ideological" and hence "abstract" (i.e., naturalized and neutral) vis-à-vis history.

3. It is important to emphasize these shifts especially for the force of historical estrangement they might exert on us, a force that recommends itself in a scholarly environment that, in accepting opera's generic unity, still endorses universalizing views of operatic history. For an emblematic moment of carelessly universal assumptions see Philippe Lacoue-Labarthe who, in his otherwise deeply thought *Musica ficta (Figures of Wagner)*, trans. Felicia McCarren (Stanford: Stanford University Press, 1994), p. xviii, seems to presume a single "metaphysical structure" as the unchanging principle of opera across its history. For a broader universalizing history, to which I will return, see Michel Poizat, *The Angel's Cry: Beyond the Pleasure Principle in Opera*, trans. Arthur Denner (Ithaca: Cornell University Press, 1992), esp. pp. 51–65. For a *locus classicus* of the universalizing approach, written, however, at a time when it offered an estrangement of its own from a different, objectivist brand of historicism and from scholarly disregard of opera, see Joseph Kerman, *Opera as Drama* (1956; rev. ed. Berkeley: University of California Press, 1988).

4. For hints as to how this substitution might work in the hands of a philosopher, with Austin and Derrida overlaid on Wittgenstein, see Stanley Cavell, *A Pitch of Philosophy: Autobiographical Exercises* (Cambridge: Harvard University Press, 1994), chaps. 2–3.

CHAPTER II
LATE RENAISSANCE OPERA

1. For a fuller discussion of late Renaissance cultural formations see my *Music in Renaissance Magic: Toward a Historiography of Others* (Chicago: University of Chicago Press, 1993). The many intriguing ideas and insights of Robert Donington concerning early opera are in my view overwhelmed by a notion of symbolism so vague as to embrace any and all constructions of meaning in operatic history and, hence, to blur the differences among them. Donington gives scant

justification, other than his confident universal application of them, for accepting his conceptions of the unconscious mind and its archetypal symbols as relevant to the late Renaissance. By imposing these more modern conceptions on all earlier opera, he obscures the earlier models of subjectivity manifested there. See for example his *Opera and Its Symbols: The Unity of Words, Music, and Staging* (New Haven: Yale University Press, 1990), pp. 5–40.

2. Giovanni Pico della Mirandola, *Oration on the Dignity of Man*, in *Renaissance Philosophy*, Volume 1, *The Italian Philosophers*, ed. Arturo B. Fallico and Herman Shapiro (New York: Random House, 1967), pp. 141–171 (see p. 143); Pietro Pomponazzi, *De naturalium effectuum causis sive de incantationibus* (Basel, 1567; reprint, Hildesheim: Olms, 1970), p. 25; quoted in Tomlinson, *Music in Renaissance Magic*, p. 203.

3. See Martin L. Pine, *Pietro Pomponazzi: Radical Philosopher of the Renaissance* (Padua: Antenore, 1986), p. 140.

4. D. P. Walker, "Francis Bacon and *Spiritus*," in Walker, *Music, Spirit and Language in the Renaissance*, ed. Penelope Gouk (London: Variorum, 1985), essay no. 10.

5. Ioan Couliano, *Eros and Magic in the Renaissance*, trans. Margaret Cook (Chicago: University of Chicago Press, 1987) p. 28.

6. Marsilio Ficino, *De vita libri tres*, 3:3, i.e., *Three Books on Life*, ed. and trans. Carol V. Kaske and John R. Clark (Binghampon, N.Y.: Medieval & Renaissance Texts & Studies, 1989), p. 256.

7. Marsilio Ficino, *Theologia platonica* 9:5, quoted from Paul Oskar Kristeller, *The Philosophy of Marsilio Ficino*, trans. Virginia Conant (2nd ed., Gloucester, Mass.: Peter Smith, 1964), p. 235.

8. Ficino, *De vita* 3:21; *Three Books on Life*, pp. 354–57.

9. *De vita* 3:21; *Three Books on Life*, pp. 358–61.

10. Gioseffo Zarlino, *Istitutioni harmoniche* (Venice, 1573; facs. reprint, Ridgewood, N.J.: Gregg Press, 1966), p. 9. The whole chapter, "Delle laudi della musica," is translated in *Source Readings in Music History*, ed. Oliver Strunk, rev. ed., ed. Leo Treitler, vol. 3, *The Renaissance*, ed. Gary Tomlinson (New York: Norton, 1998), pp. 16–21.

11. Vincenzo Calmeta, *Vita del facondo poeta vulgare Serafino Aquilano* (1504), in Calmeta, *Prose e lettere edite e inedite*, ed. Cecil Grayson (Bologna: Commissione per i testi di lingua, 1959), pp. 57–77, pp. 75–76; excerpts trans. in Strunk, *Source Readings*, 3: 43–47.

12. Jean-Antoine de Baïf and Joachim Thibault, Letters Patent and Statutes for the Académie de poesie et musique, in Frances A. Yates, *The French Academies of the Sixteenth Century* (London: Routledge, 1988 [1947]), pp. 319–22; trans. in Strunk, *Source Readings*, 3: 60–63.

13. See, among others, Dean T. Mace, who was the first to elaborate the relevance of Bembian doctrine to the madrigalists in "Pietro Bembo and the Literary Origins of the Italian Madrigal," *The Musical Quarterly* 55 (1969): 65–86; Gary Tomlinson, "Rinuccini, Peri, Monteverdi, and the Humanist Heritage of Opera" (Ph.D. diss., University of California, Berkeley, 1979); and Martha Feldman, *City Culture and the Madrigal at Venice* (Berkeley: University of California Press, 1995).

14. The standard guides to this literature in English are Bernard Weinberg, *A History of Literary Criticism in the Italian Renaissance*, 2 vols. (Chicago: University of Chicago Press, 1961), and Baxter Hathaway, *The Age of Criticism: The Late Renaissance in Italy* (Ithaca: Cornell University Press, 1962).

15. This is, I believe, what happens in Peter Kivy's account of late Renaissance musical representation, which then serves as the basis for an anachronistic perception of the "problem" of early opera. See *Osmin's Rage: Philosophical Reflections on Opera, Drama, and Text* (Princeton: Princeton University Press, 1988), chapters 1–5.

16. Quoted in Weinberg, *A History of Literary Criticism*, 1:206.

17. Agnolo Segni, *Ragionamento . . . sopra le cose pertinenti alla poetica* (Florence, 1581), p. 44; for more on Segni's views see Tomlinson, *Music in Renaissance Magic*, pp. 221–22.

18. Tommaso Campanella, *Poetica: Testo italiano e rifacimento latino*, ed. Luigi Firpo (Rome: Reale Accademia d'Italia, 1944), p. 271; for Campanella's views see Tomlinson, *Music in Renaissance Magic*, pp. 222–24.

19. Vincenzo Galilei, *Dialogo della musica antica, et della moderna* (Florence, 1581; facs. reprint, New York: Broude Brothers, 1967), p. 89; trans. in Strunk, *Source Readings*, 3: 184–89.

20. Teodato Osio, *L'armonia del nudo parlare con ragione di numeri pitagorici* (Milan, 1637), pp. 180–81; for fuller discussion of Osio's views see Tomlinson, *Music in Renaissance Magic*, pp. 224–28.

21. Jacopo Peri, *Le musiche sopra l'Euridice* (Florence, 1600; facs. reprint, Bologna: Forni, 1969), "A lettori."

22. *Il corago, o vero alcune osservazioni per metter bene in scena le composizioni drammatiche*, ed. Paolo Fabbri and Angelo Pompilio (Florence: Olschki, 1983). In their introduction (pp. 9–10) the editors assign the treatise a date sometime soon after 1628 and speculate that its author may be Ottavio Rinuccini's son Pierfrancesco (who had, indeed, edited many of his father's poetic works, including *L'Euridice*, in 1622).

23. Ibid., p. 45.

24. Ibid., pp. 45, 96.

25. Ibid., p. 63.

26. This view, articulated most notably by Nino Pirrotta in Pirrotta and Elena Povoledo, *Music and Theatre from Poliziano to Monteverdi*, trans. Karen Eales (Cambridge: Cambridge University Press, 1982), pp. 262–64, has been restated frequently by his followers.

27. For an interpretation of *Il corago* opposed to this one, one that stresses (without corroboration, in my view) the "incongruities" of sung drama "apparent" to opera's earliest audiences, see Lorenzo Bianconi, *Music in the Seventeenth Century*, trans. David Bryant (Cambridge: Cambridge University Press, 1987), pp. 175–77.

28. See Louise Clubb, "The Making of the Pastoral Play: Some Italian Experiments between 1573 and 1590," in *From Petrarch to Pirandello*, ed. J. A. Molinaro (Toronto: University of Toronto Press, 1973), pp. 45–72.

29. For the use of the word *favola* in these two general senses, one might turn almost anywhere in literary discussions ca. 1600. For an example from a writer

close to the librettist Rinuccini see two lectures by Giovanni Battista Strozzi *il giovane*: "Discorso se sia bene a poeti servirsi delle favole delli antichi" ("Discourse on Whether It Is Good for Poets to Use the Myths of the Ancients") and "Lettione dell'unità della favola" ("Lecture on the Unity of Plot") in Giovambatista di Lorenzo Strozzi, *Orazioni et altre prose* (Rome, 1635), pp. 126–38 and 148–58.

30. Louise Clubb, "La mimesi della realtà invisibile nel dramma pastorale italiano e inglese del tardo rinascimento," *Misure critiche* 4 (1974), 65–92; see p. 71. The role here of the "theorists" referred to by Clubb in obscuring supersensible realities is reminiscent of the pragmatic theorists of imitation discussed earlier.

31. Ibid., pp. 71–75; for an overview of Ficino's theories of love and their influence see Eugenio Garin, *Storia della filosofia italiana*, rev. ed., 3 vols. (Turin: Einaudi, 1966), 1:414–16 and 2:581–615; for a recent suggestive, if idiosyncratic, view, see Couliano, *Eros and Magic in the Renaissance*.

32. Richard Cody, *The Landscape of the Mind: Pictorialism and Platonic Theory in Tasso's* Aminta *and Shakespeare's Early Comedies* (Oxford: Clarendon Press, 1969) pp. 12, 23–27.

33. Ibid., pp. 30–32. For possible direct connections of *Orfeo* to Ficino's own Orphic song see Gary Tomlinson, "The Historian, the Performer, and Authentic Meaning in Music," in *Authenticity and Early Music*, ed. Nicholas Kenyon (Oxford: Oxford University Press, 1988), pp. 115–36; see pp. 126–34.

34. For the connections of Poliziano's *Orfeo* to the first opera librettos see Gary Tomlinson, "Rinuccini, Peri, Monteverdi," chap. 3, and F. W. Sternfeld, *The Birth of Opera* (Oxford: Clarendon Press, 1993), pp. 20–21, 24–25, and 55–64.

35. Francesco de Sanctis, *Storia della letteratura italiana,* ed. Benedetto Croce, 2 vols. (Bari: Laterza, 1925), 2:209.

CHAPTER III
EARLY MODERN OPERA

1. Francesco Sbarra, quoted in Ellen Rosand, *Opera in Seventeenth-Century Venice: The Creation of a Genre* (Berkeley: University of California Press, 1991), p. 45; see also pp. 42–44.

2. We might almost call this new, post-Renaissance opera "baroque," except that its historical delimitations are not those of musicologists' baroque: early modern opera as here understood does not include the court music dramas of the years around 1600, whereas it extends, if with adumbrations of a new operatic metaphysics, at least to Mozart.

3. René Descartes, *Principles of Philosophy*, 1: 53; in *The Philosophical Writings of Descartes*, trans. John Cottingham, Robert Stoothoff, and Dugald Murdoch, 3 vols. (Cambridge: Cambridge University Press, 1985), 1:210.

4. René Descartes, *The Passions of the Soul*, trans. Stephen Voss (Indianapolis: Hackett, 1989), art. 10.

5. Quoted from René Descartes, *Selections*, ed. Ralph M. Eaton (1927; New York: Scribner's, 1955), pp. 243–44.

6. Descartes, *The Passions of the Soul*, art. 34.

7. Ibid., art. 36; my emphasis.

8. Descartes, *Meditations on First Philosophy* 6; see *The Philosophical Writings* 2:60–61.

9. For Baruch Spinoza see his *Ethics*, pt. 2, proposition 7, here quoted as trans. by William Hale White, Amelia Hutchison Stirling, and James Gutman and excerpted in *The European Philosophers from Descartes to Nietzsche*, ed. Monroe C. Beardsley (New York: Modern Library, 1960), p. 173. For Geulincx see Eaton's introduction to Descartes, *Selections*, p. xxxvii. For Gottfried Wilhelm Leibniz see his *First Truths, Discourse on Metaphysics* 33, and *Monadology* 78–80 (in *The European Philosophers*, ed. Beardsley, pp. 248, 283–84, and 299). Deleuze's remark on Hume is in Gilles Deleuze, *Kant's Critical Philosophy: The Doctrine of the Faculties*, trans. Hugh Tomlinson and Barbara Habberjam (Minneapolis: University of Minnesota Press, 1984), p. 13.

10. Michel Foucault, *The Order of Things: An Archaeology of the Human Sciences* (New York: Random House, 1970), pp. 54–67.

11. Descartes, *The Passions of the Soul*, arts. 44 and 50; see also the translator's introduction, p. viii.

12. Catherine Kintzler, *Poétique de l'opéra français de Corneille à Rousseau* (Paris: Minerve, 1991), p. 371.

13. See Charles Dill, "Rameau Reading Lully: Meaning and System in Rameau's Recitative Tradition," *Cambridge Opera Journal* 6 (1994): 1–17.

14. Kintzler, *Poétique de l'opéra français*, p. 433.

15. See ibid. (for Grimarest, p. 363, for Perrin, pp. 361, 364). Abbé Dubos would articulate the general philosophy behind such positions in his view that "the richness and variety of chords, the sweetness and novelty of the melody in music should serve only to produce and to embellish the imitation of the language that belongs to nature and the passions." Quoted from *Réflexions critiques sur la poésie et sur la peinture* (1715) by John Neubauer, *The Emancipation of Music from Language: Departure from Mimesis in Eighteenth-Century Aesthetics* (New Haven: Yale University Press, 1986), pp. 61–62. The views of the French theorists seem again to repeat those of Italians at about 1600, most famously Giulio Cesare Monteverdi's injunction that the words must be mistress, not servant, of the harmonies. Again the duplication is superficial, however: formulations like Monteverdi's do not posit musical setting as a constraint that might even diminish the force and passion of spoken words. Instead, in the tradition of Platonic and Neoplatonic conceptions of song, they seek the particular amalgam of rhythm and tone with signifying words that will yield the truest, most forceful expression. Monteverdi's "second practice" is not, in comparison to the first, a limiting of music's prerogatives, but rather an attempt to extend their reach more deeply into verbal language.

16. See especially *Poétique de l'opéra français*, pp. 190–93 and 355–94.

17. Ibid., pp. 191, 395–430.

18. Ibid., esp. pp. 415–23; see also Thomas Christensen, *Rameau and Musical Thought in the Enlightenment* (Cambridge: Cambridge University Press, 1993), chaps. 6, 8, and 9.

19. See Kintzler, ibid., pt. 3.

20. See, above all, Jacques Derrida, *Of Grammatology*, trans. Gayatri Chakravorty Spivak (Baltimore: Johns Hopkins University Press, 1974); for my

readings of some of the musical issues involved, see Gary Tomlinson, "Ideologies of Aztec Song," *Journal of the American Musicological Society* 48 (1995): 343–79, esp. 345–55; and "Vico's Songs: Detours at the Origins of (Ethno)-Musicology," forthcoming.

21. See Kintzler, *Poétique de l'opéra français*, pp. 194, 277, and the whole of pt. 2, section 1: "Le Théâtre des enchantements et son système poétique."

22. The 1763 edition of Algarotti's *Saggio* is reprinted in Francesco Algarotti, *Saggi*, ed. Giovanni da Pozzo (Bari: Laterza, 1963), pp. 145–223.

23. For seventeenth-century Italianate repertories these conventions have been enumerated especially by Lorenzo Bianconi, *Music in the Seventeenth Century*, pp. 204–20, and Ellen Rosand, *Opera in Seventeenth-Century Venice*, chaps. 10–12. For scenographic conventions from 1641 through the Metastasian period see Mercedes Viale Ferrero, "Luogo teatrale e spazio scenico," in *Storia dell'opera italiana*, ed. Lorenzo Bianconi and Giorgio Pestelli (Turin: E.D.T., 1987–), vol. 5, *La spettacolarità*, pp. 1–122, particularly 45–50, 62–77.

24. For fuller development of these ideas concerning the *Lament of the Nymph* see Tomlinson, *Music in Renaissance Magic*, chap. 7; for further discussion of Ariadne's lament see Gary Tomlinson, *Monteverdi and the End of the Renaissance* (Berkeley: University of California Press, 1987), pp. 125–31; and, for a thoughtful comparison of the two works and consideration of their influence, Bianconi, *Music in the Seventeenth Century*, pp. 209–19.

25. Feind, *Gedanken von der Opera*, 1708, quoted in Bianconi, *Music in the Seventeenth Century*, pp. 320–21; Raguenet, *Parallèle des Italiens et des Français en ce qui regarde la musique et les opéras*, 1702, quoted in *Source Readings in Music History*, ed. Oliver Strunk, vol. 3, *The Baroque Era* (New York: Norton, 1965 [1950]), p. 122.

26. *Music in the Seventeenth Century*, p. 204.

27. Ibid., p. 205.

28. Jean-Jacques Rousseau, "Essay on the Origin of Languages," in Rousseau, *The First and Second Discourses, Together with the Replies to Critics and Essay on the Origin of Languages*, trans. Victor Gourevitch (New York: Harper & Row, 1986), pp. 239–95, chap. 19.

29. See *Il corago*, ed. Fabbri and Pompilio, pp. 59–61.

30. See Ellen Rosand, "The Descending Tetrachord: An Emblem of Lament," *The Musical Quarterly* 65 (1979): 346–59.

31. For an account of the emergence in the eighteenth century of antilinguistic understandings of music's effects, one emphasizing what the author sees as a reemergence of Pythagorean musical formalism, see Neubauer, *The Emancipation of Music from Language*; for an excellent consideration of the complexities attendant on conceptions of musical absoluteness across the whole of the modern period, Carl Dahlhaus, *The Idea of Absolute Music*, trans. Roger Lustig (Chicago: University of Chicago Press, 1989).

32. The expressive role of the orchestra in the passage is described by an unnamed correspondent to the *Mercure de France* on 15 June 1779; see Patricia Howard, *Gluck: An Eighteenth-Century Portrait in Letters and Documents* (Oxford: Clarendon Press, 1995), pp. 199–200. For Madame de Staël, see *De l'Allemagne* (2 vols., Paris: Garnier, 1932), 2: 91.

33. Martha Feldman, "Magic Mirrors and the *Seria* Stage: Thoughts toward a Ritual View," *Journal of the American Musicological Society* 48 (1995): 423–84.

34. Ibid., 458.

35. Ibid., 459.

36. Ivan Nagel, *Autonomy and Mercy: Reflections on Mozart's Operas*, trans. Marion Faber and Ivan Nagel (Cambridge: Harvard University Press, 1991).

37. Ibid., pp. 33–34.

38. For the emergence of such words and the new views of the emotions associated with them see, for England, Kivy, *Osmin's Rage*, chap. 9 and, for France, Joan DeJean, *Ancients against Moderns: Culture Wars and the Making of a Fin de Siècle* (Chicago: University of Chicago Press, 1997), p. 13 and chap. 3.

39. Slavoj Žižek, " 'The Wound Is Healed Only by the Spear That Smote You': The Operatic Subject and Its Vicissitudes," in *Opera Through Other Eyes*, ed. David J. Levin (Stanford: Stanford University Press, 1994), pp. 177–214, see p. 180.

40. Søren Kierkegaard, *Either/Or*, trans. David F. Swenson, Lillian Marvin Swenson, and Howard A. Johnson, 2 vols. (Princeton: Princeton University Press, 1971 [1944]), 1: 111.

41. Friedrich Nietzsche, *The Will to Power*, trans. Walter Kaufmann and R. J. Hollingdale (New York: Vintage, 1968), art. 871.

42. On these novel characters see Daniel Heartz, "Goldoni, *Don Giovanni*, and the *dramma giocoso*," in Heartz, *Mozart's Operas*, ed. Thomas Bauman (Berkeley: University of California Press, 1990), pp. 194–205.

43. For Kierkegaard's aesthetic see Terry Eagleton, *The Ideology of the Aesthetic* (Oxford: Blackwell, 1990), chap. 7. For Kerman's views, *Opera as Drama*, rev. ed., pp. 98–104. In a much more recent essay on *Don Giovanni*, Kerman has offered an interpretation of the work and its protagonist that partially rehabilitates the Kierkegaardian stance he formerly rejected. See "Reading *Don Giovanni*," in *Don Giovanni: Myths of Seduction and Betrayal*, ed. Jonathan Miller (Baltimore: Johns Hopkins University Press, 1991), pp. 108–25.

44. See Kierkegaard, *Either/Or*, pp. 62–63 and ff.

45. Ibid., pp. 63, 69. In *The Idea of Absolute Music*, p. 115, Carl Dahlhaus noted Kierkegaard's reliance in this reasoning on the "determined negation" of Hegelian dialectic.

46. Such issues inform the entire second half of "The Immediate Stages of the Erotic or the Musical Erotic," the extended essay in *Either/Or* concerned with *Don Giovanni*; see in general pp. 83–134 and specifically pp. 96–101, 106, 111, 123–25, and 132–34.

47. Ibid., p. 123.

48. Nagel, *Autonomy and Mercy*, p. 113.

49. Respectively, Nagel, *Autonomy and Mercy*, p. 116n; John Stone and Charles Osborne, quoted by Kerman, and Kerman himself; see "Reading *Don Giovanni*," p. 119.

50. Kerman understands this: his granting pride of place to "Finch'han dal vino" in "Reading *Don Giovanni*"—he devotes three full pages to it—is his deepest bow to Kierkegaard.

CHAPTER IV
MODERN OPERA

1. See Sigmund Freud, "The 'Uncanny,' " in *The Standard Edition of the Complete Psychological Works of Sigmund Freud*, trans. James Strachey, Anna Freud, Alix Strachey, and Alan Tyson, 22 vols. (London: Hogarth Press and Institute of Psychoanalysis, 1953–64), 17: 217–56; see pp. 240–41, 248–49.

2. Immanuel Kant, *Critique of Pure Reason*, trans. Norman Kemp Smith (1929; New York: St. Martin's, 1965), p. 93; further references will be given in the text.

3. Deleuze, *Kant's Critical Philosophy*, p. 22.

4. Foucault, *The Order of Things*, p. 318.

5. Ibid., p. 314.

6. Ibid., pp. 324, 327.

7. Ibid., p. 317.

8. Ibid., p. 250.

9. Ibid., p. 225.

10. Ibid., p. 229.

11. See Rousseau and Herder, *Two Essays on the Origin of Language*, p. vi.

12. These positions are evident in varying strengths in musicological discourse, too, as it grew up in the nineteenth century and continues to evolve today. For a summary account of the early emergence of the divide between the metaphysics of formalist analysis and the positivism of historical description see Lawrence Kramer, "The Musicology of the Future," *repercussions* 1 (1992): 5–18; for a controversial analysis of the persistence of the divide in mid-twentieth-century musicology, see Joseph Kerman, *Contemplating Music* (Cambridge: Harvard University Press, 1985). It is possible to distinguish a third post-Kantian choice, critical ambivalence, in which we accept both the range of Kantian critique and the lingering ambiguities of transcendentalism. This position leads toward a constantly recycling self-critique of the limitations both of objective knowledge and of a reestablished metaphysics—toward something akin, we might say in general, to a Nietzschean position. This stance has been hardest to establish in musical discourse, especially since ostensibly critical approaches have usually slipped toward either positivism or analytic transcendentalism, forfeiting in the name of "criticism" a true critique.

In any event, the idea of the "transcendental object" itself is one of the most ambiguous and difficult elements in Kant's *Critique*. For the great Kantian exegete Norman Kemp Smith, it represented a precritical holdover in Kant's mature philosophy (see *A Commentary to Kant's 'Critique of Pure Reason'* [London: Macmillan, 1918], pp. 212–19); indeed, in the second edition of the *Critique* Kant worked to eliminate references to it from his chapter on phenomena and noumena (ibid., p. 412, and *Critique*, pp. 257–75).

The foregoing treatment of natural history, economics, and linguistics summarizes Foucault, *The Order of Things*, chap. 7. In this discussion Foucault introduces a distinction that is, perhaps, a nicety not essential to his analysis. For him the newly visible conditions of economics, biology, and linguistics are not precisely Kantian transcendentals but rather "quasi-transcendentals" (see p. 250).

This is because in Foucault's view they form a counterpart—from a point beyond the object—to Kant's transcendental point beyond the subject: "They correspond to Kant's discovery of a transcendental field and yet they differ from it in two essential points: they are situated with the object and, in a way, beyond it; . . . moreover, they concern the domain of *a posteriori* truths and the principles of their synthesis—and not the *a priori* synthesis of all possible experience." (see p. 244) They seem, as Gary Gutting has put it in analyzing Foucault's argument, "to define fields of what we might term 'transcendental objectivity,' opposite poles to Kant's field of transcendental subjectivity." (Gary Gutting, *Michel Foucault's Archaeology of Scientific Reason* [Cambridge: Cambridge University Press, 1989], p. 185). But in the face of Kant's noumenon, Foucault's distinction would seem to be one without difference. For Kant the noumenon emerges from the conditions of transcendental subjectivity; yet it shows both of the features Foucault seizes on to separate it off into its own sphere. The specter of a transcendental objectivity indeed arises in Kantian thought, but like all objectivity it can only do so, as we have seen, as a product of the subject.

13. Karl Marx, *Capital*, ed. Frederick Engels, 3 vols. (New York: International Publishers, 1967), 1:56.

14. Marx, *Capital*, pt. 1, chap. 1, section 4.

15. See Frank Kermode, *The Romantic Image* (London: Routledge, 1957); the quotation is from p. 46.

16. See Ruth A. Solie, "The Living Work: Organicism and Musical Analysis," *19th-Century Music* 4 (1980): 147–56; also Neubauer, *The Emancipation of Music from Language*, and Dahlhaus, *The Idea of Absolute Music*.

17. This statement might almost serve as a free summary of Foucault, *The Order of Things*, pp. 322–28. Outgrowths of Freudianism also continue to reflect Kant's noumenal subject. The Jungian collective unconscious is an obvious case in point, one variously accompanied in Jung's thought and that of his followers by a whole modern revival of occult operation and symbolism. For a sketch of relations between Kantian and Lacanian subjectivity see Slavoj Žižek, " 'The Wound Is Healed,' " esp. pp. 184–87.

18. Freud, "The 'Uncanny,' " pp. 240–41.

19. Ibid., pp. 248–49.

20. Ibid., p. 249.

21. The specific uncanniness of the transcendental voice has been briefly described, and its emergence localized historically to the period around 1800, by Carolyn Abbate in her essay "Ventriloquism," in *Meaning in the Visual Arts: Views from the Outside*, ed. Irving Lavin (Princeton: Institute for Advanced Study, 1995), pp. 305–11.

22. Friedrich Nietzsche, *The Birth of Tragedy*, in *Basic Writings of Nietzsche*, trans. Walter Kaufmann (1966; New York: Modern Library, 1992), pp. 1–144; see p. 55. Also see below, chap. 5.

23. The issues here are exceedingly complex. They are variegated enough to accommodate, on the one hand, Wagner's wavering across his career between a musical expression subservient to words and drama and a symphonic development transcending both, or, on the other hand, Hanslick's attempt to sidestep metaphysics in his proposal of a beauty specific to musical form. See Dahlhaus,

The Idea of Absolute Music, esp. chaps. 2 and 9; for more on Wagner, see below, chaps. 5 and 6.

24. An example of the intriguing juxtapositions that can occur in this cultural climate is offered by Edward Said in *Musical Elaborations* (New York: Columbia University Press, 1991). Said wishes both to describe Western classical music as a product of local, social, performative contexts and also to maintain "a romantic view . . . that music to a consummate musician possesses a separate status and place . . . that is occasionally revealed but more often withheld" (pp. xix–xx). But the force of the second, context-transcending view seems to dominate his account. Thus, in the midst of a political contextualization of *Die Meistersinger* (pp. 40–42)—and only shortly after a strong assertion that art and life are inseparable (p. 37), he shifts to indulge in the modernist view of an independent musical aestheticism, with its attendant vocabulary and teleologies; he speaks of the "unimpeachable" aesthetic status of Wagner's music and of its "advanced" harmonic idiom that will lead to "towering" and "revolutionary" figures, such as Strauss, Bruckner, Mahler, Debussy, and Schoenberg (p. 42).

In this context of a naturalized aestheticism and the not-so-covert evaluations it enforces, when Said comes to discuss in the book's central essay the "transgressive elements" of music, he can reverse the terms of transgression as they would have been understood by the composers he discusses. Music, Said says, is transgressive precisely in its affiliations with society, "its nomadic ability to attach itself to, and become a part of, [various] social formations" (p. 70). Whereas the very notion of musical transcendence assumed in its modern form a post-Kantian ideology concerning music's ability to transgress phenomenal knowledge, that is, lived (sensory, social) experience, now, by virtue of the naturalized and transparent functioning of this ideology, music is said to transgress instead by reattaching itself to social experience.

Probably these functions of music are two sides of the same cultural coinage, and perhaps Said means for this to be implicit in his discussion. But critique needs to render opaque, and hence visible, the hidden ideology; it needs to analyze the relation between music's contact with invisible realms and its tendency toward migrating cultural affiliations. No wonder we have, from the midst of a naturalized aesthetic of transcendence, found it difficult to describe music's noumenalism.

25. Carolyn Abbate, *Unsung Voices: Opera and Musical Narrative in the Nineteenth Century* (Princeton: Princeton University Press, 1991); Guy Rosolato, "La voix: entre corps et langage," *Revue française de psychanalyse* 38 (1974): 75–94; and Michel Poizat, *The Angel's Cry: Beyond the Pleasure Principle in Opera*, trans. Arthur Denner (Ithaca: Cornell University Press, 1992).

26. See Poizat, *The Angel's Cry*, pp. 99–104.

27. Richard Wagner, "Beethoven," in Wagner, *Actors and Singers*, trans. William Ashton Ellis (Lincoln: University of Nebraska Press, 1995 [1896]), pp. 57–126; esp. pp. 65–73; for Poizat's citation, *The Angel's Cry*, pp. 77–78. As Wagner's words on the "cry of longing, as the root-element" of expression suggest, his Schopenhauerian conception of the cry is grafted directly onto his earlier views of the tonal origins of language, expressed especially in *Opera and Drama*, which in turn recycle the ideas (old-fashioned by 1850) of writers such as Rousseau and

Herder. On this latter connection see Thomas S. Grey, *Wagner's Musical Prose: Texts and Contexts* (Cambridge: Cambridge University Press, 1995), pp. 257–66. For an overview of Wagner's theory and use of the cry, and for a helpful distinction between his onstage screams and some others in opera after him, see Philip Friedheim, "Wagner and the Aesthetics of the Scream," *19th-Century Music* 7 (1983): 63–70.

28. Poizat, *The Angel's Cry*, pp. 76–77.

29. Freud, "The 'Uncanny,' " p. 249.

30. *Unsung Voices*, pp. 26–27.

31. Ibid., pp. 56, xiii.

32. Ibid., esp. pp. 119–23.

33. Ibid., pp. 120, 152, 155.

34. Richard Taruskin, "She Do the Ring in Different Voices," *Cambridge Opera Journal* 4 (1992): 187–97; see esp. pp. 194, 196.

35. See *Unsung Voices*, pp. 112–18.

36. Ibid., p. 117.

37. For considerations of mad scenes in the nineteenth-century Italian repertory see Mary Ann Smart, "The Silencing of Lucia," *Cambridge Opera Journal* 4 (1992): 119–41; also Susan McClary, "Excess and Frame: The Musical Representation of Madwomen," in *Feminine Endings: Music, Gender, and Sexuality* (Minnesota: University of Minnesota Press, 1991), pp. 80–111; and Catherine Clément, *Opera, or the Undoing of Women*, trans. Betsy Wing (Minneapolis: University of Minnesota Press, 1988), pp. 87–92. These accounts have offered, among other particulars, interpretations of the fact that depictions of altered psychic states in nineteenth-century opera are with overwhelming frequency portrayals of women. From my perspective of a widely dispersed transcendental subjectivity, this gender specificity amounts to a linkage of noumenalism to women and seems almost to mark the noumenon as a female counterpart to the male world of phenomena. Such a gesture on the part of the male creators of opera might seem at first blush to contradict the pervasive tendency within modernism, described by Andreas Huyssen, to mark "an inferior mass culture as feminine." (Andreas Huyssen, *After the Great Divide: Modernism, Mass Culture, Postmodernism* [Bloomington: Indiana University Press, 1986], p. 50.) But mass culture and the noumenal transcendentalism of high art stand in a more complex relation than this, as Marx's fetishism of commodities, first of all, indicates. For suggestions of this complexity see Huyssen, pp. 16–19, and above, chap. 6.

38. Amina's sleepwalking scene in *La sonnambula* is an exception to the earlier rule: here formal discursiveness marks not only the lengthy recitative opening the scene but the slow movement of the double aria that follows. This movement, "Ah! non credea mirarti," is a famous instance of Bellinian melodic extension, what Verdi would later call Bellini's "melodie lunghe lunghe lunghe."

39. See the shift across the pause from the *scena* to m. 1; mm. 23–24, on the way to A♭; and m. 29, initiating the move to F♭. The extraordinary six stanzas of text Piave provided for the movement are set in the following keys: stanzas 1 and 2: D♭; st. 3: to A♭; st. 4: F♭; st. 5: to D♭ minor; st. 6: D♭. (All the major-mode tonalities, it almost goes without saying in Italianate styles of this period, are laden with minor-mode inflections.)

40. Abramo Basevi, *Studio sulle opere di Giuseppe Verdi* (Florence: Tofani, 1859), p. 108.

41. "Banco! l'eternità t'apre il suo regno." This passage was transposed up a half-step in the 1865 revisions of the opera; originally it was sung at the same pitch as "Tutto è finito."

42. For Mazzini's essay see the edition of Marcello de Angelis: Giuseppe Mazzini, *Filosofia della musica e estetica musicale del primo ottocento: testi scelti da Andrea Majer, Marco Santucci, Lorenzo Neri, Abramo Basevi, Giovanni Battista Rinuccini* (Florence: Guaraldi, 1977); for the quotation here see p. 69. Further references to Mazzini's essay will be given in the text. Of a general influence of Hugo behind not only Mazzini but also the young Wagner there can be little question, notwithstanding Wagner's later lampooning of Hugo (especially in the context of the Franco-Prussian War); for similarities in Mazzinian and Wagnerian Christianity see de Angelis's introduction to the *Filosofia della musica*, pp. 28–30. For my own earlier résumé of the particulars of Mazzini's essay and views on its place in Italian musical romanticism see Tomlinson, "Italian Romanticism and Italian Opera: An Essay in Their Affinities," *19th-Century Music* 10 (1986): 43–60.

43. Wagner, "Beethoven," pp. 73–74.

CHAPTER V
NIETZSCHE

1. See the "Attempt at a Self-Criticism" Nietzsche wrote in 1886 to preface a new edition of *The Birth of Tragedy*; *The Birth of Tragedy*, p. 25. Further references to *The Birth of Tragedy* will be given in the text.

2. The issue of the fidelity of Nietzsche's use of these Schopenhauerian doctrines in *The Birth of Tragedy* has been at the center of debate over the book and its relation to its author's later thought. Two important moments in this debate, Paul de Man's "Genesis and Genealogy (Nietzsche)," in *Allegories of Reading: Figural Language in Rousseau, Nietzsche, Rilke, and Proust* (New Haven: Yale University Press, 1979), pp. 79–102, and Philippe Lacoue-Labarthe, "Le détour," *Poétique* 5 (1971): 53–76, are answered convincingly and at length by Henry Staten in the Appendix ("*The Birth of Tragedy* Reconstructed") of his *Nietzsche's Voice* (Ithaca: Cornell University Press, 1990). Staten describes how "*The Birth of Tragedy* is practically the hinge between Romanticism and everything that is post-Romantic, including Nietzsche's later work" (p. 187). Michel Haar, in *Nietzsche and Metaphysics*, trans. Michael Gendre (Albany: State University of New York Press, 1996), sees Nietzsche's break with Schopenhauerian metaphysics as coming earlier and cutting more deeply than the break depicted by Staten (see esp. chaps. 2, 3, and 8; also below, n. 4); but he also bears witness to continuities with Kantian metaphysics extending through the whole of Nietzsche's work.

3. *The Birth of Tragedy*, section 16; see Schopenhauer, *The World as Will and Representation*, trans. E. F. J. Payne, 2 vols. (New York: Dover, 1969), 1: 262–63.

4. See *The Birth of Tragedy*, section 6. Haar, *Nietzsche and Metaphysics*, chaps. 2 and 8, argues that Nietzsche, already by the time of *The Birth of Tragedy*,

had revised Schopenhauer's will from a metaphysical essence to a multiple set of forces, of dubious metaphysicality, played out in appearances and in the world—a prefiguration, in other words, of the "will to power" of Nietzsche's later writings. In Haar's view we do not need to await those later writings for the disappearance of the Schopenhauerian "radical separation between the absolute truth 'in itself' of the will and the fallacious phenomenal appearances" (p. 42)—that is, for the blurring of the distinction between phenomenal and noumenal realms. Just as Haar assimilates Nietzsche's early will to appearances and the world, so he also correspondingly argues that Nietzsche viewed music as a force immanent in will *and* the world already in his early writings; see pp. 173 ff. For more on such a view of music, indisputably present in Nietzsche's late works, see pp. 117–19 above.

5. Citing Haydn's *The Seasons* and *Creation* as examples (and instituting as a part of his ontology a common romantic complaint), Schopenhauer had condemned such mimetic music in *The World as Will and Representation*, 1: 263–64.

6. Staten, *Nietzsche's Voice*, p. 209.

7. *The Dionysian Worldview*, quoted in Staten, *Nietzsche's Voice*, p. 209.

8. See Kaufmann's introduction to *The Birth of Tragedy*, p. 13: "Unfortunately, *The Birth of Tragedy* does not end with Section 15, as an early draft did and as the book clearly ought to. Another ten sections follow that weaken the whole book immeasurably." It is not surprising that Wagner's Victorian translator William Ashton Ellis felt differently. For him these chapters were the culmination of "a work that pulses with the warm blood of genius from end to end," to be followed in Nietzsche's career only by a gradual falling-off that would eventually bring him to the nadir of an extreme "apostasy." See Wagner, *Actors and Singers*, pp. xvi, xviii.

9. Schopenhauer, *The World as Will and Representation*, Book 3, section 52 and Supplement 39 ("On the Metaphysics of Music"); see also Excursus 4 above.

10. *The Birth of Tragedy*, section 19. There is an obvious historical irony about *The Birth of Tragedy*: its linking of Wagner back to Sophocles and Aeschylus retraces a general connection that earlier composers had aspired to, but Nietzsche, following Wagner, condemns the results of these aspirations. The inventors of recitative around 1600 certainly were not trying to re-create or revive ancient tragedy, as is still usually asserted in generalizing histories of opera; but there is just as little doubt that their experiments took place in a context of considerable academic interest in Greek and Roman drama. In rejecting their *stile rappresentativo* Nietzsche marches in step with an unhistorical Wagnerian self-aggrandizement, ignoring a congruence that might otherwise have sharpened his own sense of the dichotomy between tragedy in ancient and Christian times. For a basic question that Nietzsche raised in *The Birth of Tragedy*, the question of the functions of tragedy in ancient times, was one which had exercised scholars in the late Renaissance as well. The differences in their approaches bespeak, of course, deep differences in their conceptions and embodiments of subjectivity. In this light it would be intriguing to compare any number of analyses of Aristotle's tragic catharsis from the late *cinquecento* (or indeed, for yet another perspective, from the French classic era) with Nietzsche's radically different conception. Nietzschean passages that could provide a starting point for such a comparison are *The Birth of Tragedy*, section 22; *Twilight of the Idols* (trans. Walter Kaufmann in

The Portable Nietzsche [New York: Viking, 1954], pp. 463–563), "What I Owe to the Ancients," section 5; and especially *The Will to Power*, sections 851–52.

11. The remark comes in a note on Wagner that Nietzsche did not publish; see *The Will to Power*, appendix, p. 555.

12. Ibid., p. 539.

13. See *The Will to Power*, section 1067.

14. *Thus Spoke Zarathustra*, trans. Walter Kaufmann in *The Portable Nietzsche*, pp. 103–439; First Part: "On the Despisers of the Body," p. 146.

15. See *On the Genealogy of Morals*, trans. Walter Kaufmann in *Basic Writings of Nietzsche*, pp. 437–599, 2:16.

16. Henry Staten has argued that the structure of willing itself—the pleasure derived from exercising the will to power and Nietzsche's very "insistence that will to power is an affect, a feeling, a pleasure, a pathos"—does not allow Nietzsche to escape entirely from a subjectivity with metaphysical overtones; it brings close "the most elusive problem of the later work, the question of *who* wills in will to power." See *Nietzsche's Voice*, pp. 122–29.

17. *Nietzsche contra Wagner*, trans. Walter Kaufmann in *The Portable Nietzsche*, pp. 661–83, p. 664 ("Where I Offer Objections"). In *The Case of Wagner*, section 7, Nietzsche spoke of writing a book entitled *Toward a Physiology of Art*; see *The Case of Wagner: A Musician's Problem*, trans. Walter Kaufmann in *Basic Writings of Nietzsche*, pp. 601–48.

18. At the moment in *Nietzsche contra Wagner* cited above, Nietzsche asks: "What is it that my whole body really expects of music? For there is no soul. I believe, its own *ease*: as if all animal functions should be quickened by easy, bold, exuberant, self-assured rhythms." "Where I Offer Objections" in *Nietzsche contra Wagner*, p. 664.

19. *The Will to Power*, section 1052; on the parallels Nietzsche perceived between Dionysus and Christ see Staten, *Nietzsche's Voice*, pp. 146–48.

20. *The Will to Power*, section 1041.

21. Haar, *Nietzsche and Metaphysics*, pp. 31–32.

22. "Skirmishes of an Untimely Man," section 10 in *Twilight of the Idols*, pp. 519–20.

23. "Our faculties are subtilized out of more complete faculties," Nietzsche remarks in an unpublished note. "But even today one still hears with one's muscles. . . ." *The Will to Power*, section 809.

24. In the unpublished note just now cited, Nietzsche continues: "Empathy with the souls of others is originally nothing moral, but a physiological susceptibility to suggestion: 'sympathy,' or what is called 'altruism,' is merely a product of the psychomotor rapport which is reckoned a part of our spirituality. . . . One never communicates thoughts: one communicates movements, mimics signs, which we then trace back to thoughts." See ibid. Again, as Staten reminds us, Nietzsche does not ultimately answer the question of the locus in which this biological will is experienced. Where is this "back" we trace signs to? See Staten, *Nietzsche's Voice*, pp. 124–25.

25. Nietzsche's attempt at externalization is evident again, this time with an allusion to Descartes's *esprits animaux* and pineal gland, in an unpublished note that minimizes the role of metaphysics in a sensate, embodied "spirituality": "The

most spiritual men . . . accord the senses a more fundamental value than to that fine sieve, that thinning and reducing machine, or whatever we may call what in the language of the people is named 'spirit.' The strength and power of the senses—this is the essential thing." *The Will to Power*, art. 1045.

26. "Wagner as a Dancer" in *Nietzsche contra Wagner*, p. 666.

27. *The Case of Wagner*, 7. Nietzsche goes on to contrast Wagner with Kant—maliciously but hilariously—by virtue of the shortcomings of leitmotivism: "That Wagner disguised as a principle his incapacity for giving organic form, that he establishes a 'dramatic style' where we merely establish his incapacity for any style whatever, this is in line with a bold habit that accompanied Wagner through his whole life: he posits a principle where he lacks a capacity (—very different in this respect, incidentally, from the old Kant who preferred another boldness: wherever he lacked a principle he posited a special human capacity)."

28. As is well known, Wagner would later alter this goal with the help of Schopenhauer, ennobling music as the avatar of the beyond, rather than the servant of drama. Nietzsche had conveniently ignored Wagner's pre-Schopenhauerian theory in order not to sidetrack his own agenda in *The Birth of Tragedy*; see his condemnation, quoted earlier, of conventional opera that made music the servant of poetry (p. 115). For his later view of the opportunistic about-face that Wagner made when he encountered Schopenhauer, see *The Case of Wagner*, 4 and, especially, *On the Genealogy of Morals*, 3:5: "He grasped all at once that with the Schopenhauerian theory and innovation *more* could be done *in majorem musicae gloriam*. . . . The value of *the musician* himself all at once went up in an unheard-of manner, too: from now on he became an oracle, a priest, indeed more than a priest, a kind of mouthpiece of the 'in itself' of things, a telephone from the beyond—henceforth he uttered not only music, this ventriloquist of God—he uttered metaphysics." For an overview of Wagner's shifting position on musical expression, which involved a qualified rehabilitation in his later, Schopenhauer-influenced writings, of early-romantic ideas of absolute music, see Dahlhaus, *The Idea of Absolute Music*, chap. 2, and Grey, *Wagner's Musical Prose*, chap. 1. For the relation of this rehabilitation to Wagner's view of Beethoven, see Grey, *Wagner's Musical Prose*, chap. 2 and especially p. 53.

29. "Where I Admire" in *Nietzsche contra Wagner*, p. 663; I have modified Kaufmann's translation to render Nietzsche's *Takt* as "measure" rather than "beat."

30. *The Case of Wagner*, 6.

31. Ibid., 7–8.

32. Ibid., 8, 11, and Postscript; also "Where Wagner Belongs" in *Nietzsche contra Wagner*, p. 672.

33. For Nietzsche's lampooning of the various redemptions of Wagner's plots see *The Case of Wagner*, 3.

34. Ibid., first Postscript.

35. Elsewhere Nietzsche sums up the distinction as one between "two kinds of sufferers: first those who suffer from the *overfullness* of life and want a Dionysian art . . . and then those who suffer from the *impoverishment* of life. . . . Regarding artists of all kinds, I now avail myself of this main distinction: is it the *hatred*

against life or the *excess* of life which has here become creative?" See "We Antipodes" in *Nietzsche contra Wagner*, pp. 669–71.

36. On Wagner and modernity see also *The Case of Wagner*, Preface and 5.

37. Ibid., 10; *La gaya scienza* is a reference to the Troubadours (according to Walter Kaufmann; see p. 634n), and hence an allusion to Mediterranean, non-Germanic lyric poets. Nietzsche's evocative imagery here is not completely consistent: after the passage cited above from *Nietzsche contra Wagner*, p. 669, those who suffer from impoverishment of life are said to want of art and philosophy "calm, stillness, *smooth seas*," etc. (my emphasis).

38. *The Case of Wagner*, Preface, second Postscript.

39. *The Case of Wagner*, 1; on Offenbach see *The Will to Power*, art. 834.

40. *The Case of Wagner*, 1.

41. Ibid., 2.

42. Theodor Adorno's Marxist perspective casts a related light on Nietzsche's exoticizing view of *Carmen*: for him it represents an escape from bourgeois Europe, offered not only by *Carmen* but also by many other "operas of exogamy," toward those who are "condemned to hunger and rags and suspected of possessing all the happiness which the bourgeois world denies itself in its irrational rationality." See "Fantasia sopra *Carmen*," in Adorno, *Quasi una fantasia: Essays on Modern Music*, trans. Rodney Livingstone (London: Verso, 1994), pp. 53–64; p. 54. A fuller analysis of the life-affirming significance Nietzsche found in the dance of *Carmen* might profitably juxtapose the opera with two passages of central importance in *Thus Spoke Zarathustra*, "The Dancing Song" and "The Other Dancing Song." For hints as to the direction such an analysis might take, see Staten's interpretation of these passages, *Nietzsche's Voice*, chap. 9. On Nietzsche's orientalizing in regard to *Carmen* (and that of many others involved in the creation and reception of the opera) see Susan McClary, *Georges Bizet: Carmen* (Cambridge: Cambridge University Press, 1992).

43. *The Case of Wagner*, 1.

44. *The Will to Power*, section 809.

45. *The Case of Wagner*, 2.

46. Ibid.

47. Ibid., 1; for Nietzsche's thoughts on the "great" or "grand" style and music: *The Will to Power*, sections 842, 800; also "Skirmishes of an Untimely Man," 11, in *Twilight of the Idols*, p. 521; and Haar, *Nietzsche and Metaphysics*, pp. 181–82.

48. *Beyond Good and Evil*, trans. Walter Kaufmann, in *Basic Writings of Nietzsche*, pp. 191–435, sections 254–55.

49. *The Case of Wagner*, 3; see also *The Will to Power*, p. 447n.

50. *The Case of Wagner*, 2.

51. Tchaikovsky's remarks on *Carmen* are quoted in McClary, *Carmen*, p. 117.

52. Adorno recognized this antimetaphysical fate in *Carmen*; his description of it is the essential insight motivating his essay about the opera and Nietzsche's response to it. For Adorno, *Carmen*'s music wipes away the illusion of a transcendental fate and, with it, sublime love and metaphysical meaning. This amounts to

the positing *tout court* of an anti-Schopenhauerian, Nietzschean subject. *Carmen* offers an "aesthetic refraction of passion," in which "subjectivity becomes conscious of itself as nature, and abandons the illusion that it is autonomous mind [*Geist*]." It abandons, that is to say, its fundamental claim to metaphysical stature in the post-Kantian era. See "Fantasia sopra *Carmen*," pp. 61–63. This Nietzschean and Adornian view of the "south of music" and its antimetaphysical nature might help to set apart not only *Carmen* but also other operas from the Germanic (and Wagnerian) dichotomy between high metaphysical expression and kitsch (by which such works are often denigrated). Adorno's brief appreciation of *Cavalleria rusticana* (in *Quasi una fantasia*, pp. 16–17) is noteworthy in this regard.

53. Clément, *Opera, or the Undoing of Women*, p. 48.

54. McClary, *Carmen*, p. 57.

55. *Nietzsche and Metaphysics*, p. 95. For Adorno, Nietzsche never succeeded in completely embracing this intersubjectivity, a failure made clear in his clinging to notions of subjective authenticity and genuineness. The failure also manifests itself, Adorno adds, in Nietzsche's views on Wagner's theatricalism, for in the assuming of various roles that the social view of subjectivity demands, "It is not with play-acting that [Nietzsche] ought to have reproached Wagner . . . but with the actor's denial of play-acting." The problem was not theatricality per se, in other words, but a theatricality that claims to represent, through actors' assuming of roles, "realistic" subjects as integrated and self-sufficient. See Theodor Adorno, *Minima moralia: Reflections from Damaged Life*, trans. E. F. N. Jephcott (London: Verso, 1974), no. 99 ("Gold Assay").

56. Staten, *Nietzsche's Voice*, pp. 152–53.

CHAPTER VI
GHOSTS IN THE MACHINE

1. Theodor Adorno, "De gustibus est disputandum" in *Minima moralia*, no. 47.

2. Theodor W. Adorno, *Introduction to the Sociology of Music*, trans. E. B. Ashton (New York: Continuum, 1989), pp. 72, 77.

3. Quoted by Anthony Barone from Adorno's essay "Bürgerliche Oper," in Theodore W. Adorno, "On the Score of *Parsifal*," trans. with commentary by Anthony Barone, *Music & Letters* 76 (1995): 384–97; see p. 393; a revised version of "Bürgerliche Oper" has been translated by David J. Levin as "Bourgeois Opera" in *Opera Through Other Eyes*; see p. 29.

4. Theodor Adorno, *In Search of Wagner*, trans. Rodney Livingstone (Great Britain: NLB, 1981), p. 107. For this relation of opera and film see also Adorno, "Bourgeois Opera," pp. 31–32, 34.

5. Adorno, *Sociology of Music*, p. 81.

6. Adorno, "Gold Assay" in *Minima moralia*, no. 99; see also "Monad," no. 97. For some necessary cautions in approaching Adorno's concept of the modern subject, see Andreas Huyssen, "Adorno in Reverse: From Hollywood to Richard Wagner," in *After the Great Divide: Modernism, Mass Culture, Postmodernism*

(Bloomington: Indiana University Press, 1986), pp. 16–43; esp. pp. 26–27. Huyssen is eloquent not only in rehabilitating certain aspects of Adorno's thought but also in summarizing the limitations of the theory of culture industry broached most famously by Adorno with Max Horkheimer in their *Dialectic of Enlightenment*. What follows is an attempt not to reassert the "hard" form of this theory but to suggest some of the implications of its unquestionable core—the increasing commodification of culture since the nineteenth century—for operatic culture in the twentieth century.

7. The commodity thus operates in two directions at once: it is both an objectification of subjective forces and a dissolution of the object. Jacques Derrida has captured this and other intricacies of commodification well in his recent *Specters of Marx: The State of the Debt, the Work of Mourning, & the New International*, trans. Peggy Kamuf (New York: Routledge, 1994); see pp. 148 ff and especially p. 157: "This phantasmagoria of a *commerce* between market things . . . corresponds *at the same time* to a naturalization of the human *socius*, of labor objectified in things, and to a denaturing, a denaturalization, and a dematerialization of the thing become commodity, of the wooden table when it comes on stage as exchange-value and no longer as use-value."

8. Adorno, "Gold Assay" in *Minima moralia*, no. 99.

9. See Adorno, "Theses against Occultism" in *Minima moralia*, no. 151; also "The Stars down to Earth: The *Los Angeles Times* Astrology Column," in Theodor W. Adorno, *The Stars down to Earth and Other Essays on the Irrational in Culture*, ed. Stephen Crook (London: Routledge, 1994), pp. 34–127.

10. Adorno, *In Search of Wagner*, p. 83; see also "Art-object" in *Minima moralia*, no. 145.

11. It may be true, as Carolyn Abbate has complained, that Adorno ignores in this account of Wagnerian objectification the formidable labor apparent in Wagnerian singing; see *Unsung Voices*, pp. 13–14. But he does so only to assert something Abbate herself does not question (in analyses like that of Tannhäuser's Rome Narrative; see chapter 4): that in Wagner's music dramas the sounding origin of operatic voice has shifted in large measure from the singers to the players.

12. It is in this individual anticipation of mass movements that Wagner most plainly plays for Adorno a paradoxical double role: not only as the forefather of elitist, artistic modernism but also as the harbinger of its seeming antithesis, modern mass culture. Wagner thus reveals the underground confluence of these two cultural currents. For their relation in Adorno's thinking about Wagner see Huyssen, "Adorno in Reverse."

13. George Bernard Shaw, *The Perfect Wagnerite: A Commentary on the Niblung's Ring* (New York: Dover, 1967), p. xiii.

14. Though my terms and emphases here are different, my view intersects with John Deathridge's in "Wagner and the Post-modern," *Cambridge Opera Journal* 4 (1992): 143–61. There Deathridge argues convincingly that from the late 1850s Wagner turned away from the Young Hegelian promotion of constant innovation and sheer rupture with the past that had characterized his earlier writings. He entered into a "'post-modern' reaction to his own obsession with the radically new," observable in the music dramas from *Tristan* on. The reaction Deathridge

describes is, I think, intimately connected to Wagner's nostalgic regard for a pre-Hegelian, Kantian subjectivity. The very nostalgia of this reaction signals what Deathridge deems its "postmodern" quality and what I interpret as its inability to extricate itself from the spiraling forces of the modernism it reacted against.

15. See Robin Holloway, "Experiencing Music and Imagery in 'Parsifal,'" in *Parsifal—Richard Wagner* (English National Opera Guide 34, London: Calder, 1986), pp. 23–41. For discussion of the views of Wagner and his followers on symphonic versus poetic structure see Grey, *Wagner's Musical Prose*, passim, esp. pp. 306–26, 339–42, and, regarding *Parsifal*, p. 174.

16. This dualism comprises the "new organicism" Daverio perceives, in differing balances, in *Tristan* and *Parsifal*; see John Daverio, *Nineteenth-Century Music and the German Romantic Ideology* (New York: Schirmer, 1993), chap. 7, esp. pp. 187–89 and 204–5. For Adorno and Dahlhaus see Adorno, "On the Score of 'Parsifal,'" p. 385; Carl Dahlhaus, *Richard Wagner's Music Dramas*, trans. Mary Whittall (Cambridge: Cambridge University Press, 1979), p. 155.

17. For discussion of this difference, see Carolyn Abbate, "'Parsifal': Words and Music," in *Parsifal—Richard Wagner*, pp. 43–58; see esp. pp. 44–46. For the earliest motivic analysis recognizing the generative fertility of the opening melody of *Parsifal*, see Hans von Wolzogen, "'Parsifal': A Thematic Guide through the Poetry and Music (1882)," in *Music Analysis in the Nineteenth Century*, Volume 2, *Hermeneutic Approaches*, ed. Ian Bent (Cambridge: Cambridge University Press, 1995), pp. 88–105.

18. Robin Holloway has singled this out as the dominating sonorous image of the work and provided a helpful discussion of its appearances; see "Experiencing Music and Imagery," pp. 32–39.

19. For a description of the emergence of the prophecy music see Abbate, "'Parsifal': Words and Music," pp. 44–46.

20. Holloway elaborates a similar point in "Experiencing Music and Imagery," p. 39.

21. Richard Wagner, "Religion and Art," in Wagner, *Religion and Art*, trans. W. Ashton Ellis (Lincoln: University of Nebraska Press, 1994 [1897]), pp. 211–52, p. 213.

22. Ibid., pp. 222–24. Wagner summed up both his dissatisfaction with objectified religion and his old-fashioned idealism in the quotation from Schiller he used as epigraph for his essay: "In the Christian religion I find an intrinsic disposition to the Highest and the Noblest, and its various manifestations in life appear to me so vapid and repugnant simply because they have missed expression of that Highest" (p. 211). Michael Tanner, in *Wagner* (Princeton: Princeton University Press, 1996), p. 184, interprets Wagner's opening words in "Religion and Art" as urging that we settle for art in a situation of "reduced expectations," where "religion in the genuine sense is no longer possible." This reading abets Tanner's general view that *Parsifal* is not a Christian work but only a work about Christianity (see below, n. 26), but it seems to fly in the face of the religious powers of music that Wagner describes with clarity and evident sincerity in "Religion and Art."

23. In 1885, for example, Edouard Schuré criticized *Parsifal's* "materialist theology of blood, devoid of any high spiritual feeling." Three years later Charles

and Pierre Bonnier assailed the work's "religious paraphernalia" and quoted Wagner's own Schopenhauer on the "childish stories" and "mystical machinery" by which Christianity put across its message of redemption. And Hanslick famously expatiated on his distaste for the relics, the sacred miracles, and the supernatural powers of *Parsifal*. These writers are quoted in Lucy Beckett, *Richard Wagner: Parsifal* (Cambridge: Cambridge University Press, 1981), pp. 105–11.

24. Adorno, "On the Score of 'Parsifal,'" pp. 386–87.

25. Beckett, *Richard Wagner: Parsifal*, p. 149.

26. Slavoj Žižek has recently reached a similar conclusion in an analysis of *Parsifal's* libretto informed by Kantian views of the subject and Lacanian psychoanalytic theory. For him the conundrum of the spear's powers—the fact that it alone can heal the wound it dealt Amfortas—is the key to the work. This puzzle might be read in Kantian fashion, with the wound representing the inaccessible, noumenal condition of its own healing. But this Kantian noumenon could not be objectified; Kant would be "as far as possible from allowing any finite subject to assume the role of the instrument which 'smote you' in order to enable the realization of the Good." Wagner, instead, aims for just this anti-Kantian objectification of both the spear and the subjective agent of its use, Parsifal. This reveals the extent to which Parsifal is nothing but an instrument of a greater authority, a disempowered "spokesman of mute domination." In this Parsifal anticipates for Žižek the subject in totalitarianism, perversely defining itself, in a process of "self-objectivization," as the object of others rather than as a subject in regard to objectified others. Through an analysis of the objectification of noumenal forces that involves both the spear and Parsifal, Žižek approaches a position not far from Adorno's. See Slavoj Žižek, "'The Wound Is Healed.'"

Other accounts seem to be stymied by *Parsifal's* objectivity. Michael Tanner, for example, attempts to counter at one blow all the attacks on *Parsifal's* religious character by maintaining, tendentiously in my view, that *Parsifal* is not religious at all, but rather is *about* religion. He depicts the work as antitranscendental in spirit, an incomparable study in "the psychopathology of religious belief" that is entirely immanent to human concerns and their reflection in natural surroundings. But he does so only by categorically separating off the human psyche (the object, after all, of any study in psychopathology) from the transcendental in a way that seems to ignore the whole post-Kantian construction of the subject and, moreover, to overlook the transcendental overtones apparent in modern psychological thought (especially Freudianism and its outgrowths). And he does so, perhaps more to the point, by ignoring the transcendental, antiphenomenal religiosity, with music as its Schopenhauerian medium, that Wagner plainly professed in "Religion and Art." See Michael Tanner, "The Total Work of Art," in *The Wagner Companion*, ed. Peter Burbidge and Richard Sutton (London: Faber and Faber, 1979), pp. 140–224, esp. pp. 205–18; also, more briefly, Tanner, *Wagner*, pp. 197–98.

As I have suggested, Lucy Beckett, for her part, embraces the religiosity of *Parsifal* and offers an interpretation of the work—a courageous interpretation, in its way—from within the framework of Christian belief. Faced with the objectivity of *Parsifal*, however, especially in the form of the pagan magic that resides in the grail (a magic bound up, for example, with the macabre figure of Titurel), she finds no recourse but to fall back on her belief. She proposes a distinction between this magic and the grail's symbolic representation of the incarnation, writing off the non-Christian elements as residues of the multiple sources Wagner relied on for the grail story. (See Lucy Beckett, *Richard Wagner: Parsifal*, chap. 6.) But her distinction seems circular, a differentiation of false and true magics that has no foundation outside a particular magical system (in this case Christianity) marking itself as truth. Indeed, her distinction seems almost to duplicate Wagner's own between a religion of congealed materiality, "of fetishes and idols," and one of ideal divinity. (See Wagner, "Religion and Art," p. 213.) If, as I have argued, *Parsifal* was finally unsuccessful in Wagner's aim of exalting one side of this dichotomy and suppressing the other—a failure implicit in the commodity dialectic that rules the work and manifested, in part, precisely in the reified, magical presence of the grail—then we will surely not come to a deeper understanding of the failure by posing again the dichotomy Wagner started from.

CHAPTER VII
THE SUM OF MODERNITY

1. Adorno, "On the Score of 'Parsifal,' " p. 386.
2. See Deathridge, "Wagner and the Post-modern," p. 160.
3. Lacoue-Labarthe, *Musica ficta*, pp. 121, 132.
4. Long before he wrote *Moses und Aron* Schoenberg had dreamt of a work that would retrieve remnants of authentic, ancient faith from the evils of the modern world. From the first this faith was opposed to modern materialism (not to mention Wagnerian redemption by love). As far back as 1912, looking toward the never-completed *Die Jakobsleiter*, Schoenberg wrote to Richard Dehmel:

> For a long time I have been wanting to write an oratorio on the following subject: modern man, having passed through materialism, socialism, and anarchy, and despite having been an atheist, still having in him some residue of ancient faith (in the form of superstition), wrestles with God (see also Strindberg's "Jacob Wrestling") and finally succeeds in finding God and becoming religious. Learning to pray! It is not through any action, any blows of fate, least of all through any love of woman, that this change of heart is to come about.

Quoted by Pamela C. White, *Schoenberg and the God-Idea: The Opera* Moses und Aron (Ann Arbor: UMI, 1985), pp. 65–66.

5. See Theodor Adorno, "Sacred Fragment: Schoenberg's *Moses und Aron*," in Adorno, *Quasi una fantasia*, pp. 225–48, pp. 242, 226–27; see also Adorno, "Arnold Schoenberg, 1874–1951," in Adorno, *Prisms*, trans. Samuel and Shierry Weber (Cambridge: MIT Press, 1983), pp. 147–72, 164–65; on Schoenberg's religious views and the influence on him of Schopenhauer see White, *Schoenberg and the God-Idea*, chap. 2.

6. Adorno, "Sacred Fragment," pp. 229–30.
7. Ibid., pp. 233–34.

8. See White, *Schoenberg and the God-Idea*, pp. 162, 73–76; also Paul Griffiths, *Modern Music: A Concise History from Debussy to Boulez* (London: Thames and Hudson, 1978), pp. 95–96. For Adorno the connection of such row usage to the theology of *Moses und Aron* was inevitable: "Every music that aims at totality as a simile of the absolute has its theological dimension." He adds, "The absolute determination of every [musical] detail makes [the work] resemble willy-nilly the manifestation of the absolute, and this remains true even when . . . it denies that essence can become manifest." See "Sacred Fragment," p. 234.

9. Adorno, "Sacred Fragment," pp. 228–29, 244–45; and "Arnold Schoenberg," pp. 156–57; see also "Sacred Fragment," p. 245: "The sheer density of the construction becomes the medium in which the ineffable can manifest itself without usurpation."

10. White, *Schoenberg and the God-Idea*, pp. 160–225.

11. Adorno, "Sacred Fragment," p. 241.

12. Lacoue-Labarthe, *Musica ficta*, pp. 129–32.

13. See Adorno, "Sacred Fragment," pp. 231, 246. For Adorno's summation of the problematic persistence of older expressive ideals through Schoenberg's oeuvre see "Arnold Schoenberg," p. 161 f: "Something in Schoenberg, perhaps allegiance to the command cited in the text of the choral pieces op. 27—'Thou shalt make no graven images'—seeks to eradicate the depictive-aesthetic features of music, the imageless art. At the same time, this feature characterizes the idiom in which every one of Schoenberg's musical ideas is conceived. He laboured under this contradiction to the very end."

14. From "Composition with Twelve Tones"; quoted by White in *Schoenberg and the God-Idea*, pp. 31–32.

15. The latter quotation is T. J. Lustig's, in Henry James, *The Turn of the Screw and Other Stories*, ed. T. J. Lustig (Oxford: Oxford University Press, 1992), p. xxiii; he quotes Felman on p. xv.

16. It may be true, as Vivien Jones has maintained, that James's later novels "explore and demonstrate the modern sense that we are locked within our individual consciousnesses with only our own subjective perceptions to rely on" (see Patricia Howard, ed., *Benjamin Britten: The Turn of the Screw* [Cambridge: Cambridge University Press, 1985], p. 7)—but only if we qualify the view of consciousness she seems to broach. The inaccessibility of solid truth to the consciousnesses that James depicts is a product of their instability, of the indefiniteness of their boundaries, which James in turn reflects in their constant, fluid reformulation under the force of the interactions in his dialogue.

17. What indeed would it mean for a sound such as singing to be illusory in the fashion of a visual mirage? Composers in the modern era seem rather strictly to associate the singing of their operatic ghosts with material presence. After his death, the Commendatore sings only from a monumental body of stone; romantic ghosts, such as Wagner's Dutchman and Meyerbeer's Bertram in *Robert le diable*, sing in bodies indistinguishable from those of the mortals around them, their ghostliness being discovered in the workings of the plot rather than in some disembodied appearance they present. In Verdi, leaving aside as precisely antispectral the divine, angelic voices from on high in *Giovanna d'Arco* and *Don Carlos*, we might note two negative confirmations of the principle: the identity of

the ghostlike figure at the end of *Don Carlos* is left famously undecidable (is he the monk from act II, whose music he shares, or the ghost of Charles V?) while an unequivocal specter, the ghost of Banquo in *Macbeth*, sings not a word. Meanwhile, a most-famous of diabolical operatic ghosts, Samiel in Weber's *Der Freischütz*, speaks but does not sing—a distinction that probably should be considered in connection with his offstage invisibility.

18. For some early critics see Howard, *Benjamin Britten*, p. 56; for Britten's insistence that the ghosts sing, see p. 46. For Kerman's thoughts, see *Opera as Drama*, pp. 224–25; for Brett's, see Philip Brett, "Britten's Dream," in *Musicology and Difference: Gender and Sexuality in Music Scholarship*, ed. Ruth A. Solie (Berkeley: University of California Press, 1993), pp. 259–80.

INDEX

Page numbers in italics refer to illustrations.